100 THINGS SEAHAWKS FANS
SHOULD KNOW & DO
BEFORE THEY DIE

John Morgan

TRIUMPH
BOOKS

Triumph Books and colophon are registered trademarks of Random House, Inc.

Library of Congress Cataloging-in-Publication Data

Morgan, John, 1982–
   100 things Seahawks fans should know and do before they die / John Morgan.
      p. cm.
    ISBN 978-1-60078-399-9
   1. Seattle Seahawks (Football team)—Miscellanea. 2. Seattle Seahawks (Football team)—History—Miscellanea. I. Title. II. Title: One hundred things Seahawks fans should know and do before they die.
   GV956.S4M67 2010
   796.332'6409797772—dc22
                              2010017780

This book is available in quantity at special discounts for your group or organization. For further information, contact:

Triumph Books
542 South Dearborn Street
Suite 750
Chicago, Illinois 60605
(312) 939-3330
Fax (312) 663-3557 | www.triumphbooks.com

Printed in U.S.A.
ISBN: 978-1-60078-399-9
Design by Patricia Frey
Editorial and page production by Prologue Publishing Services, LLC
All photos courtesy of AP Images unless otherwise specified

To Alanya, for everything

Contents

1 Living XL

Super Bowl XL. Ford Field, Detroit. Seahawks versus Steelers. First quarter, kickoff...

Josh Scobey secures it just inside the 3, then stutter-steps, sprints behind up-man Maurice Morris. XL is on; Seattle ball. The Seattle machine, all short routes and pull blocks, pistons made of linemen, gears made of wide receivers, is easing into first. First snap, three-step drop, Matt Hasselbeck to Darrell Jackson for a too-easy seven yards. The Seahawks will punish soft coverage until stopped. Then we'll beat you over top.

Mike Holmgren has a plan, and it's working. For the first series, Jackson is unstoppable. Another pass launched before Jackson can finish his cut. Reception. Holmgren gets the MVP involved. Shaun Alexander charges behind Sean Locklear, cuts in, puts a hand on Chris Gray's hip, and the two jog for eight. Jackson again, running an out, and it's another easy first down as Hasselbeck rainbows it in. Holmgren envisions a masterpiece, and his medium is offensive linemen. Ryan Hannam then Walter Jones then Steve Hutchinson pull sequentially and fan toward the sideline. Shame Alexander only runs for one before collapsing on the ball.

"Could this be real?" I'm standing. I'm shouting at the TV set. I'm shouting at my girlfriend's parents' TV set.

SEA!—HAWKS!

No. Nononono—not yet. Incomplete. It's third-and-9. It's third-and-9. Seattle sets three wide, split backs, and Pittsburgh responds with a 3-3 nickel. This is the game? It feels like the game.

Matt Hasselbeck drops back to pass during an early drive near midfield in Super Bowl XL against the Pittsburgh Steelers.

It's the first quarter. It's the first quarter. It feels like the whole game in the balance.

Snap.

Locklear and Gray pop; Lock slanting in while Gray slides out to contain the edge rush. Clark Haggans stunts in and tears through the inside shoulder of Locklear. Steelers swarm the edge, and Hasselbeck can feel it all closing in. He's hardly through his seven-step drop before he's attempting to step up, step out of pressure; steps into a sack by Haggans instead.

Okay. Okayokayokayokayokay. So high and now so low, but it was a good drive, and we can pin 'em back. Pin 'em back, Rouen. Pin 'em—ah, crap. Touchback.

The crowd is roaring. Al Michaels says it's 80 percent Steelers fans. They cheer their team right into a false start. Hahaha. Backed up—get after it, D! Chuck Darby slices in and falls behind the line. That's bad. Leroy Hill knifes in and wraps, stopping Willie Parker for no gain. Is that Lofa Tatupu appearing from the pile? Putting a shoulder in? Damn right. *Ta! Tu! Pu!* And there he is again, charging hard from the third level and blowing up the Steelers screen. How you like third down, Pittsburgh? Uh-huh. False start, again. That's another five. Okayokayokay. Yes. Yesyesyes. It's third-and-19. Seahawks rush three. Bryce Fisher edge rushes to perfection and nearly sacks Ben Roethlisberger at the 1. Ben scrambles, slides into a charging Tatupu for 10. Punt time. That's the D. That's the D that made the difference, that got us here.

Punt. Warrick, headliner of D-Jack's draft class but a castoff now, motions hook and ladder then shimmy-shakes for minus-2. A lot of noise and little production, that's Peter Warrick.

Let's power this up. Power it up. Put it away. *Seahawks! SEA!*

Alexander motions from the backfield to wide left. Yeah, that's not fooling anyone. Hasselbeck takes the snap and pitches to Mack Strong. Hannam cut blocks. Jones straight abuses Joey Porter. Hope you weren't planning on participating in this play, Joe-Joe. Strong starts his giddy-up but is tripped up by Kimo von Oelhoffen. Shoot. Shoot. If they awarded yards for execution…. Morris motions wide. Jones smacks around Kimo this time. Hasselbeck surveys, sees nothing, tucks and runs for nine. That's right, improvise. Show those quicks. Make them respect the legs, Matt.

My heart barely beats before Hasselbeck finds Jackson for 10 and the first. Drive alive. Madden is prattling about Holmgren never wanting Alexander to be the lone back. Seattle breaks three wide, split backs. Morris motions wide, leaving Alexander as the lone back. Haggans charges, Alexander "blocks," curls, and "receives." Bobble, bobble, and not even the presence of mind to drop the ball before falling to the turf for a loss of two. Damn it. Damn it, Shaun. Damn it. Where have your hands gone, Shaun? Damn it. Away from the action, Robbie Tobeck is making sure a Steeler remembers him. We scrap in Seattle, too. This is ain't Rams football. This ain—

Okay. Okay. Hasselbeck to Bobby Engram for six. We're back on that brink. It's third down. Here we go. Here we go. Hasselbeck drops, targets Jackson, and connects for 18—

Holding? Bunch a damn bull. Wait, no, that's holding. Gray stabs an arm under James Farrior and clotheslines the charging linebacker. Argh.

That's bad. Third-and-16. Drive has a sword hanging right over it. A steel sword. Heh. *Er.* Seahawks break three wide, two on the left, and the Steelers counter with a wacky 3-2 look. Get that crap out of here, Lebeau. Hasselbeck drops, Steelers rush three, Hasselbeck launches and…*nooooooooooooooooooooooooooooooooo!*

Dropped. Hasselbeck's pass falls between Jackson and Joe Jurevicius and nearly into Ike Taylor's mitts. But he drops it. Confusion. Route confusion or something.

Punt.

Hines Ward motions wide left into the left slot. He's trying to draw Marcus Trufant into the pile and thus create a short edge for Willie Parker. Seahawks read it, strong safety Michael Boulware runs down to cover Ward. Dude's gonna be good. Kid has all the tools. Snap. Parker blasts left, attempts the edge but is dropped by a charging Trufant. Attaboy.

Steelers pick up six on the next attempt. Shoot. Still, third down, third down, get them off the field. Hawks rush four, and Roethlisberger targets Ward slicing through a disorganized zone. The pass drops in low and incomplete. Two Pittsburgh drives. Two three-and-outs.

SEA!—FENSE!

Ball back in the good guys' hands. Ball back where it belongs. Seahawks line surges into the Steelers' front three, and Alexander runs for an easy four. Seahawks pick themselves up and set. Hasselbeck takes a three-step drop and zips it to Jackson. He has inside position on Taylor, receives and burns by him. That's good for 20. Reset. Reset. Hasselbeck drops back, sits in a comfy pocket, and finds Vicious coming back on a hook route. Joe extends his long arms away from his frame and pulls in the catch. Quietly, Mack Strong makes the play. Seattle's line pushed hard left, and only Strong was left to pick up blitzing linebacker Haggans. He engages and runs Haggans around the pocket, never dropping his block for a second and keeping Hasselbeck free of pressure.

Seahawks are driving, on the 16, about to punch it in and pull away in the first. Okay, not pull away, but establish that vital early lead. And then pull away! I'm standing. My future wife has abandoned the insanity for someplace quiet. She's about to hear my anguish pour through the walls.

End of the first quarter...to be continued.

2 Walter Junior Jones

The differences between a typical left tackle and a legendary tackle are both great and subtle. Few fans train their eyes on the position, preferring, most naturally, to follow the ball carrier and the "action." We usually notice an offensive tackle on two occasions: the chagrinned, bent, and idle pose taken by a beat blocker. This is colloquially known as the "Winston Justice"—referring both to the man and the moral concept of fairness as applied to overhyped clods. The Winston flashes before an end or linebacker explodes into the quarterback.

The other is rare and sweet. Walter Jones made half a career out of locking down and driving back ends. He drove Patrick Kerney like a plow, tearing open a hole for Shaun Alexander to jog through. Jones' dominance was cartoonish at times. He could drive an end into a linebacker and create a time-based sculpture, *Pile: Portrait of Man Defeated.*

Walter Junior Jones, workout warrior. He ran a 4.75-second 40 at the 1997 NFL Combine. That became a kind of suffix. He wasn't the best offensive tackle of his class. That was Orlando Pace. Pace went first overall to the St. Louis Rams. That designation of second-best became a kind of prefix. Second-best left-tackle prospect, Walter Jones, who ran a 4.75/40 in the 1997 NFL Combine, was drafted sixth overall by the Seattle Seahawks.

The sixth overall pick in the NFL draft is hugely expensive. In the late '90s rookie contracts hadn't exploded, but the salary cap was commensurately smaller. A top 10 pick is a vital resource granted only the lowliest of teams. Bad teams build from them. Bad teams are sunk by them. Good teams have built from them. Their ranks are a who's who of great all-time players: Peyton Manning,

Walter Jones, the Seahawks' best-ever player and probably the greatest left tackle in NFL history, blocks a Raiders linebacker during a blowout 31–3 loss at Oakland–Alameda County Coliseum in October 2000.

Bruce Smith, John Elway, Kenny Easley, Eric Dickerson, Lawrence Taylor, and on and on.

It was an auspicious start to his NFL career, but one earned dogging it through the C-circuit. Jones was a proud community college graduate. Jones spent two seasons at Holmes Community College in Mississippi before transferring to Florida State. He only played one season of Division I football. Typically, that makes a player risky, and maybe Jones was. Luckily for Seattle, Dennis Erickson, Randy Mueller, and Bob Whitsitt were interested in big action and bold moves.

Seattle had two picks in the first round after trading Rick Mirer. It had moved up to No. 3 to draft Shawn Springs and wanted to maneuver up to No. 6 to nab Jones. It would be costly, and the Seahawks' ownership was in flux. Peter King related the fateful conversation that brought Jones to Seattle:

> Aware that anti-Seahawks sentiment at the state capital was running high, Whitsitt warned his boss. "You could be out of this in three days. Dennis and Randy think they can move up and get this great tackle, but it could really push your costs up. If they get Springs and this tackle, it could cost $13 million in signing bonuses alone."
>
> "What did we say when we got into this?" Allen replied. "If we're involved, we're involved. Are we still involved?"
>
> "Yeah," Whitsitt said.
>
> "Then we have to do it," Allen said.

Paul Allen was in, and with his backing, Seattle was about to add its best player ever.

Seattle had spoken with the Jets about trading for New York's sixth overall pick. The deal was: No. 6 for No. 12 and the Seahawks' third- and sixth-round picks. It fell through. The Jets backed out and instead traded with Tampa Bay. Seattle was sure Tampa had moved up to draft Walter Jones, but general manager Rich McKay, Tim Ruskell's then-boss and mentor, called Seattle and offered to trade back. Somehow, the pick had become cheaper in translation. Seattle packaged its No. 12 and third-round pick for No. 6. The sixth-rounder they kept as a result became Itula Mili.

Jones missed two games in September with an ankle injury. He missed two games in November with an injury to the other ankle. I am sure some people were pretty concerned. They likely would have been panicked had they known that a kidney condition kept Jones from taking strong analgesics. But it was an aberration. Jones would not miss another game because of injury until injury ended his 2008 season and, with it, his career.

He was good and he knew it. Jones made quarterbacks better and running backs great. He helped 41-year-old Warren Moon make an improbable Pro Bowl in 1997. Jones blocked for Trent Dilfer's best years as a pro. He helped a sixth-round pick develop confidence and lead the Seahawks to their first and only Super Bowl.

For it, he wanted to be paid. Mike Holmgren and later Bob Whitsitt complicated the situation and pushed it to the brink. Seattle franchised Jones in 2002. He wasn't happy. He held out through training camp and into the season. Finally, he signed and reported before Week 3. It became a yearly tradition. Seattle would not extend a long-term contract that satisfied Jones; the Seahawks would franchise Jones to retain him, he would hold out through training camp, then return for the season. It became a joke. Jones was nicknamed "the Franchise."

Holding out didn't hurt his play. He established himself as a perennial Pro Bowler and, along with Pace, put left tackle on the map. The position became a respected building block, and linemen's salaries skyrocketed. Nowadays left tackles are more highly valued than running backs. If salary is the measure, in 2009 the top five offensive tackles were more highly paid than the top five corners and the top five wide receivers, and were behind only defensive ends and quarterbacks. Left tackle has become a building block, but also a position of superstars. Fans talk up big blocks and pancakes. They brag about footwork and drop steps.

Flashier moments earned Jones a reputation among fans, but every-snap steadiness and consistency earned Jones a position among the greatest offensive tackles to ever play. He allowed zero sacks in 2004. Zero. Jones had it all. He could move, he could control, he could pull and wage total war on a defense. He was a superstar and a lunch-pail player. Jones kept it simple, yet astonishing. For 12 seasons, he broke huddle, took his position on left end, put his hand down, sprung up, and blocked out the sun.

3 The Atypical Prototype

Since his retirement, Steve Largent's three major records—receptions, receiving yards, and receiving touchdowns—have all been bested. His record in receptions has been bested 19 times. His record in receiving yards has been bested 11 times. His record for receiving touchdowns has been bested five times and tied once, by Tim Brown.

Breaking Largent's record is not a key to Canton. His receptions record is now little more than a signpost in a good wide receiver's career. Contemporary receivers Derrick Mason, Muhsin Muhammad, and Hines Ward have all passed Largent, and only Ward has any shot at the Hall of Fame. And Ward would enter because of his team's success rather than his own.

Even his more sterling record—receiving yards—was quickly eclipsed by contemporaries like Henry Ellard and James Lofton. Lofton was inducted into the Pro Football Hall of Fame, but after five years of eligibility. Ellard is still very much on the outside looking in.

Largent is perhaps the greatest beneficiary of the Mel Blount rule. Largent was always an adept route runner who had deceptive speed, but in the bruising mid-'70s pass environment, he struggled to get open. He had 87 receptions in his first two seasons, despite starting 27 games. He caught 71 in 16 games in 1978. Only two strike-shortened seasons stopped him from surpassing 60 the next 10 seasons. It's easy to see his place within history, his steadily fading place on the record books. Couple that with his known tools deficiencies, and it creates a warped portrait of the player. Make no mistake, Largent was great, just maybe not great in the way some Seahawks fans want him to be.

Largent was a great value and great story. Seattle acquired him for an eighth-round selection. The Houston Oilers saw him as too small and too slow and planned to cut him. Seattle acquired him, played him in Week 1, and Largent caught five passes for 86 yards and never looked back. Apart from being an underdog, he was handsome and white in a sport that was steadily not, and at a position that was almost exclusively black. Maybe it didn't matter.

It did matter that he was the first star on an expansion team that not only lacked stars, but much of anything to root for. His quick success earned him a spot on the All-Rookie team. His third season, he went from good to great, and the Seahawks followed, posting their first winning record. He had refined his style. His yards per reception were dropping, but his receptions skyrocketed, and so did his value.

Largent was a possession receiver before that took on pejorative connotations. And as atypical as he was when he was drafted, he unwittingly became the prototype for the modern receiver. In the run-first game that had dominated the NFL before 1978, running was the backbone of an offense, passing a high-risk/high-reward means to cash in. Coaches said, you run to pass, and play-action

Steve Largent, the prototype of the modern-day possession receiver, heads to the end zone on a touchdown reception during a preseason game against the Minnesota Vikings in 1986.

was a staple of every offense. Largent was not fast or tall, but reliable. He ran precise and deceptive routes and caught whatever came near him. In many ways, he was the forerunner for Jerry Rice, and Rice a continuation of the prototype he had developed.

See, Rice wasn't fast either, and he wasn't tall. Yes, he was athletic, but athleticism wasn't his calling card. Rice was a receiver you could run an offense through. Unlike Largent, he had a coach who embraced that. Rice became the embodiment of the new NFL, where passing would rule, but Largent was the prototype.

The skills he possessed, even today, define truly valuable receivers. Descriptions of Largent are full of apologies. Even his Hall of Fame profile is overrun with excuses and qualifiers. It starts,

"Steve Largent, a 5'11", 187-pound wide receiver with only average size and speed but armed with exceptional determination and concentration…" As if, after all these years, coaches and voters are still scratching their heads—*how the hell did that guy beat us?*

I won't argue his determination and concentration, but it's a little insulting to the hundreds of corners, safeties, and linebackers to argue Largent was simply more determined. No, Largent was better. He was an innovator. Instead of outrunning his opponent, instead of outmuscling, outjumping, out-whatever, he beat them through skill. He read secondaries like Fischer read a board, and struck mercilessly at weaknesses. He honed every route to be indistinguishable from another. He caught everything, earned trust with every quarterback, became a master of detail and bedeviled opponents by attacking vulnerabilities they had never considered.

Maybe it's the insecurity of being great but never sensational, of being Hank Aaron instead of Mickey Mantle, but Seahawks fans struggle to make Largent somehow more than he ever was, and in so doing, diminish him. Largent was a first. He couldn't play in the modern NFL, but he couldn't, because he helped make it. After Monet, every failed portrait artist became an Impressionist. After Largent, every slow receiver with smarts and great hands became a possession receiver.

4 Second-Quarter Mania

Super Bowl XL. Ford Field, Detroit. Second quarter…

Robbed. Door kicked in, drawers rifled through, heirlooms stolen, violated, robbed. The Seahawks were robbed of a touchdown. Did Darrell Jackson extend his arm? Maybe. Okay, certainly. And did that action create separation between him and defender

Chris Hope? Yes. Yes. But was it really severe enough to warrant a penalty? Of course not. Right?

My lunatic fan brain accepts no quarter. The officials are compromised. Cull the lot.

I am enervated with frustration. Seattle's drive slumps. Mike Holmgren burns a couple plays running the ball. Shaun Alexander strings the run wide, then wider, then out of bounds. Kimo rides Walter into Shaun on second down. It is third-and-23. Third-and-not-worth-trying. Third-and-don't-screw-up.

Seattle splits four-wide, two a side, and Pittsburgh responds with a 3-3 nickel. Hasselbeck receives the snap, drops five, pump fakes over the middle, and launches hard toward the end zone! D.J. Hackett is isolated in the corner. The kid with hops. The Seahawks' now and future secret weapon. He stops, soars, but mistimes his leap and is falling as the ball arrives. Rookie Bryant McFadden swats it away. Time for Brownie. Josh Brown nails it to put Seattle up three.

That word, *ambivalent*, I feel it. It isn't ambivalent, *meh*. Or ambivalent, *yeah!* But ambivalent, what? Would a Super Bowl win's good be better than a Super Bowl loss's bad? It was like Pascal's wager. If I believed in this team until now, whether I could know if they would win today or not, I could achieve the only satisfactory end: a win I never doubted. Right?

The Seahawks were the third team in history to prevent its opponent from achieving a first down in the first quarter. Al Michaels told me that. So maybe three wasn't so bad. Seattle was shutting down the Steelers' offense. It was winning drives even if it had only three to show for it.

My little pep talk is halted by the resumption of play. Pittsburgh returns it to the 20 and sets two wide, two tight on the opposite side. Seattle is in a base 4-3. The receivers are bunched. For some reason this concerns me. D.D. Lewis is turned around and upside-down covering Cedrick Wilson on a simple curl route, but Lofa Tatupu storms downhill and forces the incompletion with a hard shoulder tackle.

Jordan Babineaux tips away a bomb to Hines Ward, and the Steelers are buried under third-and-long. Yes? Yes. Yes! Defensive football. It's...unexpected. It's...taking a while to embrace. It's...*awesome*. I'm standing again. I'm shouting weird things at the TV. Sentences peppered with Seahawks and the unknown names of Steelers' mothers and ancestors. A guttural "SEA!" erupts from my lungs, and I know this isn't making a strong impression on the future in-laws, but I'm damned if I care.

Pittsburgh is four-wide, shotgun. Seattle is in a 4-1 dime package. Seattle stunts its line: Darby around the blind side and Wistrom up the gut forces Roethlisberger to scramble. Tats breaks coverage and truncates Ben's scramble. He stops, plants, and fires deep. The ball rainbows errant over Tru in lockdown coverage on Nate Washington. Seahawks force another three and out. I'm not drinking but I'm plenty drunk. It's all irrational and reactive and incomprehensible and impassioned. It's fandom at its fringes.

Chris Gardocki outputs his coverage, and Warrick receives and breaks free to his right. *Go. Go. Go.* Thirty-four yards—

Oh! No!

Flag. Frickin' Pruitt. Frickin' Pruitt. Frickin' officials.

Chris Gray fires forward, and Alexander runs for five. Hass overshoots Engram high and to the right, and it's third down. Seattle splits four wide, two a side, and the Steelers show a 3-3 before settling into a 4-2 nickel. An NFL game has about 11 minutes of actual game action, leaving hours of agonizing anticipation. Lot of life's best things are like that. What'd that junkie say? All pleasure is only relief?

Snap. Pitt sends five, retreating the right end into coverage. Chris Hope fires through the interior, and before Mack Strong can engage and pancake the chump, Hasselbeck is on his horse, rolling to his left. He strikes to Joe Jurevicius on an in, and it's good for 15 and another heartbeat in my strangled chest.

Hutch fires out and owns Larry Foote on an otherwise unremarkable run. Alexander trips in the hole and falls forward for three. He nets five off right tackle. This time Steve Hutchinson loses his block, and James Farrior slices in for the stop. It's third, but it's manageable. It's third, but it's not a crisis third. It's third, but Hawks only need two to convert.

Ryan Hannam motions right to create trips off right tackle. Steelers are in a 3-4. Hasselbeck drops five steps and waits a beat before zinging to Jerramy Stevens. Stevens is free after running a post corner toward the right flat. He catches, plants two feet, and begins to turn before Hope punches the ball free with hard, helmet-first tackle. It's a clear fumble but not called, and I'm caught between praising the Lord and damning the devil. Goddamn, Stevens. Goddamn you! Thank you, merciful God. But damn, Stevens. Damn his hands. Damn his illegitimate children, should he have any. Damn. Damn. Damn. Thank God that wasn't called.

Every moment hangs like a flare. Tom Rouen's punt hangs high and expertly drops and bounds up at the 1. Scobey is in position to down it, but looks disoriented, punches the air, whiffs, and the ball tumbles past for a touchback. I damn his mother. I do. Then I forgive. Then I ball my fists. Then I sit.

"And Jerome Bettis is in the game for the first time!" The crowd explodes.

Ben runs play-action then rolls right. Bryce Fisher alone reads the action and pursues Roethlisberger into the right flat. Ben eyes Hines Ward and flings it wild out of bounds. Marcus Tubbs pursues Bettis and drops him after two. Little known fact about Jerome: he sucks. What's that, you say? He doesn't? In fact, he's Hall of Fame bound? Oh, no. No. No. He's worthless.

I pull myself back from the brink. Maybe I don't care too much, but these conversations would seem saner if they involved two people. I think.

Seattle has forced third-and-long, and, swallowing my consuming hatred for the Bus for a second, I recognize this is a good thing. This is an essential thing. Pittsburgh fans four wide receivers tight. Seattle responds with a 3-2. LeRoy Hill is in a sprinter's stance, barely hiding his blitz, and the rookie is unprepared for the snap. His blitz fails, and he's barely to the line when Ben fires toward Antwaan Randle El. Ah, hell. Trufant closes and bats the ball loose, but El recovers and runs away and past the magic yellow line. Nearing a great play, Trufant breaks cover and allows the first. Tatupu cuts across to make the clean-up tackle. Balls. Ball almost loose, but recovered, balls on your mother, brother. Argh.

All but Marquand Manuel break contain, and the Steelers punish Seattle's aggressive defense with an end around to Hines Ward. I'm sitting. Manuel is sitting. Manuel is injured. Manuel is Seattle's back-up free safety, pressed into action after starter Ken Hamlin's season ended on the other end of a street sign. Third-string safety, that's encouraging. In comes Etric Pruitt.

Steelers break, I don't know—two wide? Seahawks something-something. Some guy runs behind the line before the snap. Lofa is slapping hips and getting the linemen over the proper gaps. Like it matters. Here goes nothing. Ben fakes play-action. Rolls. Underthrows! Boulware's on his horse! He's under it! Jumps!

Yes! Interception!

Michael Boulware is running "over" coverage but reads Ben's pathetic wobbler right out of his hand and breaks contain to play the ball. It's all expert stuff. Awesome. Stupendous. I didn't say *stupendous.* I said something *cool,* like, "Bad. Ass." That play was bad. Ass. Boulware is a badass. Seahawks! Seahawks! Seahawks! Seahawks gonna be badass champions of the world. *SEA!*

To be continued.

5 The Promise of Mike Holmgren

Head coach is the closest most of us will ever relate to a famous football professional. Yeah, a lot of us mucked it up in the trenches, threw a moonraker spiral that dropped over the receiver's right shoulder, intercepted a pass and didn't realize it until we were burning the return, did something heroic, did something natural that's unnatural, were great for a second and got it. Got what it's like to be a great athlete. But as we aged, we lost that. Away from organized sport. Watched as our bodies declined. Became just average guys.

And so the head coach, scrawny and short, tall and rotund, sunken-shouldered and glowering—that's us. Our window into the world of professional football. We can decide whether to go for it or kick the field goal. We can watch the clock and plan timeouts. We can know when it's time to drop the veteran down and start the rookie. We can feel the thrill of the perfect play call. We can be the coaches we admire, but we could never be Kenny Easley or Shaun Alexander or Jim Zorn.

Mike Holmgren was the second great head coach in Seahawks history. Like Tom Flores, his greatest triumph came before joining the Seahawks, but like Chuck Knox, he brought glory to a team without much. *Hope.* That dangerous word.

Seattle acquired Holmgren the way any benighted franchise acquires talent above and beyond its standard: with a truckload of cash and promises of unprecedented power. Holmgren had built a consistent contender in Green Bay. That's not the truth-truth, but sometimes unvarnished facts deceive. Green Bay built a consistent Packers contender. One that didn't vanish when Holmgren left town. But Holmgren was the embodiment of that organization. He brought to Seattle a piece of the most accomplished team in the history of American football.

January 9, 1999. After a stinging wild-card loss to the San Francisco 49ers, Mike Holmgren signed an eight-year, $31 million contract to become Seattle's head coach and executive vice president. He would make the meal and pick the ingredients. He was the man or, as he would come to be pejoratively known, "the Big Show."

The Holmgren hire can be appreciated in a factual sense. Holmgren was a gifted disciple of Bill Walsh, and Walsh was the most revered coach in football at the time. His West Coast offense was powering many of the best offenses in football, including the still potent 49ers Walsh had long since left, the current Super Bowl–champion Denver Broncos, and Holmgren's own Super Bowl XXXI–champion Packers. Holmgren had served as quarterbacks coach and offensive coordinator of the 49ers during their dynasty and had earned a reputation as a quarterbacks guru. He molded Brett Favre into a young legend and before him had coached Joe Montana and Steve Young. Many thought Young was a failure before joining San Francisco. He was later inducted into the Pro Football Hall of Fame.

Or the Holmgren hire can be appreciated for what it really was: a promise from new owner Paul Allen that rebuilding was over and the Seattle Seahawks would again be a relevant football team.

Montana was Montana when Holmgren was still coaching at Brigham Young. One could argue Montana was Montana when Holmgren was still an assistant coach at Oak Grove High School. Young was an achievement, but whose? Walsh casts a long shadow. Coaching for him did not mean adopting his greatness. Nor does coaching Favre give Holmgren a piece of Favre's greatness. Coaching is like that: esoteric. We appreciate it from the outside, from the results, but we rarely know exactly what a coach does, if their decisions are correct or if their and their team's success or failure happens independent of their actions.

Holmgren could have failed. He could have failed to bring the greatness that had defined his professional career to Seattle as many high-profile coaches have done after changing teams. Paul Allen did not ensure Seattle success. He ensured Seattle relevance. He ensured that Seattle would not just stay in the Pacific Northwest, but that the Seahawks would fight hard to be the best team possible.

Holmgren did not fail.

6 The Rise of Matt Hasselbeck

"Dil-fer! Dil-fer!" roared from the seats of Husky Stadium. It was a bad day to be Matt Hasselbeck. It probably ranked alongside that day he first noticed his forehead waging an inexorable campaign on his hairline. It was a bad season to be Matt Hasselbeck. He was later benched in favor of Trent Dilfer.

Seahawks Nation apologizes.

If Bobby Engram was Mike Holmgren's masterstroke as a general manager, Matt Hasselbeck was his single most important move. It was an inside deal. Seattle acquired Hasselbeck for the NFL equivalent of a bag of chips—and not fancy, small-batch, kettle-cooked chips—no, no, the kind that succeed based on shelf placement and an association with one's childhood. I'm talking Cool Ranch Doritos—off-brand. Seattle traded its No. 10 overall pick and a third-round pick to the Green Bay Packers for Matt Hasselbeck and the No. 17 overall pick. As fate would have it, that 10th overall selection turned into megabust Jamal Reynolds. Seattle's pick turned into Steve Hutchinson. No adjectives necessary.

Matt Hasselbeck lets fly in the second half of Seattle's 24–21 overtime win over the New York Giants on November 27, 2005. Hasselbeck's long, uphill struggle to be the No. 1 quarterback culminated in the team's drive to Super Bowl XL.

Hasselbeck had the rare honor of starting his first year under Holmgren. Holmgren was always a veterans-first coach, and the team had signed Dilfer in the off-season. Dilfer had the musk of winner about him after riding the Baltimore Ravens' historically good defense and special teams to a Super Bowl. But while Holmgren loved veterans, he loved his guys even more, and Hasselbeck was definitely one of his guys. Holmgren scored, finding Hasselbeck in the sixth round of the 1998 NFL Draft. He had cut Hasselbeck in favor of Rick Mirer, but after trading Mirer to the Jets for what would become a fourth-round pick,* Hasselbeck was signed off the practice squad.

Hass was a bit buried in Green Bay. A little-known Mississippian who never got hurt, Brett Something, never got hurt, or got

---

*No, seriously.

hurt but emasculated his rivals with unprecedented toughness, or played through pain, warriored up, and, most importantly, just had fun. Out there. Just had fun out there. Which didn't allow Hasselbeck to have any fun. Out there. He might have been having a blast from the bench.

Holmgren fleeced his former home and brought the best quarterback in Seahawks history to Seattle. That was March. Holmgren reassured his new quarterback of the future by signing Trent Dilfer. That was August 3. At the time, Holmgren downplayed the significance of signing Dilfer by saying, "We have young quarterbacks, and I've been looking for a veteran quarterback. It has very little to do with Matt Hasselbeck. Matt's our quarterback." And he would continue to be Seattle's quarterback for, oh…about eight more weeks.

Mike never lost faith in Hasselbeck, but we can be forgiven if he was the only one. It was Dilfer mania in Seattle after he replaced an injured Hasselbeck. Seattle upset Jacksonville and Denver at home. Of course, "upset" is a matter of perception. Jacksonville was a year removed from a 14–2 season and thus had the luster of a contender. By 2001 they were a mediocre team that finished 6–10. Denver had finished 11–5 in 2000, but would finish 8–8 in 2001. Dilfer had won against teams Seattle could be expected to win at home against. And he had played decent football against defenses that weren't.

But fans in the stands are essentially a seated mob, and though Hasselbeck returned and performed ably against a stifling Dolphins pass defense, the Seahawks still lost. They lost Hasselbeck's next start, too. Washington was an even better pass defense, and Seattle was playing on the road.

"*Dil!—*"

Seattle snuck out a win against Oakland, but Shaun Alexander and his 266 yards were the easy stars.

"*—Fer!*"

Trent knew something about winning. He knew it involved outscoring one's opponent. In Baltimore this involved handing off to Jamal Lewis and watching from the sideline as his defense committed sanctioned homicide. Occasionally, Dilfer would grab the ball by its laces side and attempt to "spiral" the ball forward, but this radical practice was discouraged by head coach Brian Billick. Too risky. Football players were not awarded style points.

How this could possibly translate to Seattle is better discussed by the mob. I think they might respond with a hearty:

"*Dil!*—"

Hasselbeck suffered a separated left shoulder in Week 14, and after weeks of bad play, bad sacks, and losing, Holmgren started Dilfer in his stead. Seattle won each of its next two games. Seattle finished 5–7 in games Hasselbeck started. It finished 4–0 in games started by Dilfer.

"*—Fer!*"

7 Dangerous Words

Super Bowl XL. Ford Field, Detroit. Second quarter (continued)…

I spoke dangerous words. Dangerous, regrettable words. I saw my girlfriend and said, "We might win this."

What could I do? Tension had ebbed. I was smiling. I was sinking into the couch.

The kid had stepped up, reached out, and plucked perfection from the sky. Michael Boulware. Former linebacker. Former human being. Ascension to godhood. Bless you.

Seattle takes the ball, has the lead. Shaun Alexander blocks, and there isn't a surer sign of triumph. Hasselbeck rolls right and finds Bobby Engram curling back to the ball. It's easy. Three easy. Not flashy or big, but productive. Enough to keep the Seahawks rolling. Alexander runs behind right guard, and though Mack Strong loses his block, Shaun coasts for an easy four. Easy. Easy.

It's third down. Third-and-manageable. Third-and-easy? Third down, nevertheless. Third down, and I am edging up, getting up, tensing up, standing up, and balling my fists. Seattle splits three wide, split backs. Pittsburgh is in a 3-3 with Troy Polamalu edged up, playing a hybrid linebacker/defensive back. Snap. Alexander throws a good block. All right. Strong runs left and quick curls. Reception. Turn, run, tackled over the marker. First—

But it's a bad spot! That's a bad spot. *That's a bad spot.* (It really was a bad spot.)

Seattle is short. A fraction of a ball's length, a third maybe, the space between the laces and the point, but short. Michaels and Madden are talking temptation, the temptation to go for it, but the need to punt. They mention momentum. Seattle has it, but would give it away if they couldn't convert. The Seahawks are on their own 26, and a failed conversion almost guarantees the Steelers a field goal. That's the lead, damn momentum, that's 21 minutes of winning football given up. So Holmgren makes the obvious call. The right call.

It really was a bad spot.

Tom Rouen of unfortunate name and coming infamy, kicks it low and short, and El, Antwaan Randle, fields it with bad intentions. Niko Koutouvides knocks him airborne, and a wave of blue bats him hard and into the ground like an Ichiro single. It's good, but it's not good. It's scary. All that smiling, and now I feel like a fool. Seattle barely touched it before giving it back, and the hard realization dawns that nothing is even half done.

It's Tatupu-Hill on the next two plays. Lofa hitting Willie Parker behind the line, and LeRoy finishing the job. Lofa smacking down the fullback and LeRoy knifing in for the tackle. Love these kids. Listen to me. Love 'em.

Steelers continue their customary strategy of run-first, pass if they must. Seattle has forced them into another third-and-long. Pittsburgh spreads four wide receivers tight, two on a side. The formation looks like wings or a crescent. Roethlisberger is in shotgun. Seattle responds with six defensive backs, Tatupu, and four down linemen.

Fisher pressures, and Seattle looks golden, but Ben evades and flips to a *wide-open Hines Ward*! Ward continues running toward the right sideline then redirects upfield for 12 before Marcus Trufant tracks him down. How was that? Where was that? How did that happen?! Replay shows Trufant getting picked on the left and Ward streaking free underneath. Tru recovers, but after the fact.

It's the Steelers' second third-down conversion of the game, but it feels like Armageddon. I'm gripping. I'm pissed. I'm scared again, and it can't be reasoned away. Parker runs for one. Wistrom raps from under the pile. Cedric Wilson exploits the seam and receives for 20 in front of Trufant. Roethlisberger pumps and delivers, but it tumbles harmlessly from Ward's fingertips. Catch, and it's a touchdown. Dropped. A funky screen pass to Bettis is brought back on offensive pass interference. The penalty du jour.

It's second-and-20, and I'd feel good but I don't. Wistrom, all eleven billion dollars of him, flies around left end and drops Ben for eight. It's third-and-28, and I'd feel confident but I don't. Pittsburgh empties the backfield. Seattle rushes three. Wistrom bends around left tackle Marvel Smith, clubs down Smith's arms, and flashes free before Ben steps up. That puts Smith smack in the middle. It's worrisome. It gets worse. Roethlisberger runs toward the left flat. Wistrom attempts to separate but falls on his face. Roethlisberger sees this and stops, plants, surveys, and fires toward Ward. Ward is running away from Boulware. He catches for 37. *He catches for 37!* The drive isn't alive, it's amuck. Steelers on the Seahawks' 3.

I collapse into a sit. The next two plays happen. I notice, but I don't. Seattle hasn't folded, but…

Kill the Ref

Seahawks fans would be less sensitive about spotty officiating if it had not become part of their team history. Super Bowl XL was not even the first time Seattle suffered a phantom touchdown scored by a quarterback.

Seattle was still in the 1998 playoff hunt. They were up 31–26 with 20 seconds to play against the Jets at the Meadowlands. The Seahawks had forced fourth-and-goal. That is when Vinny Testaverde ran a quarterback sneak that was stopped visibly short of the goal line. However, head linesman Earnie Frantz declared it a touchdown. Making matters worse, the crew then convened and, rather than overturn a categorically bogus call, confirmed the ruling. Seattle lost 32–31 and missed the playoffs by one game.

The play became an embarrassment for the NFL. Unlike XL, there was no ambiguity, replay showed Testaverde down well short of the goal line. The league responded by voting instant replay back into place, but the damage was already done for Seahawks fans and coach Dennis Erickson. Erickson was fired that off-season.

It's third-and-short, and I want to care so much I begin to again. It's third-and-short, but Seattle has stood tall, defended their end zone, recovered, and attacked. Bettis is in. I hate his face. I hate his beard. I hate his eyelashes. I hate "the Bus." I hate Detroit for birthing him. I want this play not to end with a stop, but a fatality.

Pitt plays three tight ends, two backs in an I formation. Seattle has five down linemen and three linebackers. It's smashmouth football. A battle of wills. And while I sit back, Seattle muscles up. It's third down, and I don't need to try to care. I can see the whole ballgame in this snap.

Ben takes the snap, motions pitch to Bettis, keeps. Bus flies forward and blocks out Tatupu; Roethlisberger leaps, stretches, falls. Short? The line judge runs up the goal line and suddenly, for no apparent reason, raises his arms: touchdown.

It can't believe it. It's reviewed. I don't see it. It's being reviewed. I don't see it break the plane; D.D. Lewis drives him back. I feel worried excitement. I don't know the right call. Does he break the plane? Can we know? Why the hell did Mark Perlman rule it a touchdown? Now it can't be overturned. It's not overturned. Touchdown. Play confirmed. I'm freaking out.

Seattle pieces together a miserable two-minute drill, and I'd be damned if I noticed a second of it. Didn't Darrell Jackson break the goal line before he stepped out? This isn't right. The pass-interference penalty from earlier that cost Seattle a touchdown seems sinister in retrospect. That was a huge swing. Why rule it then?

A drive happens. It's fractured and futile and flashes before my eyes, but not remembered. The Seahawks stall, needlessly burn clock, kick, miss the field goal.

It's halftime. That spot and those holds and that touchdown. Ford Field is caving in on us. I pass Alanya a look that says this isn't normal anger. This isn't consolable anger. This is stay-the-hell-away rage. I'm pacing. I'm plotting. I'm, I'm, I'm—

To be continued...

Chuck Knox

I had heard about Seattle's rain, its gray, its dreariness. I had read about it being so far from civilization that back in the 1800s businessmen on the East Coast would ship women out there by boat so the lumberjacks would have someone to talk to. It sounded like the perfect place to get my kind of job done.

—Chuck Knox

I admit, I find coaches to be the least interesting part of football. I not only do not hold most NFL coaches in particularly high regard, I think many are little more than meddlers who attempt to force a system on players often completely incompatible with that system. Many coaches are vengeful, cutting kickers after missing one crucial field goal. They have favorites and arbitrary standards for what is good football and what is not. They were raised on football, and that can give them a limited scope on life. Jack Patera was known to deny players water during practice, and that practice has since killed. Some overvalue practice and play clearly overmatched players because that play is assignment correct. They have doghouses, and their doghouses are built on sand.

Had I been cognizant during the tenure of Chuck Knox, I doubt I would have appreciated him very much. He favored running the ball at the very eve of the passing revolution. That earned him the name "Ground Chuck." I would have choked on those words. He was swaggering and opinionated and old-school fiery—which is to say he had a temper—and more than a little stuck in his ways.

Yeah, I'm the last person who should write an appropriately gold-tinged and fawning retrospective on Chuck Knox. But I must, and I'm sure Chuck would have none of my sniveling. Would he?

No, he would not. See, Chuck was Greatest Generation. He forged steel. His father was a steelworker and beat the hell out of his son. His father was an Irish immigrant with a drinking problem, and as Knox put it, "His pride put him in constant need of a fight to prove himself. But he didn't know who or how. So he fought me."

It was regular Horatio Alger bull, but real. And so it was dirty and fraught with lucky breaks and near misses. Chuck coached high school and built the Ellwood program. He became an assistant at Wake Forest and then Kentucky. He was hired to coach offensive line under Weeb Ewbank with the Jets, left New York in 1967, and missed his only chance to win a Super Bowl ring.

All that struggling and overcoming made him relatable. He had an ease and confidence found only in those who have consistently overcome. Knox was hard, but he cared. He did that most essential thing that any great coach must do, he motivated.

The AP named Knox Coach of the Year in 1973. He took a 6–7–1 team and turned it into an instant playoff contender. The Rams won 12 games in 1972 and finished in the playoffs every one of Knox's five years. Despite all that, he warred with owner Carroll Rosenbloom. Two strong men, two old football minds, destined to battle from the start. Knox took a million-dollar offer from Ralph Wilson and signed to coach the Bills.

Buffalo became a home. Chuck failed to turn around the Bills his first year as he had done with the Rams, but he did eventually. In his third year, Buffalo broke into the playoffs, and Knox won his second Coach of the Year.

Knox was successful, but he was never very popular with his bosses. Rosenbloom thought "Ground Chuck" was boring an unimaginative. Maybe he was right, but running reigned in the early '70s, and Knox brought the Rams unprecedented success. Just not a Super Bowl. Wilson thought he spent too much. No owner in NFL history has had tighter purse strings.

On the eve of his final year under contract with the Bills and at an impasse in negotiations, word found Seahawks general manager and interim head coach Mike McCormack that Knox wanted out of Buffalo. He opted out, signed with Seattle, and the rest, the rest is Seahawks history.

In his first season, and with Seattle closing in on a victory, the Seahawks began to edge the sideline, ready to run onto the field and celebrate. Knox was worried that if Seattle incurred a penalty for rushing the field, that the opponent would get another play. I'll let him tell the rest:

I screamed, "Get back! Get back!" I saw a huge body run past me, and out of instinct I turned and slugged him. It was Mike Tice, a tight end about a foot taller than me and 50 pounds heavier. I landed my punch directly in his gut. He doubled over. I looked up to see a couple pairs of eyes get like fried eggs. Everybody shut up and ran back. Once Tice caught his breath, he stumbled back, too.

"Coach," he said, gasping, "you almost knocked me out!"

"No, I didn't," I told him. "If I had wanted to knock you out, I would have used my right."

What makes me want to look back at this grizzled old survivor, loved by his players, relatable, successful, successful in Blue, and want to judge him? Want to discredit him? Modern arrogance, I guess.

Knox was wholly and beautifully of his time, and because of that, Ground Chuck and Hard Knox is exaggerated by some, and held up by others as some lost Golden Age. Truth is, Chuck was never the hardass so many wanted him to be.

One of his first moves upon signing with Seattle was to provide water for players during practice. Crazy, huh? That sounds less hard and more rational. He had what he called an "open door–closed door policy." His door was always open to anyone, and when that person entered, the door closed behind him. Not for some epic shout-off or act of intimidation, but to ensure privacy.

Knox was old-school, but not the caricature often portrayed. He feared heights. The press compared him to General Alexander Haig, continuing the worn but persistent football/war analogy. It's a stupid analogy. Knox wasn't compelling young men to die for the abstract concept of country. He was compelling rich young athletes to perform seven-on-seven drills. And he did so through a system of fines, not fear.

Knox removed contact from practice, instituted "thump" drills. He thought pitting his own team against itself only doubled the chance of injury. How practical; how rational. He embraced a style of football that reigned in the '70s, and as the complexion of football changed, his offenses became less potent. But he constructed a heck of a defense.

Knox was known for his clichés, and compared to Patera, he was warm and approachable. He had a TV show and a radio show. He made the hard decision to start Dave Krieg after Jim Zorn flat-lined. The two would never admit it, but I think they were kindred spirits in a way. Krieg started for Milton College. He went undrafted but stuck with Seattle. The school would close permanently before Krieg ever started. Two Midwest guys who took the long path to success.

Knox grew up in Sewickley, and he grew up poor. He was born into the kind of life sociologists deem a vicious circle: poor, beaten down, uneducated, and ready to give his children the same. Knox worked 19 years to become a head coach in the NFL, and I'm sure there were countless times a bad break or a bad decision could have derailed him.

He brought success to the Rams but was fired for being too conservative. He brought respectability to the Bills but couldn't squeeze out a new contract. He lucked into Seattle, and Seattle lucked into him. He finished out with the best winning percentage in franchise history, gave Seahawks fans a time to be proud, a time of hope and prosperity, and maybe Knox didn't win the right way—certainly not the modern way—but he won.

I can respect that.

9 Disintegration

Super Bowl XL. Ford Field, Detroit. Halftime…

I walk outside. Alanya hesitantly follows. She lights a cigarette. I don't smoke but take a couple nervous drags, anyway. I give her the lowdown. Somehow things crystallize in the retelling. It doesn't feel like Seattle is losing, but it sure feels like Seattle will lose.

I walk in. Steve Young says something about Seattle not getting the calls. It feeds an ugly, suspicious notion that is growing, branching out across my brain. I am starting to pace and then stopping. Starting long enough to know it's foolish, creepy. Stopping only long enough to feel compelled to begin again.

It's Steelers ball to start the half. Al Michaels mentions that Marquand Manuel is out for the game. Etric Pruitt is now Seattle's surviving free safety. This is bad.

Ben Roethlisberger takes a three-step drop and slings it toward Hines Ward running a curl in the right flat. It's underthrown, but Ward slides to get under. He drops it. Cool. It's a subtle reminder nothing is done, nothing is decided. Seattle is containing the run. Roethlisberger is struggling. The Seahawks offense has been inches away. Pittsburgh aligns three wide receivers left, tight end right in a peculiar unbalanced formation. Seattle counters with nickel. Before the snap, Ward motions right.

Things start to unravel in a hurry. Kendall Simmons and Max Starks blow back and turn Rocky Bernard. Starks pulls forward and engulfs Lofa Tatupu. From the left, Alan Faneca is pulling around and through the right hole. He pancakes LeRoy Hill. Seahawks are dropping fast, and Willie Parker is just entering the hole. Michael Boulware sprints from the third level but over-pursues left.

Oh. No.

Parker hits the hole. The right is cleared out. Pruitt attempts to fly over from the deep left, but he takes a bad angle. Parker, fast. Willie Parker jogs into the end zone. He doesn't look fast at all. I don't feel angry. Quite worse. I feel defeated. It's too decisive, too fast, and maybe it's the nicotine, but I feel light-headed. ABC shows replays, but there is not much too see. Everything breaks down. Bernard is bullied and turned, and then it's all giant offensive linemen engulfing spritely linebackers.

Seattle ball. Alexander juggles, drops. Morris receives. Mack Strong runs past Troy Polamalu for the first. Alexander breaks it wide for 21. Hannam, Engram blocking like champs. Seattle sets two wide, Jerramy Stevens tight right, I formation. Pittsburgh counters with a vanilla 3-4 look. Stevens angles right to avoid the jam and then streaks free up the seam. Hasselbeck motions play-action, plants, hits Stevens in the hands—*dropped!* No. *Nooo!* Dropped. Again. Dropped.

The line slides right, and Alexander runs straight past the exposed left edge. It's a good run. I don't care. It's a good run.

Pittsburgh sends the safety blitz, and Strong misreads, blocks left. Hasselbeck throws a desperation fade toward Darrell Jackson, but Jackson gets spun around, can never find the pass, and it drops into the right flat, incomplete.

Brown misses the field-goal attempt.

Steelers take the ball with good field position and proceed to begin to put the game away. Ben hits Ward for 15. Bus runs for six. Incomplete. Tatupu and Pruitt blitz, but Ben finds Ward springing free for 16. Ward pushes off Herndon so hard that Herndon is sent reeling backward. It's ugly and unfair and unflagged, but I'm flagging, and it doesn't feel outrageous so much as inevitable.

Bus runs opposite a blitz for 12. That's embarrassing. Bus dodges right for four. Pruitt is rah, rah, slapping his big gloved hands together. It stinks of overcompensation. Boulware pops through a blocker and hits Bettis for no gain. It's third down, baby. Third down. And I am not optimistic.

Pittsburgh calls a timeout, retakes the field in a confusing and unorthodox formation. *That's bad*, I think. It starts with two wide receivers right, a tight and slot back left, and a running back deep, but motions the back into the left flat. Empty backfield. Seattle is in a 4-2 nickel. Verron Haynes' motioning attracts Tatupu, and he follows him into the flat.

Snap.

Seattle collapses the pocket around Roethlisberger, and he lobs a floater right.

Herndon breaks underneath. Intercepts it! Intercepts it! Intercepts it! Sprints down the right flat. Looks free to the end zone. Has Blockers. Has Blockers. Bernard is to his right, but, but... Crap. Pulls up with a hamstring. Bryce Fisher is pacing Herndon and cuts in front to *throw Ben Roethlisberger to the turf*. But he cuts off Herndon, and the return is stopped.

So what?! I'm I'm—

Yes!!

HAHAHAHAHA.

Oh, my, oh, my God. *Yes!*

It's like, it's not over, and it's not won, but suddenly, it's not lost, either. Herndon, you glorious bastard. Andre Dyson goes down, and you show up like a mother.

Seahawks cornerback Kelly Herndon (31) intercepts an errant Ben Roethlisberger pass intended for Cedric Wilson near the goal line and runs it back for a big gain in Super Bowl XL.

Alexander cuts back left for four. Engram runs an angle route, but the ball eats him up and bounces away incomplete. Jackson runs a post, picks out Polamalu, and Hasselbeck throws a perfect touch pass even Stevens can catch. He hauls it in, cradles it in the end zone, *touchdown.*

We were on the brink. We were done. We were within seconds of falling behind 14, maybe 18. But Herndon and Hasselbeck, and now it's 14–10. I'm a little giddy and a little exhausted, and a little wary to celebrate.

To be continued…

10 Et Tu, Hutch?

We at Guard and Guard pride ourselves in the perfect production of perfect football guards. Our products match their time period and our buyers' needs without flaw.

In the era of barnstorming we made Walt Kiesling. He was big, indefatigable, tough, and master of such contemporary tools as the strike, wedge, and eye gouge. We used state-of-the-art pneumatics to power his punishing piles of pummeling punches. Powered his motor with leaded petrogasoline and set his chronometer to Swiss time.

For George Halas we produced our first and only biomechanical model, the Dan Fortman 5000. Forman had the fresh face, smarts, and underdog grit of an American GI, and as our brave soldiers fought trench to trench and island to island, Fortman fought in the trenches on an island.

We do not just build at Guard and Guard. We retrofit. Weeb Ewbank sent us Jim Parker in summer of '62, and we started right away dismantling his tackle machinery and refitting him for guard play. We installed an atomic hand punch, jet-powered uncoiling action, high-fidelity sonar, and a positive attitude toward authority.

We built Tom Mack tough and Russ Grimm technical. We built Larry Allen to giant proportions for Jimmy Johnson, and Johnson was so happy he had us build his entire offensive line. We built every great guard in American Football history, every enshrined guard and every Canton snub. We built each with only one goal, to make them better than any guard we had made before.

So when Mike Holmgren contacted us in the winter of 2001, we knew our challenge was very great. Holmgren wanted the build, breadth, and agility of the best tackles, but the tenacity and fight of the meanest centers. He needed feet and vision like a running back, but the gifted hands and coordination of a wide receiver. He needed the head of a quarterback and the heart of a fullback. He needed to be quicker, more agile, stronger, and more precise than any guard we had made before, and he was.

And he was Steve Hutchinson.

• • •

What a great way to remember Hutch. He was—is, too. Steve Hutchinson is one of the greatest offensive guards to ever play football. Wherever he's played, that team's running game took off. He blocked for the last years of Ricky Watters and helped make Shaun Alexander. He travelled to Minnesota and made Chester Taylor a name, before maybe making Adrian Peterson an all-time great. What a great way to remember Hutch, if only I could.

Hutchinson is undoubtedly one of the greatest Seahawks to ever live. It pains me to write that, as it surely pains most Seahawks fans to read it. Hutchinson is undoubtedly one of the greatest Seahawks to ever live. As I write this, he is a Viking. This time next year, he will have played more games in Purple than Blue. Hutch is a great player and a great villain.

Seattle acquired Hutch with the draft pick it acquired in the Matt Hasselbeck trade. It was a good day to be Mike Holmgren. It was a better day to be a Seahawks fan.

Guard is an atypical selection so early in the draft. Coaches see it as an inferior position to offensive tackle, but Hutchinson was a rare talent at guard. He started 45 games for Michigan State and is reported to have not allowed a sack in his final two seasons. Hutch was a strong pass protector, but it was his elegance and versatility at run-blocking that makes him so special.

He was great, everything I detailed above, now a seven-time Pro Bowl selection and a six-time first-team All-Pro. Hutch got away, and the blame can be spread. Tim Ruskell exposed him when he never should have. As blind as Holmgren could be to defense, Ruskell could be equally blind to the importance of offense. Arbiter Stephen Burbank betrayed the intent of the transition tag and defied the league by honoring the clause. The Vikings will forever be detested even if it's somewhat unclear exactly who designed the poison pill. It could have been Hutchinson's agent, Tom Condon. If it was his agent, he did it serving Hutch.

Steve Hutchinson wanted out of Seattle. Seattle had finished its most successful season in franchise history. He was paired with a legendary left tackle, Walter Jones, blocked for an MVP running back, Shaun Alexander, and played for a coach who appreciated him as much any coach could: Mike Holmgren. Hutchinson still wanted out, desperately. Whether he conceived the ploy or not, he approved of it, and accepted a lengthy and surely frustrating process that could have failed, because he did not want to be a Seahawk anymore. Seattle offered to match the contract, even restructured Jones' contract to negotiate the poison pill, but it didn't matter. If you believe in team and loyalty and that if a team wants you and is willing to do anything to succeed with you, you stick with them, then only one person truly deserves the blame for the loss of Steve Hutchinson: Steven Hutchinson. He did not want to be a Seahawk

Tobeck vs. Spencer

Robbie Tobeck is a revered player whom I did not include, because I did not know how to evaluate him. Tobeck was the center for the great 21st-century Seahawks offensive lines. He was always rewarded with glowing and unfalsifiable praise for his leadership and smarts. I could not help but think that almost any center could have led Walter Jones and Steve Hutchinson.

My major gripe is not with Tobeck, but rather the shadow he cast. Tobeck was 30 when he joined the Seahawks. Understandably, he was more experienced and better understood the game than young understudy Chris Spencer. However, fans did not question Spencer's knowledge or experience, but his intelligence. Tobeck is "cerebral." Spencer an "athlete." The translation: Tobeck is white and Spencer black.

That is not Robbie's fault. I think I would have included him on this list if his Seahawks career had been longer or if I ever truly believed he was that good. Tobeck was a journeyman who settled into a late-career prime. He was everything a good center should be: hard-working, nasty, and healthy. Having watched both, I think Spencer is already the better player.

anymore, and no matter what Ruskell missed, or Condon schemed, or Burbank decided, that is why Steve Hutchinson will enter the Hall of Fame a Viking.

Tez

The shortest path to the quarterback is a straight line. But that path is blocked. When that path is taken by Cortez Kennedy, it has to be double- and triple-blocked.

I could write this entire book about Tez, his dominance, how teams had to commit most of their offensive line just to stop him, and how he made even miserable surrounding talent look good. If you never saw him, imagine Albert Haynesworth—now make him healthy, now humble, now better. Much better. Imagine that, and

Cortez Kennedy, "Tez," became one of only three players to be named NFL Defensive Player of the Year while playing for a losing team, in 1992.

you will understand his parameters, if not the player. You will get just how incredible Tez was, but you will not be able to witness him.

Somehow I don't think Tez would appreciate a long, fawning expository breakdown of his career. He was all about the shortest path to effectiveness. He was all about efficiency and domination. Instead, let's just consider his inhuman 1992. That was the season that Cortez Kennedy won Defensive Player of the Year. Seattle finished 2–14. The offense was historically bad. It was starting a Stan

Gelbaugh, a Kelly Stouffer, and sometimes even a sentinel known as Dan McGwire. It was "Raiderized," and in early '90s lingo that meant crappy.

The Seahawks line was decrepit. Joe Nash and Jeff Bryant were both 32. Nash would struggle on for a few more seasons of mediocre play. Bryant was a year from retirement. On his right was Tony Woods. Woods was a run-of-the-mill, undistinguished end who stuck and stuck, but never did much. Kennedy was in the center, playing the one-tech. He was like a red giant in some cold, empty solar system.

Nash and Bryant were undersized artifacts from a formerly good defense. They were great players, but they were not the kind of talents that you imagine aging gracefully. Tez had 20 pounds on any of his linemates and was expected to anchor, give the interior ballast, substance.

The Seahawks were outscored 312–140. Game after game, the defense was battling against its own offense. The offense was last in yards, last in points, and last in first downs. That translated to short fields, clock-killing drives, and little rest between series. Any human defender couldn't hope to stand out on such a miserable team.

Tez did not stand out. No. He stood atop the corpse of the Seahawks offense and dominated. He had 14 sacks. Fourteen. He had a sack in 11 games. He sacked in blowout losses. He was unstoppable. Crazy enough, sacks were not even his game.

He was named the NFL Defensive Player of the Year. He became only the third player ever to win that honor on a losing team, and the other two, Reggie White and Lawrence Taylor, played for teams that were each only a game short of .500. The why is both simple and complex. Most basically, players on losing teams rarely get recognition. Whoever is actually the best, national awards are more about the most noteworthy. Pro Bowls and MVPs and Defensive Player of the Year are awarded to the best players among the best teams.

It wasn't just that, though. Defense depends on offense. Taylor played in close games. Only two were lost by eight points or more. He was able to get his 7.5 sacks because he faced quarterbacks who had incentive to risk a sack if it meant making a play. Not surprisingly, five of his 7.5 sacks came in games the Giants won.

Tez dominated against teams that had every reason to run, check down, or throw it away. The Seahawks were behind so often, for so long and without any hope of recovery, they actually faced the least number of passing attempts in the entire NFL. A team that couldn't create a drive with God's hand still somehow got off the field on defense.

Canton is obsessed with team achievements and statistics. It only sees Kennedy as a very good player who peaked early, but never played for a very good team. That is stupid. He was great, singularly and incredibly great. Kennedy was not just one of the greatest defensive tackles of his generation, he was one of the greatest defensive tackles to ever play. His 1992 is every bit the achievement of Peyton Manning's 2004, Jerry Rice's 1995, or Chris Johnson's 2009. He transcended his team. He deserves a transcendent honor.

12 The Modest Champion

Matt Hasselbeck always seemed a hair away from greatness. He could squat where legends lived. His Northwest pale complexion, nasally voice, and subtle jaw line gave him the look of a sidekick rather than a leading man. Brett Favre looks carved from marble. Hasselbeck has an oval face that wore frustration better than triumph.

Frustration followed him into his second season in Seattle. His uneven performance had lost him the starting position to Trent Dilfer. It must have been jarring to go from sixth-round pick buried behind Favre to quarterback of the future to Dilfer's backup in less than a year. There was pride in being Favre's backup. That position could describe almost any quarterback in the league. It had once described Mark Brunell, and Brunell became a Pro Bowl starter. There was pride in being a starter. A starter could fail, but he was always the man. Everyone on any football team anywhere knows their starting quarterback. He is the nucleus of the team. The leader.

There was no pride backing up Trent Dilfer. Even in his Super Bowl–winning season quarterbacking the Ravens, Dilfer earned titles like "game manager" and "worst starting quarterback to ever win the Super Bowl." It was not like Dilfer had arrested the position from Hasselbeck through eminent skill, either. Look at Football Outsiders DYAR rankings for 2001, and you will find Dilfer wedged between Ryan Leaf and Rob Johnson.

Leaf It Be

Seattle flirted with one of football's greatest busts when Mike Holmgren signed Ryan Leaf in 2002. Leaf was probably the most famous bust of our time. He was the loser in one of the great pre-draft quarterback controversies of all-time, when leading up to the 1998 draft pundits debated who had the better potential, Leaf or Peyton Manning. The funny thing is, most actually thought Leaf had the higher ceiling. Manning was the safe pick.

He not only busted and busted in the shadow of perhaps the greatest quarterback ever, but he did so publicly and embarrassingly. Holmgren signed him, thinking that with time to heal and the pressure off, Leaf could finally reach some of his potential. He attended Seahawks minicamp and was finally producing something he hadn't since his rookie year: good press. But just a few weeks later, Leaf called it quits. One has to wonder what Matt Hasselbeck thought about the signing.

Dilfer was at an age, and the Seahawks had the kind of surrounding talent that, had he been able to stay healthy, he could have taken the starting position and run away with it. What a horrible thought. Human frailty saved Seattle from human fear, and Mike Holmgren's plan to start the proven veteran ended temporarily when Dilfer sprained his MCL in the Seahawks' first preseason game. Hasselbeck did not win the position back. In fact, his preseason was lousy and plagued by the same problems that benched him the year before. He was not confident in Holmgren's system and could not execute it at game speed. Suddenly, Hasselbeck was not just being outplayed by Trent Dilfer, but every quarterback to don the blue. Aged Mark Rypien, Jeff Kelly, and Ryan Van Dyke had little trouble besting Hasselbeck's five interceptions and seven sacks in just 54 drop backs.

He carried that momentum into the season. Quarterback rating thought Hasselbeck was an All-Pro, but quarterback rating spits some funky opinions. He threw for 155 yards in 32 attempts, a very Dilfer performance, and after matching touchdowns in the first quarter, Oakland ran away with it the second. They built a 28–7 lead that Hasselbeck was powerless to overcome.

So it was back to the bench and back to backing up Dilfer in Week 2. Dilfer did what he always did: put up a palatable stat line while doing little to help his team win. Much to the shock of people who buy into garbage stats like quarterback record, the quarterback who never did anything to win, but won anyway, started losing. This is where I would like to write that Hasselbeck rode in on a horse named Destiny and finally seized the position from Dilfer.

Instead, Dilfer suffered a torn Achilles tendon and was placed on injured reserve. The infallible coaching hierarchy, determined by skill, unadulterated by favoritism or superstition, was again fixed through injury. This time, though, when Dilfer went down, Hasselbeck stepped up. The accuracy that had always enticed blended with confidence in the system, and everything Holmgren could have hoped for began to show itself. He was making quick decisions and trusting his arm.

Dilfer could have never led the 2005 Seahawks to the Super Bowl. Hasselbeck was probably the most irreplaceable part on that team—as a quarterback typically is. Alexander got the record and the MVP, and because of that, Steve Hutchinson and Walter Jones were finally recognized as the best guard and tackle playing in the NFL, but great running teams come and go. The Seahawks were a great team. They had the best offense in the NFL by DVOA, a balanced offense, but their passing game was more than twice as valuable per play than their run game.

It was not a great receiving corps. Joe Jurevicius was a thirty-something journeyman receiver. Much is made about Jerramy Stevens' talent, but his value was locked into his position rather than his play. When Seattle set with a tight end off right tackle, teams were forced to commit to the run or face certain failure. Stevens was often running free up the seam. If he had any kind of hands, he could have been a great receiver, but even in 2005 he was not anything close. I am not sure Seattle would have suffered too much if Stevens had been replaced with Ryan Hannam.

It was a mediocre group, truly. There was depth when Darrell Jackson was healthy, but Jackson was a No. 1 receiver in name only. It was a mediocre group that Hasselbeck breathed greatness into. All the struggles, the hard work, the failure and breaks, had turned him into a confident and adroit West Coast quarterback. He achieved greatness through his offense, if never independently of it. Eventually, even Holmgren began to trust him. Hasselbeck knew how to audible, and that made the Seahawks' offense even more deadly. He carried the team through the divisional round, when the run stalled and Alexander left with a concussion. He was his best in the NFC Championship. Hasselbeck was agile, decisive, and consistently, improbably accurate. If it wasn't greatness, if it wasn't immortality, it was the closest Matt Hasselbeck ever came.

13 The Improbable Legend

Dave Krieg broke from obscurity to hard-scrabble his way onto the Seahawks' roster and into starting. His college folded before he was named official starter. He was undrafted, one of many. Everything in his life resembled every snap Krieg ever took: an ordeal.

Krieg attended Milton. He was the seventh-string quarterback, which begs the question: what tiny college has the funding to keep seven quarterbacks? Apparently Milton was a prodigal bunch, because they closed down in 1982. Before they shuttered their doors, they gave the Seahawks one of their all-time great players.

He probably couldn't have been but a Seahawk or a Buccaneer. Milton was the kind of starting point that could obscure any talent, and the truth is, though he crafted himself into a good player, he was never that talented. Milton sent tape to Seattle, and the Seahawks were happy to improve upon stirring Sam Adkins.

His career started out predictably: Krieg stepped into an August 14, 1981, preseason game against the Cardinals, threw two touchdowns to put Seattle up 21–20, and then, when the Seahawks fell behind again, fumbled a snap from center to just about end it. Krieg could throw, and Krieg could scramble, but as often as not, he only scrambled himself into peril. He'd had one regular-season appearance in 1980, and before he ever completed a pass, he took a sack.

Krieg gave Seattle their first quarterback controversy when he started in place of an injured Jim Zorn. It was a typical quarterback controversy. Zorn was better, but Seattle won in two of Krieg's three starts. Fans loved the competition, and the media made it a regular story, but between Jim and Dave, it was a lot of hot air. There were pointed quotes. Then the offensive coordinator made the diplomatic claim that Krieg could "do anything Jim Zorn could do," and you know that inspired a few heated barroom debates.

He ended the season as the Seahawks' starter and did enough to fuel the controversy. Had I been alive at the time, I think I would have backed Zorn. He had accomplished more with less, and was still very much a young man. He had a meaningful advantage in adjusted net yards per attempt, and unlike Krieg and his small sample, did it against all opponents. Then again, Krieg did it against two top 10 defenses.

History would have proved me a fool, because the difference in ability would soon become glaring. The two would duke it out in the 1982 preseason, with Krieg winning. He started in Week 1 and Week 2 and took sacks like Rob Johnson in cement shoes. Fourteen

Dave Krieg, in action in a game against the L.A. Raiders in October 1984, beat out fan favorite Jim Zorn in 1982 and went on to pass for more than 26,000 yards and 195 touchdowns in his 12-year tenure with the Seahawks.

I Just Can't Quit Sacking You

The inimitable Pro-Football-Reference.com Blog (www.pro-football-reference.com/blog) is a great source for historical analysis and trivia. They looked through their game logs and created a list of the great all-time sack pairings. No, this is not Montana to Rice, but more like Bruce Smith to Ken O'Brien. Smith sacked O'Brien 17 times in his career.

Notable to Seahawks fans are both the players that most victimized Dave Krieg and the Seahawks that victimized others. Derrick Thomas sacked Krieg 15 times. Second to Thomas was Leslie O'Neal, who took down Krieg 14 times. O'Neal was also the scourge of Rick Mirer, and sacked the Golden Boy 10 times.

The Seahawks did a little damage themselves. The greatest pairing was Jacob Green and John Elway. Green took down Elway 13 times. That has to satisfy.

sacks in 74 attempts would be enough to convince most coaches to call for the hook, but Krieg wasn't benched. He was injured. An injured thumb put Zorn back into the fight. He responded by trading sacks for picks, and barely completing over 50 percent of his passes.

Everything started anew when Chuck Knox took over. He appointed Zorn the official No. 1 and put the controversy to rest. But where the controversy might have been fabricated in the past, it was real and vital in 1983. Zorn was suffering "quick-decision symptoms," which manifested as an inability to throw an accurate pass. His completion percentage was the worst of his career, and he was matching touchdown for interception. Eventually, Zorn burned every excuse, and his 4-for-16 showing against Oakland and then 1-for-8 start the next week against Pittsburgh ended his day and ended his starting career, respectively. Krieg did that thing coaches need a player to do before they can trust them: he won. He won five of the next eight and then led Seattle to their improbable playoff run.

After that, the controversy was over, and Krieg became the Seahawks' starting quarterback for good. He fought a perennial battle of improvising and attempting too much, which led to him taking sacks and losing fumbles, and forcing throws he couldn't make and giving up interceptions. Fans like to cite Krieg's quarterback rating: he finished at 81.5, ahead of contemporary John Elway, but ignore that quarterback rating does not count fumbles or sacks. Of course, Elway had many of the same problems. Compare the two, and only two things truly separate them, longevity and postseason success.

Was Dave Krieg a great quarterback? I watched enough archived footage to know he could be thrilling, precise, and tremendously effective, but also nerve-wracking. Seattle never surrounded him with much offensive talent, though. In 1994, three years after leaving Seattle and then with Detroit, he took over for an injured Scott Mitchell and had the best season of his career. Players don't peak at 36. Not even Dave Krieg. So what happened? Well, he went from Ground Chuck to Barry Sanders and Herman Moore. He had Lomas Brown protecting his blind side, which helped him keep his happy feet in check. The Lions got hot, and Krieg guided them into the playoffs. There they would meet Mike Holmgren's Packers and lose a nail-biter.

It makes you wonder. If Krieg arrived on a wave of hype, if he had surrounding talent as Joe Montana had, or a system that allowed him to distribute the ball instead of hand off and chuck, would he have made it? Would he have a plaque in Canton? By statistical measures, he was not so far, and he brought a level of competitiveness to Seattle never seen before, but he mostly went unrecognized. The sacks were a problem, and Krieg fed his blockers to the dogs far too often, but they weren't definitive. I guess it will just go down as another what-if. For a guy who did so much with so little, who accomplished so much from such modest roots, who was so good and yet waited years to even be honored by his own team, I imagine a little missed recognition is all in a life's work.

14 Mike Holmgren, GM

On balance, he succeeded almost as well an any Seahawks fan could hope. He lost battles but, with a little help, won the war. Mike Holmgren ended as Seattle's all-time leader in wins with 86, led Seattle to the playoffs in six seasons and five straight, and to this day, its only Super Bowl appearance.

It took a little while.

Holmgren replaced much disrespected head coach Dennis Erickson. Erickson was actually building something of a contender. His 1998 Seahawks had a better point differential than any of Holmgren's first four iterations. It had a talented defense that Holmgren dismantled. Erickson added Walter Jones and Shawn Springs. Holmgren added Lamar King. General manager Mike Holmgren was the first employee Seattle had to fire to become a contender again, but it took a lot of blunders to determine that.

As I mentioned, Holmgren headlined his first draft with Saginaw Valley State defensive end Lamar King. King was a big man. Draft experts projected him as a strong-side defensive end. Against a right-handed quarterback, typically the strong-side end is the lesser end. Pass rush is traded for presence. It is not an absolute. Reggie White spent most of his career attacking from the strong side. But it's typical, and White was atypical in almost every way.

King was never quite the bust he was made out to be. Exaggerated expectations and replacing a legend lost King and Holmgren the PR battle, but he had a not-terrible career for a 22nd overall pick. King started his second season but battled injuries. Those injuries never stopped and, like Brian Bosworth, eventually cost King his career. He left the league a young man. Holmgren had little to show for his first ever pick. It became a trend. If King was only a modest failure, the rest of Holmgren's draft made up the difference. The closest it came to producing a regular starter was Antonio Cochran, and Cochran was a fringe starter. His next draft was similarly thin. It produced two very good players, Shaun Alexander and Darrell Jackson, but no other starting-caliber talent. Alexander was selected along with Chris McIntosh, and McIntosh retired just three seasons later. Hardly a failure by Holmgren, McIntosh suffered recurring neck injuries that ended his career.

I could go on. Holmgren found some success, suffered some bad luck, made some blunders, and never was able to fill out a roster, but the problem wasn't that Holmgren was outstandingly incompetent, but that under Holmgren, the Seahawks' power structure was monolithic.

Consider Ahman Green. Green was selected by Erickson the season before Seattle hired Holmgren. Holmgren didn't like him. He had the stink of ex-coach on him. In 26 attempts in 1999, Green fumbled twice. As a head coach, Holmgren couldn't tolerate that. As a general manager, Holmgren should have been able to see through his own frustration. It was 26 attempts, so small a sample

Sawed-Off Shotgun

Mike Holmgren was always a very conservative coach. He did not like trick plays and rarely implemented them into the playbook. When Pittsburgh ran a reverse to Antwaan Randle El that ended in a touchdown pass, the play was a staple in their playbook and well-known enough that Madden hinted at it the drive earlier. Seattle seemed unprepared, and they probably were, because their own passing game never practiced it against them.

Perhaps more telling was his reluctance to implement the shotgun in Seattle's offense even as the formation became an essential part of the modern offense. In his final season in Seattle, he began dabbling in the semi-modern formation. As if to prove his reluctance, the Seahawks mostly snapped out of what is called the "pistol," a sort of half-shotgun, half-dropback.

it's hardly a sample at all. Holmgren couldn't see through it. He made snap judgments like a coach. That's bad business.

Holmgren was fed up with Green and wanted to cut the talented young back. He was talked into trading him for pennies on the dollar. When all was said and done, Holmgren traded away an All-Pro rusher for a second-string and soon-retired corner. He had too much power and too much responsibility; the power made him irrational, and the responsibility made him sloppy.

Could he have been an effective general manager if he was just a general manager? Maybe. That theory is being tested as I type this. Holmgren assumed the position of team president of the Cleveland Browns. He is inheriting a loser, but a talented loser, and though I didn't want him back in Seattle, I wish him the best in Cleveland. But Paul Allen wanted head coach Mike Holmgren, and general manager Mike Holmgren was a compromise and an experiment. It was a failure.

Seattle fell to 7–9 in 2002, and pressure mounted for general manager Mike Holmgren to step down or head coach Mike Holmgren to be fired. He assented, begrudgingly. Holmgren was never very happy with Bob Whitsitt. Goodwill born through Super Bowl XL was quickly burned through, and his relationship with Tim Ruskell was adversarial. I think he wanted to be the boss. Now he is, but somewhere else. Which is too bad, because if General Manager Mike Holmgren was failure, Head Coach Mike Holmgren was a smashing success.

15 Final

Super Bowl XL. Ford Field, Detroit. Late Third quarter…
Seattle forces a three-and-out sometime between my breaths.

Rocky Bernard is doubtful to return.

This stuff is important, but it's just flying by. The whole game is flying by. It's deep in the third, and I don't know whether I am anticipating or dreading the conclusion. I kind of want to close my eyes and look up and see Matt Hasselbeck hoisting the Lombardi.

Stevens drops another, and I'm done, just finished with Jerramy Stevens. It's his third drop of the game. Whatever it is that supposedly excited the Seahawks about Stevens, I am ready for it to excite another team. For all his potential, he's a sink, a cipher, an unfilled position on most plays.

The camera zooms on Alexander just in time for him to flinch violently, drawing the flag. Running back false start. That's keen. Hasselbeck overthrows Joe Jurevicius, and then Holmgren burns a play with a pass to Strong underneath. Punt.

John Madden says it's about time the Steelers run a gadget play, but they don't. Tats tips it away to put Pittsburgh in second-and-long. Roethlisberger scrambles, drops his throwing shoulder into D.D. Lewis, but is stopped short of the first down. Pressure, throw away, and then a punt. It's a tight game and a tight score, and every little play seems magnified because it is. No small error is okay. No missed opportunity, no broken concentration, no blown assignment is okay.

Peter Warrick does not field the punt, and it rolls deep, deep down to the Seahawks' 2.

Alexander powers up the middle for five. Matt runs play-action and then breaks free for the first. It's awesome. I love Matt Hasselbeck. It's stupendously, tremendously gutsy and smart and valuable because it gets Seattle out of jail.

Fresh downs on the 15. Hasselbeck rolls left and finds Hannam for three. Hannam for nine on the right. Alexander Duplo blocks, and James Farrior nearly fights right through him, but Hasselbeck is poised and precise and keeps the drive clicking. Then it's a perfectly timed pass to Engram that he curls, receives, and extends for 21. That should be the end of the quarter.

But it's not. Seattle attempts to squeeze in a play, and it looks lost from the start. Hasselbeck drops, lobs toward Jurevicius, and it floats incomplete as the clock expires. It never looks right. It looks panicked. The quarter ends.

Nose tackle Casey Hampton tracks down Alexander after five, and that just doesn't feel right. Third down. Seattle splits trips right, wide receiver left. Pittsburgh is in a 3-3 nickel. They blitz, but Mack Strong steps up and seals off the pressure. Hasselbeck looks left, center, left, and then finds Engram wide open on the right. He receives and sprints upfield for 17. Alexander runs for six. Alexander runs for five and the first. Sean Locklear is beat badly off the edge, but Hasselbeck steps forward and zings it to Stevens! Catch! Seahawks on the 1!

Penalty.

Flag, holding. It's not clear on the replay. Does he grab the pads? Does it matter? The penalty means everything. It's a 28-yard swing. From one to go for a touchdown to first-and-20 on the 29. My stomach is stirring, and a cinch is closing about my temples, and I'm cussing myself for caring so much, but cussing the NFL double. This isn't right. It's not even anger I feel now, but ganged up on, hated.

A play later, Hampton throws Robbie Tobeck down with one arm and sacks Hasselbeck. Mike Holmgren attempts to surprise with his never-surprising draw play, and Alexander puts Seattle in better position for a field goal.

Third down. Hasselbeck looks left, throws to where Ryan Hannam is supposed to be, isn't, but Ike Taylor is. Interception. Throws to where he thinks Hannam is supposed to be? Overthrows Jackson? Throws it directly at Ike Taylor for an easy interception. Hasselbeck runs left, throws a shoulder into Taylor, stopping the return, and it's flagged. Flagged—unjustifiably, incorrectly flagged.

Flagged…

…flagged.

What happens next? I don't know. Football.

• • •

…Roethlisberger pitches it to Haynes, Haynes hands it to Antwaan Randle El, and El zips it to Ward for the score.

• • •

…Hasselbeck scrambles, cuts in, fumbles! The ball is recovered by Pittsburgh. Of course, the ball is recovered by Pittsburgh. It's reviewed. We know which way this is going. Oh. Overturned. Golly, the semblance of fairness.

Drive falters, ends, dies, writhes, curses its God, and clutches it heart and extends its arms and legs and thrashes and then gets real stiff.

Steelers get the ball back and run a long, back-breaking, clock-control drive.

Punt.

Seattle needs to score to tie. Seattle needs a touchdown and a field goal. It's academic. Get in range, kick the field goal, and then pin your hopes on an onside kick. It's academic. Play the sidelines, control the clock, take your shots, and know you will probably lose, but that you can't beat yourself.

1:51 remaining—Hasselbeck finds Stevens over the middle for six. What the f—?

Between snaps, Darrell Jackson is nowhere, lost. Seattle sets, and Jackson runs long across the field, finally positions himself in the slot.

1:28—Hasselbeck finds Jurevicius dragging across the deep middle, he hits, bounces off Hope, twists, stumbles forward, and is tackled.

1:05—Throw away.

1:00—Hasselbeck scrambles left, stops before crossing the line of scrimmage, surveys, sees nothing, sees Mack Strong, tosses errant across his body. Strong looks bewildered. Strong looks unprepared. The ball falls incomplete.

:52—Hasselbeck throws it to…somebody. Seahawks are not finishing their routes. It's fourth down.

:47—Engram for 13. Run up, clock it.

:35—Spike.

:34—Hasselbeck throws into the right flat, and the bad decision is saved when Alexander characteristically cannot hang on.

:27—Hasselbeck finds Stevens in the right flat for three, and instead of diving to get out of bounds, Stevens attempts to break it upfield, before being wrapped and futilely laying out toward the sideline. The official swings his arm. The clock runs. Bill Cowher smiles.

:08—Hasselbeck targets Stevens just short of the goal line. Stevens drops the pass.

I find my girlfriend, look her in the eye, and swear to never watch football again.

16 Go a Week Without

This is not a suggestion, by the way.

Seattle was bad. Ugly, uncompetitive, old, injured, bad, and weeks, months out of the race. The Cowboys and Eagles were playing what amounted to a regular-season playoff. The winner won the NFC East and was in. The loser went home.

I live in the Portland area. Seahawks football is a given, I thought. I live in Washington. Seahawks football is a right of geography, I thought. My local Fox station disagreed.

I got Cowboys-Eagles. I got competitive, high-caliber playoff football, and I was out of my mind mad. I searched everywhere for a feed, but found nothing but jumpy, blurry, lagging garbage. I was without a car. I could not, could not watch my Seahawks. I was forced to watch competitive, high-caliber playoff football, and I was freaking out.

Seahawks football had become a constant. As surely as I could pour water from my tap and get light by flicking a switch, the Seahawks appeared 20 times (or more!) a year, and I was going to be there for every second of it. When that tap went dry and that switch flicked without effect, I realized I needed to see the Seahawks to live. I just couldn't, wouldn't stand a week without seeing even the absolute worst, most broken, and bad performance by my beloved team.

Maybe I am crazy. I encounter fans all the time who sacrifice Seahawks football to get out, shop, live, see chick flicks. Many more will never admit it, but they don't tune in until and unless the season turns out good.

Missing that day was an audit of my fandom. I could have enjoyed a competitive game, I guess. I could have turned the TV off and done something. But with something I wanted so bad torn away from me, denied me, I realized surely and truly then that every Sunday, until I die, when the Seahawks are on, I know where I want to be. I know were I need to be. I know where I will be.

The Seahawks are a great story. It has twists and turns and suspense and great characters I may never meet but nevertheless love. Losing even one game was like having pages torn out. Maybe Week 17 of the 2008 season was little more than an afterword on a tragedy already wrought, but losing that game was missing one final chance to be with that group of characters that I had followed and loved. Tragedy is compelling, victory is soaring, but each is as essential as the other. I did not want to lose a moment, a second, a sentence of the story.

Months later I found a copy of the game and sat down and watched Darryl Tapp and Brandon Mebane and Josh Wilson and drank a beer. It was something stolen, out of time, and stripped of context, returned. It couldn't matter less. I cherished it.

17 Paul Allen

Team owners are not known until they do something boneheaded or selfish. Jerry Jones, the old oil tycoon, is known for being his team's de facto chief executive. Unlike most, he's made it work. Al Davis is known now for his quotable press conferences, decrepit appearance, and string of bad decisions. Jones is surely selfish, but his passion is sincere, and he wants the Cowboys to be good as much or more than any fan. Davis tries, but it's likely the game has passed him by. His emphasis on height-weight-speed and tools like raw arm strength have become a tired punch line. Still, Jones and Davis are good owners, owners who love football and their team and exist within their community instead of exploiting it.

Other owners, like Bud Adams and Robert Irsay, are more notorious than known. Both squeezed their home cities, demanded civic support impossible for the depressed economies of Houston and Baltimore, respectively, and then, despite political concessions, moved their team anyway. For a sports fan, nothing burns like losing a franchise. No loss, no injury, not even the sulfurous smoke that surrounded XL, can possibly hurt like losing a franchise, because hope is the impulse that keeps a fan's heart beating, and no loss can kill hope, except loss of life. Men like Clay Bennett are killers. Like Elizabeth Bathory, they steal life from others thinking they can own it themselves.

Men like Paul Allen are not heroes but the compassionate common citizen—simple but given great means. They are more than philanthropists, because they do not simply give charity but breathe life into a city.

Allen was born in Seattle. Like a lot of us, that might not have seemed so important at the time, but it painted the rest of his life. He attended private school, befriended Bill Gates, and so forth. You can read about it almost anywhere. It's one of the great nerd-buddy romps of the latter 20th century. Kids meet, buy DOS, get wealthy, become despised, nevertheless become more wealthy, buy yachts, sports teams, museums, maybe pine for lost innocence, give money away, lose money, have others take pleasure in their steadily declining fortune, etc.

Allen stepped into the lives of Seahawks fans on the eve of the most important spring in team history. The Kingdome was crumbling, killing people, and though building a new stadium is never practical, fans knew it was new stadium or SoCal SeaBrahs. Seahawks owner Ken Behring was posturing. He had no connection to Seattle. He had moved Seahawks operations to Anaheim, California. He was big-game hunting and had an entire city in his sights.

The NFL forced Behring to move his operation back to Seattle and offer the team to a Seattle-area investor. In mid-April 1996 Allen bought an exclusive option to buy the Seahawks. The projected value of the team was $200 million, and a year later, Allen would pay just that to buy the team outright.

18 Emerging from Still Watters: The Rise of Shaun Alexander

It was too easy. It always was. Too fluid. Too easy. Effortless in the pejorative.

WTF, Shaun Alexander? You quittin' on us?

201 Yards in the Snow

One game that has always defied the neat picture of Shaun Alexander in decline is his 201-yard performance in Week 12 of 2006. It was a strange night in a lot of ways. It was the first time it ever snowed in Qwest Field. Alexander was returning from his foot injury, but he wasn't rested and ready. That would seem to be the knee-jerk thought: that maybe Alexander could play well as long as he could get an occasional break.

That seems dubious. He had rushed 17 times the week before and averaged 2.2 yards per rush. He should have been more rested then and, facing one of the league's worst run defenses, able to do whatever it is some thought he could do with fresh legs.

My guess is that the snow just slowed everyone down a little bit. He was still a better back in 2006 than he would become in 2007, and with a little slickness, a little loose footing, his vision and decision-making overcame his vanishing speed. It was not vintage Alexander. He needed 40 carries to top 200. And on a busted foot, I always thought it was reckless of Mike Holmgren to run Alexander so hard, but however I try to explain it, he really was good, and without that performance it is unlikely the Seahawks would have made the playoffs.

He jogged through the ACC, all grin and grace. Never looked muscular or pounding or even breakaway fast. He graduated out of the Combine. He was Alabama fast or Alabama strong or just God-given good at running the football.

He came into camp and outclassed the aged Ricky Watters. Watters was still flitting about the league, clinging here and there when a wise coach could be seduced. Holmgren got it. Guys like Watters who could receive and rush created scheme versatility. A yard rushing was worth a yard receiving. Alexander split touches. Watters wringed his once abundant talent. He produced. Alexander amazed.

How can a guy running so slow get down the field so fast? How can a guy who doesn't fight break so many arm tackles? How is a guy as gentle as Alexander ever going to intimidate a defense?

By smiling right into the end zone.

Mike Holmgren teased him in 2000. Alexander excited in the snaps he got. A start and 11 carries against K.C.: 74 yards, quality runs none longer than 17, but a fumble. Back to single-digit carries, young man. Dropped a 50 burger second go round against the Chiefs, but fumbled. Again. Back to the bench, kid. Maybe you can flash a little something in Week 17, it's been a long season: 8.4 yards per carry with none longer than 17, that's enough to warm Qwest on a drizzly winter day. Or start it shivering.

Shaun Alexander takes the ball and looks for a hole during a 28–24 victory over the Tennessee Titans at Nashville in December 2005. Alexander rushed for 1,880 yards and 27 TDs en route to an NFL MVP Award and Super Bowl XL.

Or shouting. Watters started in 2001. The promising rookie was waiting in the wings, and only Holmgren fully understood why. His heart sank when Watters was diagnosed with a cracked right shoulder. Watters was the steady vet who kept Seattle afloat. Seattle was still sinking fast. Watters' injury was another terrible blow to a team that squeaked out a victory in Week 1 and then was blown out in the following two weeks.

Holmgren should have been singing, but coaches are a stubborn lot. Alexander took his first start of the season and second start overall and rushed for 176 yards and two touchdowns. One hundred seventy-six yards! *Seattle won! Boom!* One hundred forty-two in the next game. Then a downer: 87, 60. Loss, loss.

If Watters could start, maybe he should. The kid showed some magic, but teams were catching on.

266!

Yards!

And not just against some so-and-so, but against the playoff-bound Oakland Raiders. The second-to-last playoff-bound Oakland Raiders team before Al Davis' death.* It was the fourth-highest rushing total ever, only behind Corey Dillon (ahem), Walter Payton! and O.J. Simpson!

Alexander didn't have the bruising style of Sweetness or the slashing style of the Glove, but he did have that effortless grace, knack for cutback lanes, and blinding smile. He was his own rusher. The very first Shaun Alexander.

So, after all that, and even with some dwindling production and Watters' return to health, it took some kind of stones for Holmgren to start Watters in Week 14. We're told coaches are paid to make the hard decisions, but how often do they really just make the easy decisions hard to swallow? Seattle won easily against an inept Cowboys team, a team led by none other than Quincy Carter, but it certainly wasn't starting Watters that did it. Watters didn't

---

*Just a hunch.

somehow force Carter into completing 14 of 33 passes for 135 yards and a pick. He didn't shut down Emmitt Smith or sack Carter four times. No, he ran for a 104 yards on 28 carries. Watters finished his day and his career with a broken ankle in the fourth.

Shaun Alexander never fought to start in Seattle again.

19 Curt Warner and the Vanishing Breed of Dominant Backs

What can you say about Curt Warner that you can't say about a Mack Truck? Warner don't run outta diesel.

Warner hails from a dying era of back. Backs who weren't zone-blocking backs, or scat backs, or even feature backs, but backs who were the physical embodiment of pounding the rock. Who took the ball and then, with whatever peculiar blend of freakish athleticism, strength, quickness, agility, or speed they had, humiliated the grown men around them.

He did all sorts of things wrong. Technically wrong. He carried the football like a mugger carries a purse. He initiated contact without incentive of extra yards. That cost him. He missed his second season with an ACL tear. He had an unusually short career, just five seasons as a feature back; short even for a short-lived position. And when he went out, his era of back sort of went out with him—guys like Payton, Campbell, and Brown. Men who could physically dominate their peers but still outrun them. Guys who could break a tackle by breaking the tackler. Warner could man-slap 32-year-old Woodrow Lowe without losing balance. Cut. Go.

Shaun Alexander has the numbers, but Warner was likely the best back in Seahawks history. The kind of back you build an offense on. The kind of back, when he's on, you hand the ball to

Curt Warner tries to beat a defender to the corner during a 34–21 Seahawks victory over the L.A. Raiders at Memorial Coliseum in October 1983, Warner's sensational rookie season.

and marvel. The kind of back who makes Ground Chuck appetizing. Warner could best good run defenses and abuse bad ones.

In his rookie season, Seattle rode Warner right to the AFC Championship Game. In the divisional round, he dropped 99 on Denver in a blowout win over the Donkeys. Notched 113 against the Dolphins the next week and scored the game-winning touchdown. When Warner lost his mojo in the Black Hole, gaining only 26 on 11 carries, Seattle's offense followed. The Seahawks were down by 20 at halftime and were blown out by the eventual Super Bowl–champion L.A. Raiders. It didn't turn out to be the worst thing Tom Flores ever did to the Seahawks.

All that pounding added up, and Warner popped his ACL in the first week of the 1984 season. You can replace the tendon, but you can't ensure the player returns the same. Warner was so good, it can be easy to ignore what he lost. He did lose something though, a little agility maybe, a little glide. Something.

He returned and earned three more thousand-yard seasons. In another, he fell 15 yards short after missing three games. Good had replaced great. The numbers, yeah, the numbers were there. Warner could stumble into the numbers even at his most ground down and beat up. The production was gone, though. Warner was a shadow of himself by 1989 and lost from the league partway into 1990.

So it goes.

20 Aftermath

Super Bowl XL. Final: Steelers 21, Seahawks 10.

I swore off football forever. My fandom flagged. A season of ecstasy punctuated by 15 exclamation points killed one penalty at a time. I held my head, wanted to yell. Probably did. Surely yelled. I

Win Probability: 0

A minute and a half into the fourth quarter, a six-yard run by Shaun Alexander pushed Seattle's win probability in Super Bowl XL over 50 percent for the first time since the second quarter. They would maintain that slight advantage for about 30 seconds of game clock. Sean Locklear's hold knocked them down to 44 percent. Casey Hampton's sack pushed them down to 38 percent. It was the interception by Ike Taylor that really killed them.

It is not a surprise. Seattle was well within field-goal range and still had some small chance at scoring a touchdown. The interception cost them three points if we assume Brown would have been able to kick the field goal. It cost them field position, especially following the bogus low-block call on Matt Hasselbeck. It just about cost them the game. In barely more than two minutes of game clock, the Seahawks' chances of winning Super Bowl XL plunged from 55 to 14 percent.

stood, wanted to punch something, kick something, destroy something, looked about my future in-laws' house, sat back down, held my head. Outrage became heartburn became heavy legs became defeat. My hopes flagged.

Half of all Super Bowl teams lose. Perceptive little factoid there, huh? And when it's over, it's tempting to wish it never happened. Why feel so good only to feel so, so bad? There are blowouts and grinders, games that were closer than the score, comebacks, failed comebacks, and historic comebacks. A kid named Namath once promised the whole shebang. Got himself enshrined with that moxie.

Blow a team out and, however anticlimactic, there's something about it that sings to a man's soul. Any team can win a Super Bowl, but embarrassing your opponent is like cuckolding your boss. It's triumph with icing. Dust off that jersey and wear it out, because for a few months you're not just king, you're destroyer. You hate me, but you fear me more.

Getting blown out births perspective. Maybe it was just worth it to get there. Team never had a shot, anyway. Maybe it was all just a dream awaiting interruption, but a sweet dream; a sweet few months of stolen bliss. Can't complain about achieving so much with so little, right, pal?

Grind it out and win the way your elders want. Maybe it's morbidly bad football, 11 minutes of action deactivated. All pile-ups and dropped passes and timely penalties and lucky breaks, but whichever way your team lands, it was manly football, unadulterated by flash, bang, whiz, touchdown! Touchdown! Touchdown!

Make a comeback and win without winning—or win! The Titans were thwarted at the 1, and however much that stung, and I'm sure it stung like Tabasco on a scratched cornea, the savor lasted long after the finish. That's a team that fought every damn down and nearly hustled their way past a better opponent. Builds character or some such nonsense. Rams won, but Titans earned respect.

Or you can watch your team stripped of glory, one yellow blur at a time. No one wants to complain here, no one wants to be sour, but, damn it, I was sour. I was complaining. I was pissed. I didn't want apologies; I wanted conspirators. I wasn't looking for explanations; I was looking for mortal rage, the kind that topples governments and burns buildings.

So that was XL, the aftermath, as known by one fan, but what about XL the game? Was it all ugly penalties and Steelers standing around the Lombardi Trophy? Was there never hope, never a thing worth watching, nothing but dross, nothing but loss?

No. No. No, no, no, nononono—can't let my bitterness blind me. It was indeed sweet for a series, a quarter. Right? Maybe. Right? I needed to know, so I rewatched it, second by second, gut out of it, cognizant of the outcome, with new eyes maybe, right?

Right. It was not savory, but it was not fixed. Seattle did not win, and they were in fact beat. They fought hard, though. They very well may have been the better team. It was a great game, dramatic, and the Steelers did not pull away until the very end. It was better seeing the Seahawks lose again, but I could finally see the loss was bitter, but not the game. The game was epic.

21 AFC West

The Seahawks were born into the NFC, but grew up in the AFC. Older fans still harbor rivalry between the Seahawks and the existing AFC West, while many younger fans see the division as alien as the NFC North. I straddle the line somewhat. I know and loathe the NFC West, but I understand still-lingering enmity for the AFC West. It might not matter anymore, the way that Arrowhead rocked, or how it became dead quiet thanks to Marty Ball; Dan Fouts, Don Coryell, and the true West Coast offense; the Black Hole; Elway, but it matters as history, as roots, as part of being a complete Seahawks fan.

The American Football Conference was comprised primarily of the remnants of the AFL. The history of the American Football League is complex and cool and better left to another writer, but noteworthy to Seahawks fans because its original rivals were all AFL originals. The Los Angeles Chargers became the San Diego Chargers. The Oakland Raiders emerged after the Minnesota Vikings joined the NFL. The Dallas Texans became the Kansas City Chiefs, the AFL's most successful franchise. Denver were Donkeys all the way back to their foal days.

The Seahawks began life in the NFC but switched in their second season. The NFL wanted the Seahawks and Buccaneers to play each other twice, and each of the other teams in the NFL once. So they did. As it turned out, the Bucs ended Seattle's losing streak at five. Tampa would lose its first 26 games.

Seattle faced its first division opponent in Week 3 of the 1977 season and lost 24–13 to the Broncos. Oakland smacked Seattle around in Week 8, and San Diego edged the Seahawks in Week 11.

Seattle finally beat a division rival when they clipped the Chiefs at Arrowhead. Kansas City finished 2–12, but I am sure losing to the expansion Seahawks hurt extra.

It was a trend. From the time the Seahawks joined the NFL to the time Marty Schottenheimer took over in Kansas City, the Chiefs had two winning seasons and one playoff appearance. They were blown out by the Jets in the 1986 wild-card round. The Seahawks never developed a very strong rivalry with Kansas City. It was a token rivalry, but 13 years of bad football and losing took the piss out of it.

Oakland was different. The Raiders were good, very good. They were closer geographically, and years of winning had created pockets of Raiders fans in Seahawks country. Had Oakland and later L.A. smacked around and demolished Seattle, it wouldn't be a rivalry, but the oppressed meekly cursing the oppressor. It wasn't that, though. It was good football, meaningful football, and for years.

Oakland crushed Seattle in 1977. The Seahawks lost by 37 points. Seattle then won the next four games. Seattle finished 9–7 both seasons on the strength of those victories; and those losses kept Oakland out of the playoffs. The Raiders would win the next five, but three were within a touchdown. The losing is what mattered, and although it was exciting football, in the end it was just another loss. Seattle was fading, and Oakland was emerging, and the young rivalry seemed destined for obsolescence.

Then came Chuck Knox and 1983.

The Raiders had moved to Los Angeles prior to the 1982 season. Al Davis was turning heel. He had lobbied unsuccessfully for luxury boxes to be added to the Oakland Coliseum and responded by signing an agreement with the owners of the L.A. Coliseum. The move went to an NFL owners' vote, and needing three-quarters approval, Davis got none. The relocation was defeated 22–0. Davis filed an antitrust suit, spent eight days on the stand, had his character run through the media wringer, won anyway, packed up, and moved the Raiders to L.A.

Seattle was suddenly not just fighting a division rival, but against the forces of evil. During the trial, the prosecution presented an interview with Davis in which he revealed his boyhood fascination with Adolf Hitler. It was later disallowed, but the damage to his character was done.

Knox put an end to rebuilding. He decided whatever had been built previously probably wasn't worth building again. Seattle started hot but fell to 3–3 after a close loss in San Diego. Being at .500 has a nervous feeling to it. You're one step away from Heaven or Hell.

Seattle next faced the 5–1 L.A. Raiders at the Kingdome. Jim Zorn was still starting. He had been underappreciated for his success on a piecemeal offense. He was falling apart at the seams. Steve Largent was out with a knee injury. The Seahawks netted two passing yards. Two, on 16 attempts. Two, 13 yards forward, 11 back on a sack. Two—2—two yards passing, and only 153 total.

But won.

Seattle's defense scorched L.A. for eight sacks, six fumbles forced, five recovered, and three interceptions. Paul Johns returned a punt for a touchdown. Zorn scrambled for a score. Curt Warner rushed for a score and Dan Doornink another, and Seattle, improbably, impossibly, won, beating the Raiders 38–36. They beat the Raiders again two weeks later.

Seattle squeaked into the playoffs, made a surprise run, and met the Raiders in the AFC Championship Game. The Seahawks' rivalry with the Broncos revolved around John Elway. Horseface deserves and gets his own essay.

I never detected strong rivalry between Seattle and San Diego. The two teams never managed to be good in the same season. The Seahawks were building a loser when Don Coryell turned the Chargers into the most exciting offense in the NFL. Seattle was respectable in the '80s, but the Chargers became mediocre—too good to laugh off, but never good enough to make a rival. Seattle was sifting through the rubble of rebuilding when the Chargers rebounded briefly under Bobby Ross, and once Ross was forced out and San Diego was back to seasonally hiring and firing coaches, Seattle was getting good again.

Seattle's two lasting AFC West rivals were Oakland and Denver. Oakland was the scheming, cutthroat spawn of overlord Al Davis, good rivals to any club, but especially the Seahawks. Denver was the pious sons of John, and equally revolting in their own way. Elway backers evangelized the West and suffered no heretic, so it was always kind of special seeing Denver be just good enough to get blown out in the Super Bowl. Rivalries, they lose currency over time, and nowadays most Seahawks fans think little about Davis or Elway or the drama of travelling to Mile High or the Black Hole, but they never lose importance, and for every Seahawks fan, there should be some vestigial bile somewhere deep inside that still burns for the Broncos and Raiders and Chiefs and Char—well, maybe not the Chargers.

22 Shaun Alexander, Middle Years

Alexander finally fought his way into starting. Wait, no, that's incorrect. Ricky Watters busted up his ankle and was placed on injured reserve. He happened to be an unrestricted free agent. Lucky us. I know it angers some when common sense is applied to the arcane decision-making of coaches—NFL coaches are next only to doctors and admirals in never having their decisions questioned no matter how foolish, but coaches should be questioned. Unchecked power is an evil without qualification.

Shaun angered some with his breezy running style, bad hands, and unwillingness to block. The middle years for Shaun Alexander were all about good stats, great running, and a lot of bad football between his touches. It wasn't very popular to question Seattle's young superstar. He was good-natured and sweet. He was active in the community and the team's only real face. Never mind he was the team's third-best player and fourth-most important. Never mind that his backup, Maurice Morris, and fullback, Mack Strong, bested him as a receiver and bested his yards per carry. He was Smilin' Shaun Alexander!

That is how the middle years go. The young stud had settled in, and as the prestige of youth and novelty wash off, the familiarity-bred contempt settled in. His play bristled some, his running frustrated others, his personality could grate, and in that oh-so-modern way, his religiosity was just too much.

The thrown ball bemused him. Holmgren wanted a dual threat. What he got was a reluctant receiver who wasn't so much bad at receiving as disinclined to bother. He was targeted a ton but never did much with it, and by his third season starting, the targets started to vanish, too. Alexander never threw more than a perfunctory block. Football fans want blood, but Shaun was content to play.

That bled into his rushing style. Alexander was not a power rusher, and he didn't bust through blockers. At its heart, football is entertainment, and the polite-acquiescence out of bounds can never replace the *crack* of bodies smashing with the force of a car crash. Of course, football fans don't have to wake up Monday morning with that beat-by-a-tire-iron feeling, either.

Alexander was someone who would tell you about his humility. Or so it felt. Who wore his achievement and good deeds on his sleeve and made those achievements and good deeds reflect poorly on him.

He believed in predestination, and for good reason. Predestination tends to be controversial when applied to children born with HIV, but wears like an expensive suit on millionaire professional athletes. When his career began to sag, Alexander

Hitting the Wall

The reason most could not tell that much had changed in Shaun Alexander is that the skill Alexander had lost is almost imperceptible to the human eye. As Chuck Knox recognized in 1984, it doesn't take much lost quickness before a running back is too slow to reach a hole. Franco Harris was constantly hitting a pile, and rather than fire the offensive line, the Seahawks decided to fire Franco.

That is exactly what plagued Alexander. He was never the fastest rusher, but he was quick and lived off his initial burst. He had lost enough by 2006 that he couldn't reach the hole before it was already closing around him. Or, too often when he could get himself into the hole, he would attempt to cutback as he always had, and his burst just wouldn't let him. He would be tackled in the pile.

Running backs can run 40 yards in under five seconds. They run the five yards it takes to get to a hole in less than a single second. Alex had lost literally fractions of a second, but those fractions were enough to take a man from the pinnacle of success to complete failure. He is far from alone, though. Every year another rusher hits that wall, and the vital speed/quickness that made them a professional abandons them.

attempted to treat an untreatable broken bone in his foot with prayer and was convinced it would work. It didn't.

Of course it was all nonsense—a portrait of a man through a media filter that changed as its audience did. The bad brushed to the side when Alexander was contending for rushing titles and scoring touchdowns in bunches. We want to know the ins and outs of heroes until they're not heroes anymore. Without reason but prominence and exposure, Alexander was a role model. You too could be Shaun Alexander if you work hard, thank God, and win the genetic lottery.

Alexander did his best in the way he thought best and achieved more in his field than most ever will. He made three straight Pro Bowl appearances, was named All-Pro in 2005, won the league MVP that same year, and tied the single-season record for rushing touchdowns (before LaDanian Tomlinson broke it the next year). Critiquing how he rushed is akin to chastising Pablo Picasso for abstraction. It was beautiful. It just was. It was a time of pride and glory for Seahawks fans, Mack Strong, Walter Jones, Steve Hutchinson, Robbie Tobeck, Chris Gray, Sean Locklear, and Mike Holmgren. We all fed a little bit off what Shaun could do. We all drank in his talent and pumped our fists when he scored and scored and scored.

It was the middle years, the glory years, the years Alexander was so great fans could take him for granted. It ended like fireworks: all fire and ash.

23 The Hidden Zorn

The history of a football team is the history of its players, and the Seattle Seahawks' quarterback history started slinging the ball backward. The sixth Ring of Honor inductee in franchise history was a lefty; his chemistry with the first Ring of Honor inductee, Steve Largent, downright sinister.

Jim Zorn is lost in a nostalgic fog. Seventies-era Seahawks fans might have missed Zorn's excellence. Modern fans see his stats and figure he was a placeholder. He was neither a loser nor a placeholder but arguably the second-best quarterback in team history—arguably, the best. He didn't have Dave Krieg's longevity, but he didn't fumble like fumbling scored points, either. He didn't have Matt Hasselbeck's success, but he didn't line up behind Walter Jones and Steve Hutchinson, either.

No, Zorn was thrown to the wolves. Expansion franchises chew up and spit out quarterbacks like they chew up and spit out head coaches. The two represent the face of the franchise, and when the franchise loses, fans want to punch that face in the face. Tampa started with Steve Spurrier. He retired after one season. Then they tried Gary Huff. Huff was a Chicago quarterback. Carolina turned

The Seahawks' first star, Jim Zorn, looks downfield during the franchise's first regular-season win, a 13–10 whuppin' of their expansion counterparts from the NFC, the hapless Buccaneers, on October 17, 1976, at Tampa Stadium.

to rookie Kerry Collins. Collins turned to the bottle. Houston selected David Carr first overall. Carr left a few million neurons on the football field.

Zorn was like Mark Brunell. Brunell didn't have a great arm, wasn't prototypical, and didn't ride into Jacksonville on a wave of hype. He wasn't even supposed to be the starter. The Jaguars' first overall pick in the expansion draft, Steve Beuerlein, was supposed to take the fall. He was experienced at that. Cornelius Bennett once sacked Beuerlein so hard it was immortalized in a painting. He was destined to be an expansion quarterback.

Brunell was built to succeed on an expansion team. He was smart and mobile and won in ways that chagrinned as much as defeated his opponents. He wasn't a pure pocket passer but wasn't a scrambler, either. Brunell was an opportunist.

Zorn was that, but better. His career, shorter, but his peak, higher. What is commonly misunderstood about Zorn is that his career began in one of the most hostile periods for passing in NFL history. Before the 1978 season, something commonly referred to as the "Mel Blount rule" was passed. Blount is a Hall of Fame cornerback who played for the (hated) Steelers. He was known for his extremely physical style. The rule commonly bearing his name banned defenders from contacting receivers after five yards past the line of scrimmage. It remade the league.

By efficiency, using the Hidden Game of Football standard, a statistic that includes net yards lost on sacks, rewards touchdowns, and debits interceptions, 1977 was the worst season in post-merger history for throwing the ball. Teams averaged only 4.7 adjusted yards per attempt. In other words, it was a league full of Rick Mirers. From there, efficiency rose dramatically, through the '80s, '90s, and on through the modern game. Teams now average roughly 6.5 adjusted yards per attempt. From his second year through his fourth, and again in his sixth, Zorn performed well above league average. And unlike Krieg or Hasselbeck, he did it despite little surrounding talent.

He did it with bootlegs and smart scrambles, and that essential expansion quarterback ability, toughness. He did it with trick plays and outlet passes, and a brotherly bond with Largent. He did it with resolve and canny, abilities that made him a great quarterbacks coach two decades later. He did it ugly, but he did it, and left it all on the field. Zorn fought like 10 devils and had nothing to show for it but the victory. He piloted Seattle's first two winning seasons. It aged him. He was fading fast by his late twenties. Zorn brought respectable football to Seattle, and when the Seahawks franchise was ready to catch up and make a run of its own, Zorn had to step aside because he had given all he could give.

24 Zero

Zero was not recognized as a number for most of human history. Early civilizations understood zero—"void" or "null"— as a placeholder, but not as a number. It was first recognized as a number by the Indian mathematician Brahmagupta. Before then, one would never count zero. How could one count to zero?

One *could* count down to zero. But what number to start with?

566: Walter Jones starts opposite rookie Will Smith. The first-round pick would eventually establish himself as one of the best players on the Saints' first Super Bowl–winning club, but on this day, he's just an overmatched kid. Jones slaps him around, locks him down, and blows him up. Matt Hasselbeck stands tall, but his Seahawks are shut down. 565, 564…

537: Jones faces off against one of the greatest defensive ends of his generation, Simeon Rice. Rice had 30.5 sacks over the past two seasons, appearing in the Pro Bowl both years. In Super Bowl XXXVII he sacked Rich Gannon twice and helped harass him into five interceptions, en route to a blowout win for the Bucs. A surefire candidate for Canton, shut down by Walter Jones. Jones holds the edge and provides blind-side protection when no other protection can be found. Hasselbeck is sacked five times, but not once by Rice. Rice cannot even record a tackle.

506: The Seahawks return home against the collapsing 49ers. Jones smacks around Brandon Whiting. Two games later, Whiting plays his last game in the NFL. Ever wonder why 49ers fans hate Terrell Owens? Whiting and a fifth-round pick was their prize for trading one of the best wide receivers in football.

The Seahawks embark on a bye week. I envision Jones following around Hasselbeck, pancaking solicitors, drive-blocking WashPIRG members into nearby WashPIRG members and generally creeping out Sarah Hasselbeck and terrifying Mallory and Annabelle. The quest for nullification is an unyielding task.

473: Next came the hated Rams, Seattle's first NFC West rival. The Rams had been great but were fading. The Greatest Show had turf burn. Marshall Faulk was in his twilight. Marc Bulger had replaced Kurt Warner. It seemed like a shrewd move for a season, but time was testing that theory, and fast. Jones squared off against future Seahawks hired gun Bryce Fisher. Fisher was a low-profile guy but entering his prime. He would have 8.5 sacks that season and another nine for the 2005 Seahawks. He would get shut down that day. Jones would mirror his every movement and trade clubs with counterpunches. Seattle couldn't win that day but started out like a contender. The Seahawks led 27–10 in the fourth quarter, but a defensive collapse sent it into overtime. Seattle lost but won the division. They were beginning their run of dominance behind a tackle who could block out the sun.

437: To Foxboro and to face the reigning and future Super Bowl–champion Patriots. Jones faced a young Richard Seymour. Seymour was in his prime. His mix of size and athleticism was special, and Seymour was one of many irreplaceable parts in the Patriots dynasty. He could fight through two offensive linemen and still challenge plays in the backfield. Seymour was a star. Walter Jones more anonymous than known. The *Boston Globe* asked Seymour what separated Jones from other tackles, and he said with a smile, "Their contracts." Two tackles and zero sacks later, maybe he would revise that estimate. New England won, their 20th consecutive victory, but Seattle fought hard, fought against a 17-point deficit and within three by the fourth quarter, and scared the Patriots. Scared them, and as for Jones, gave their brash superstar something to remember.

384: Seattle had traveled to Patrician New England and fought hard against the Patriots but lost. They were 3–2 but had the mix of high highs and moderate lows of a developing contender. Two thousand four was a tease. The Seahawks were developing something special, but as quickly as they could excite, they would crush your spirit. The Arizona Cardinals were not good. They were bad, very bad, and without their best player, Anquan Boldin. Seattle should have exploded into Sun Devil Stadium and left only atomic shadows in their wake. Walter Jones did, batting around right defensive end Peppi Zellner as a lion would a shrew, and sending another veteran end to his premature retirement. Zellner never played another down after the 2004 season. But Seattle was awful. Matt Hasselbeck was gruesome. Maybe the recent signing of Jerry Rice gave him the yips. He completed 14 passes in 41 attempts and threw for four interceptions. Seattle lost, fell to 3–3, and everyone was just a little worried about Hasselbeck.

342: Seattle picked themselves up, traveled home, and talked themselves into bringing their best against the 1–5 Carolina Panthers. The Panthers were "better than their record," a victim of the "Super Bowl losers' curse," who "had to be taken seriously" and "couldn't be underestimated." The Panthers were, eventually, a good team again. In late October they were still reeling from the loss of Steve Smith. Jones was matched against a fading Mike Rucker. Rucker had been a Pro Bowler in 2003, but at 29 was already losing a vital step. He peaked at 12 sacks in 2003, but had just a split sack to that point in 2004. Jones didn't dominate, and Rucker was able to stay active, but he did shut him down. Seattle won and again crawled over .500.

311: Seattle traveled to San Francisco. Jones had left his brand on Whiting and was instead matched against Tony Brown. Brown recorded half a sack, but not against Jones. He was a defensive tackle playing out of position. Jones had the power to pop and the quickness to do it twice before Brown blinked. Seattle dropped 42 on the 49ers and then traveled to St. Louis for a rematch.

280: Jones got his second go at Fisher and finished him off. I am sure the two had some kind words to exchange next season. Fisher: "I am honored to play on the same team as you, Walt." Jones: "Do I know you?" Jones did his job, but Hasselbeck completed only 15 passes in 36 attempts, and Seattle fell again to their division rival.

244: It was Trent Dilfer versus A.J. Feeley in an epic struggle for terrible. The Dolphins were 1–8 but took the fight to Seattle. Jones squared off against Jason Taylor, and Taylor squeezed out half a sack, but from the strong side. Jones polished up and pushed the Dilfer-Hawks through to victory. It was victory and continued pursuit of the NFC West or loss and shame, agony, and irrelevance.

213: Shame, agony, and irrelevance rode in on a train from Buffalo and broke open a can on Qwest Field. Hasselbeck threatened to forever humiliate anyone who ever supported him with another POS showing. Jones would not abide. He squared against another emerging talent, Aaron Schobel, and shut him down, allowing only a tackle assist. Drew Bledsoe reminded Seahawks fans that beating New England had brought them Rick Mirer, and the score was lopsided enough that J.P. Losman made an appearance. It was a shameful day for the Seahawks, but Jones quietly kept the streak alive.

173: Then it was hosting Dallas and dropping a bomb on Marcellus Wiley.

131: To Minnesota to drop another pile on Lance Johnstone.

94: At New York Jets, Bryan Thomas held without a stat.

58: Home and another clobbering of Bertrand Berry.

31: Seahawks battle the Falcons for their playoff lives and the NFC West title. It's a close game, and the two teams battle back and forth until Seattle takes a third-quarter lead that holds through the fourth and to victory.

0: Jones completes one of the most incredible runs in NFL history, shutting out pass rusher after pass rusher and helping lift Seattle to the playoffs. What is the number zero? In this case, testament to 566 snaps of doing everything right.

25 Visit Qwest

I had a punched-in-the-kidneys feeling from living the high life late into the late night with some Bears-fans family of mine. I was standing beside Shrug. We were in Qwest. My back hurt and my blood felt full of broken glass and a headache was peaking over an ibuprofen wall.

You would never know I was deliriously happy.

My dad was a mechanic, and a nefarious pay system known as the flag system kept us in perennial poverty. He wasn't real good with people, either. So it was bad jobs and unemployment. We never had money to go to football games. We didn't have the money to go, much less attend.

Tickets are expensive. Parking is expensive. Food is expensive and bad. I started to feel faint, and so I bought some nachos. I was sort of packing it down to try and stay standing. The chips were chips, but the cheese sure wasn't cheese.

I walked back and nodded at Shrug. We continued to not say much. He had season tickets and knew the regulars, and there were some head nods and small talk, and I wasn't brooding but could have been mistaken for as much. Shrug was doing me a solid for writing on Field Gulls. It was my second game at Qwest and only the second football game I had ever attended.

Qwest is beside Safeco. You pay and park and get out, and all around there are Seahawks fans. I think that is the moment I first felt really happy to be there. I am satellite fan. I live a few hundred miles from the team, and in Portland there is a mix of civic pride and neutrality that makes it no more a Seahawks city than Portland,

Grass: Safer Alternative or Gateway Turf?

The Seahawks pioneered FieldTurf in the NFL. Paul Allen paid to install it in Husky Stadium, and players were so impressed, he installed it in Qwest, too. Astroturf was famous for causing fluke injuries and shortening careers. FieldTurf was a welcome improvement. It still is nowhere near as safe as grass.

A study published March 11, 2010, indicated that one of the most severe injuries an athlete can endure, a complete tear of their anterior cruciate ligament (ACL), is 88 percent more likely on FieldTurf than on natural grass. On top of that, serious ankle sprains are 32 percent more likely.

Health is an essential part of winning football. Injured players perform worse, and when a player is lost, most teams lack the depth to adequately replace him. Allen introduced FieldTurf because it was better than the alternative, but if players are still endangering their health by playing at Qwest, it creates a significant disadvantage for the Seahawks. Not only are they more likely to lose their own players, but they are less likely to attract free agents.

Maine. I've looked for Seahawks bars, and you'll find some in Vancouver, but Portland is fiercely independent.

That kind of sucks, honestly. When the Blazers get going, it's the talk of the city. Not like local news, which I couldn't give a flip about, but on the tongues of the people. People care and know what's up, and it's vigorous and tangible. Portland is a Blazers town. Exclusive.

I feel very distant from Seahawks fans. There are some in the area—pockets—but there is never mania or crippling disappointment. The Portland area sports shows almost revel in the team's failures. They thumb their noses at Seattle. It's a Boston–New York vibe, but less abrasive, more passive-aggressive.

So when you walk toward Qwest on game day and all around you there are jerseys and excitement and whole families schooled in Seahawks tradition, it's like nothing else. You can tell people are up for this, and they are locked in, and there's nowhere else they'd rather be and all that jazz. Maybe it's a cliché, but when it wraps around you and permeates your senses, the original thought is alive again. You don't feel so stupid for caring so much about something so abstract as a professional football team.

I can't remember exactly where our seats were. I have been near the field and I have been up high, and either has its charm. Something about the live experience, the speed, but also the authenticity, reconnects you with the sport itself. On TV, you are seeing football as television show. There is running commentary and updated information and shifting camera angles, and after a while you do not even feel like you are watching a football game but a football show.

From the stands, it is up to you what you see. You surely do not see it all or well. The mystery feeds the excitement. Everyone around you bleeds Blue, so it's a partial crowd. A mob, really. You don't really think through if a penalty was right or not, only who it affected. There is a collective spirit, and it's partisan. Who will cast the first stone? Why, I'd be honored.

It was a great game. Seattle won. I will forever remember, late in the fourth, Seahawks up seven, Chicago ball, watching Patrick Kerney come free around right end. There was a bad feeling about that drive. Bernard Berrian had made a miracle one-handed catch, and big plays trigger panic in a crowd. Kerney came around right end and fought through a double team. Rex Grossman was holding the ball away from his body and absently plodding toward the left flat. Kerney closed, stripped, and Darryl Tapp recovered. Qwest erupted. That pretty much ended it.

I recorded the game and rewatched it and that play many times, but the memory that persists is the memory from the stands. The angle, the tininess of the players so far away, the stillness around me, and the way everything seemed to develop so slowly. I can still recall perfectly within my mind, but it's like a silent film, grainy, jumpy and short. Yet it sticks like nothing I have seen on TV ever has. Just a few seconds, but as important to me as XL or the NFC Championship.

26 Learn to Love a Rookie

Tim Ruskell had his guys. They needed to be virtuous, preferably soft-spoken, and God-fearing. They needed to be from a major conference, and if that conference was the SEC or PAC-10, ever the better. Mostly, they needed to scout well. A Ruskell guy could be too slow, too small, a workout blunder, but they had to shine on the field. They had to play football.

It was a surprisingly controversial approach to building a roster. Ruskell was always at odds with fans and media types who wanted bigger, stronger, and faster Seahawks, but circa April 2007 he was

Me! Bane! and the Art of Nicknaming

I have a real thing about nicknaming players. I end up typing the same names so much that eventually I just go nuts and start calling them something else. I think nicknaming is a kind of art. A good nickname should be concise, specific, and fresh, but also in some important way match the player himself.

I got to calling Brandon Mebane "Me! Bane!" because I would sit by myself watching tape, and Mebane would stir something inside me, and I would just shout it out like that. "*Me! Bane!*"

The worst thing that can be done is forcing a nickname. A website I respect, Kissing Suzy Kolber (kissingsuzykolber.uproxx.com), decided to nickname Chris Johnson during his record-setting 2009. They decided on Zulu Cthulhu. I cannot fully express how awful and stupid that is. Why would someone opt to say "Zulu Cthulhu" instead of Chris Johnson? It's long, it's forced, and the literary reference has no connection to the actual player. A nickname must be natural, but maybe most importantly, it must make sense to you. The only way it will ever stick is if you believe in it yourself and continue to use it no matter how stupid others find it.

high on his horse and impervious to most criticism. Back then, his controversial stance of drafting good football players instead of good athletes was spoken of in the reverential tones afforded ahead-of-their-time thinkers and artists. How quickly that changed.

Brandon Mebane was too slow and too small and wouldn't survive the jump in competition. I was sure of it. Rest assured I was on the Internet within minutes, registering my disgust throughout the world. It was 2007, I was young and foolish and didn't know half as much about the NFL as I wanted to, or wanted people to think I did. My opinions were one part my own and two parts the garbled nonsense proclaimed on high by the great media megaphone.

Stupid as I was then, I didn't take my opinions for fact. There was no John Morgan brand to sell, no need to sell an overweening, helmet-headed public persona, no need to don the false pretense of expertise. And so, I wasn't fond of the Mebane pick, but I was open. Two years later, Brandon Mebane was my go-to jersey on game day.

It started in preseason 2007. If you don't watch the preseason, start. Watching kids battle their hearts out for a chance at Sunday football is compelling. Mebane was compelling. He smashed through a double team and forced Charlie Whitehurst to lob a panic throw toward the sideline. He drove Paul McQuistan into Dominic Rhodes and blazed the trail to a Darryl Tapp safety. Late in the fourth quarter, he bullied through a Packers double team and engulfed rusher Corey White.

Whitehurst, McQuistan, White—it wasn't an all-star cast of victims. It was the preseason, and most football fans would rather mow their lawn than suffer four quarters of jobber football. But it was the beginning of something special.

Mebane made the 53-man with ease but was buried deep on the depth chart behind Chartric Darby. Soon I was on a crusade. Darby was Old Man Football, a respected veteran, a seasoned pro, and about a thousand other vague clichés, but he wasn't Mebane's equal, and he didn't deserve to start over the kid. But football, however much we would like it to be, is not meritocratic. Starters have inertia. Darby was the starter for the Super Bowl–champion Tampa Bay Buccaneers. He started most of the season for the Super Bowl–bound Seattle Seahawks.

That prestige doesn't force double teams and it doesn't stuff rushers. It doesn't do much but populate a fan's memories and inform a coach's superstitions. In fewer snaps, Mebane was doing more. Through my love of Mebane and honest desire to see him entrusted with more, I was learning the game and learning to love it more. I could see what made a good defensive tackle through what Mebane did. His first step was lightning-quick. His power, lower center of gravity, and active hands kept the pile moving backward and stopped rushing lanes from forming.

Opponents needed to double- and sometimes even triple-team him, and that freed other defenders to run to the ball carrier or attack the quarterback.

Brandon Mebane was doing special things, and I wanted to spread the word. I recorded games and watched snaps in slo-mo. *Me! Bane!* was born. I was a crusader who would rather die on my sword than leave my work unfinished. People needed to know about this kid, his power, his presence, his passion, and his deserved place as a starter.

As these stories often go, Mebane earned his spot not through eminent ability or my tireless prosthelytizing, but by chance. Darby was injured six games into the 2007 season and placed on injured reserve. Mebane was the next man up. He stepped in, and not coincidentally, the Seattle Seahawks' defense took off. The run defense became stifling, and the pass rush able to take over a game.

The winner wasn't Seattle or Ruskell or even Mebane. The winner was me. I developed a bond with a player through a common cause. From being an unknown to being a young stud, on the lips of head coach Mike Holmgren, announcers of all ilk, and eventually, even the local media. Brandon Mebane has yet to make a Pro Bowl and maybe never will. He's not a star; he's my favorite Seahawk ever. It just took some time, some work, and some devotion.

You'll never love a team until you're truly a part of it, and though I will never line up in the trenches, never grab the game-winning touchdown, break tackles to the end zone, strip-sack and recover for six, or jump a route and high step to pay dirt, I did my little part to become a part of Seahawks Nation. And after months of spreading the word, years of pumping his name, I know, once you've fallen in love with that player, seen him from obscure mid-round draftee to young star, you're hooked. You're a Seahawks fan forever.

27 The Student

Lofa Tatupu is more than a great middle linebacker. He is a star. Diehard football fans may care as much about their team's stars as they do their team's assigned parking spaces, caring only about winning and who helps the team win, but a star has value that transcends the gridiron. There are hard, cold truths: stars sell jerseys, and Tatupu has sold his share. There are strategic considerations: Tatupu gives Seattle a national presence, and that makes Seattle more attractive to free agents. There is something else, though. Tatupu can be a hero, an entry point for fans young and old, someone to care about beyond his football contributions, someone to admire.

Tatupu embodies what fans want. He is not the biggest or most athletic player, but he plays with intensity and fire. He is not the most ostentatious player. Tatupu is the anti-Boz of Seahawks history, arriving not hyped but derided and proving his doubters wrong rather than right. Tatupu is a vocal leader, and people are attracted to leadership to a fault. Do Tatupu's manic gesticulations and booming commands put Seattle in a better position or make the Seahawks more aware? We may never know, but a defense needs a leader, if not to command them then to give purpose. Fans understand this instinctively. Humans understand this instinctively. It's an ugly shame sometimes, how even the basest leader can rise in a vacuum, so smart, dedicated leadership like Tatupu's is revered.

He transformed Seattle's defense his rookie season, or so it will forever be remembered. Tim Ruskell transformed Seattle's defense, patching holes at end, tackle, corner, and obviously linebacker, but Tatupu became the face of Ruskell's greatest achievement. As opinion of Ruskell soured, Tatupu continued strong, became independent of that first success, and if a complement to a good team in 2005, Tatupu became essential to the 2007 team that won because of its defense.

All that, the shine, the reputation, the beginnings of a legend, does not do Tatupu the player justice. He is more than just a figurehead; he is a great, maybe one day enshrined, middle linebacker.

Tatupu is a connoisseur's tackler. No, he doesn't always wrap. And yes, since bulking up, his arms have retreated into his thickening torso. But unlike flavor-of-the-week middle linebackers who tally great tackle totals on struggling teams, Tatupu's contributions are constant, precious. At its heart, the tackle is both a good and misleading stat. It is good because it is concrete. A tackle is something we can fully understand and witness on a football field. Something more abstract, like pass defended, is up to the scorer's interpretation. Did the defender deflect a long completion to force a punt? Did the defender misread an errant pass and bat away what should have been an interception? Was the defender just nearby an uncatchable pass? Pass defended doesn't account for any of that, tells us nothing about why the pass targeted the receiver in the first place, or the quality of the coverage. It doesn't even inform us exactly what happened. So a tackle is a tackle—concrete—but a tackle is not of equal value to any other tackle, no.

Lofa tackles downhill, striking a rusher at the earliest point possible, taking efficient angles and if not always wrapping, almost always slowing, jarring, facilitating his team's collective gang tackle. Many linebackers produce huge tackle numbers by landing thrift tackles that do not help their team. Consider, a rusher runs left, behind left tackle. Tatupu attacks the gap between the tackle and the guard and attempts a difficult tackle behind the line of scrimmage. If he succeeds, the tackle not only stops the ball carrier, but stops him for a loss. Now consider another middle linebacker. He does not attack the gap, but takes a long angle to the left flat.

Instead of attacking the ball carrier, he corrals the ball carrier, capping his run but not stopping the play from achieving success. Yes, he sinks the tackle, and if he always pursues like this, he will amass many tackles, but they are bad tackles that do not help his team.

Tatupu attacks. By storming through gaps and tackling downhill, he pushes the rusher toward the sideline, turning the sideline into a defender and moving the rusher in the direction no rusher ever wants to run: laterally. Tatupu attacks. He doesn't always target the rusher at all, but works in concert. Tatupu excels at jamming the lead blocker into the hole and creating an uncontested path to the rusher. Tatupu and LeRoy Hill double-team backs like few linebacker duos in the league.

Tatupu is a smart and versatile pass defender. He drops deep but adjusts quickly to plays underneath. His read and reaction time are so good that his field speed is excellent. He doesn't blaze—Tatupu is not a burner, never will be—but he appears in pass lanes and punishes quarterbacks with poor vision. On one exceptional afternoon, Tatupu intercepted three passes from quarterback A.J. Feeley. The final came with the game in the balance. He intercepted a pass from Jake Delhomme in the NFC Championship Game. On each, Tatupu did the same thing: hid out in a zone, disappeared from the quarterback's read, then burst into the throwing lane, and undercut the route. That incredible anticipation not only feeds his field speed, but his return ability. For a guy who was considered too slow, his average interception return is remarkable. Brian Urlacher shot up the boards when he ran a 4.59-second 40. Tatupu dropped after a 4.83. Yet Urlacher has averaged only 15.9 yards per interception return, and Tatupu 22.9.

That is the essential Tatupu. He is not the greatest athlete, but he's gifted. He is not the hardest hitter, but he's jarring. He is not the fastest player, but he's quick. He is the most prescient defender I have ever witnessed. Tatupu turns tired tropes about being a film junky, about being cerebral, and fulfills them. He does not claim but plays with undeniable, unimpeachable football intelligence.

28 2005 NFC Championship Game

Matt Hasselbeck was quick, evasive, and could make accurate throws on the move. I barely remember the 2005 NFC Championship Game. It was such a thrill, and Seattle was up so much so early, the whole day became a merry blur in my memory. I remember being unbelievably happy. I remember Seattle shutting down Steve Smith. I don't remember much else, and I wanted to. So I sat down with my notebook and started rewatching every play, frame by frame. What was it that Seattle did that Carolina couldn't stop? Was it just Smith? Surely not.

Seattle did lock down Smith. The Seahawks bumped him off the line and doubled him over the top. It was not a novel strategy,

Mr. January Goes Cold

The Carolina Panthers' Jake Delhomme had the highest postseason quarterback rating in NFL history when he took Qwest Field on January 22, 2006. In 2003 he was clutch against the Cowboys, sensational in St. Louis, solid at Philadelphia, and hung 323 on the New England Patriots in a three-point Super Bowl XXXVIII loss. He then blazed into the 2005 playoffs, cutting up the Giants and dropping 319 on the Bears in compiling an overall passer rating of 108.4. Midway through the third quarter of his NFC Championship Game against the Seahawks, his rating stood at 1.6. He eventually boosted it with some garbage-time stats, but finished with an embarrassing 34.9.

Maybe the Seahawks broke his brain. Mr. January struggled from then on, playing in only one more postseason game, another blowout loss against Arizona, in which Delhomme threw five interceptions and finished with a 39.1 rating.

though. New England had attempted the same method in Super Bowl XXXVIII, but Smith was still able to receive for 80 yards and a touchdown. Moreover, Jake Delhomme passed for 323 yards and three touchdowns. New England assigned multiple players to slow Smith, succeeded somewhat, but could not succeed in slowing the Panthers' passing attack.

Seattle grounded the Panthers' attack by controlling the middle. Rocky Bernard had the best game of his career. He consistently tore through the Panthers' interior, shut down passing lanes, and pressured Delhomme. Delhomme tried to slide outside the pocket and, in doing so, opened himself to exterior pressure. Bernard had two sacks and another discounted when Seattle accepted a holding penalty. Delhomme couldn't step into his passes. He doesn't have the kind of quick release or cannon arm to overcome interior pressure, and pressure was on him every time Bernard was in.

Alexander was at his drunken-boxing best. People underestimate just how quick, agile, and, yes, powerful Alexander was. He never looked like he was working hard, but that is because he's a natural. Alexander would weave and cut three times to make one yard. There was better blocking and better holes, but Alexander was at his absolute peak. He was nothing like the back that would return next season. It must have been frustrating for opposing defenses. The lines he would take were outrageous. I started charting his path, and he wasn't north-south, he wasn't east-west, he wasn't one cut and go, Alexander was running a squiggly line. He broke arm tackles because defenders would get seasick tracking his progress. It was all ankle-breaking, floating, and effortless-looking, but awesome.

The greatest story of the NFC Championship Game was Hasselbeck. Maybe it's the baldness, the perennially worried face, the modern dodderer some confuse his former self with, but I forgot how athletic and graceful Hasselbeck once was. He wore out

Hasselbeck and that Clown from Carolina

In the 2005 NFC Championship Game, Matt Hasselbeck faced his former head coach at Boston College, Dan Henning. Hasselbeck had had a bit of a rocky relationship with Henning. He benched Hasselbeck and questioned his leadership. He thought Hasselbeck was too subdued. Hasselbeck retorted, "You should wear big red shoes and a big red nose because you are a clown!" Get him, Matt.

It's fitting then that Hasselbeck found his perfect match in Mike Holmgren. The Big Show was a big dog, and I think he preferred a quarterback who followed more than led. I wonder if Henning felt pride or anguish watching Hasselbeck tear through his Panthers. I imagine pride.

Julius Peppers. He stepped through pressure, could pass from any position, could begin a rollout, sense an end coming free, abort, and throw with zip. Hasselbeck was once an athletic and intelligent scrambler. He had great footwork and made honest-to-God open-field moves. He was confident in his reads and could throw all over the field, just supremely in the moment as only the greatest can be. Hasselbeck had the perfect mix of touch and zip, and his passes appeared in windows he'd never think to attempt anymore. He was a different man. A younger man. Decline denial only seems more odorous after watching just how great he once was.

Mike Holmgren frowned and frowned and frowned until Craig Terrill hit Smith from behind and forced the game-ending fumble. That was Mike, and that was the attitude he fostered in the entire team. Seattle ran away with the game, but to see their scowls, to see their intensity, their frustration with every minor failure, you would think they were being beat. Holmgren motivated by making players believe perfection is possible. In its pursuit, something so close was attained.

This game is like candy for a Seahawks fan. It didn't have the in-the-moment intensity of XL. Tom Rouen made it interesting, too interesting, when he punted a line drive to Smith and created an easy touchdown return. That was short-lived. The defense was on it. Lofa Tatupu was quick and limber and could as easily shoot a gap and drop Nick Goings for a loss as jump a route and pick a pass. He did both before Goings led with his helmet, knocked Tatupu woozy, and knocked himself out of the game. Lofa continued, but there was a kind of before and after.

It was the greatest moment in the history of Qwest. The greatest triumph in Seahawks history. It was easy like an Alexander run. It squiggled and sawed its way past defenders and led to paydirt. The season ended with a lot of heartbreak and disappointment. It ended with maybe more frustration and outrage. Before all that, there was a moment when every Seahawks player was at their very best, and the plan came together like never before and perhaps never again.

29 Ruskell

No figure in the history of the Seahawks is as controversial as Tim Ruskell. Ruskell is associated with the highest high and blamed for the Seahawks eventual collapse. He is polarizing. He once provoked irrational trust and eventually provoked irrational hatred.

Ruskell was the first real general manager to share power with Mike Holmgren after Holmgren stepped down. Bob Whitsitt nominally filled the position from 2002 to 2004, but was a confessed basketball executive. He was there to enable and aid Holmgren, not to challenge him, and if his tenure was marked with less of the sloppy roster mismanagement that undercut Holmgren, it wasn't particularly more successful. Ruskell was an old scout, a football mind of Holmgren's equal. He was Holmgren's foil.

Holmgren knew offense, and Ruskell understood defense. He cut his teeth in Tampa Bay and made his reputation helping Rich

McKay assemble the great turn-of-the-century Bucs defense. Holmgren had built the core of a great offense, but his defenses were consistently rotten. He had little eye for defensive talent. His lone defensive triumph was drafting Rocky Bernard in the fifth. Bernard would become an excellent interior pass rusher and an essential part of the 2005 Super Bowl team. Apart from Bernard, Holmgren's legacy on defense was replacement-level linebackers better suited for special teams, busts of all kinds, weak free-agent classes, and lost talent.

Things didn't get better with Whitsitt. Trader Bob could contest Holmgren, but he couldn't match his football acumen, and what should have been collaboration and compromise became meddling and rancor. The Holmgren-Whitsitt classes lacked Holmgren's high-end talent, but matched his depth. In other words, they were mostly bad. When Seattle eventually collapsed many years later, it was these classes, so devoid of talent, that hurt them most.

From End to End

Julian Peterson was a defensive end at Michigan State but became a linebacker in the pros. He started his career in San Francisco and was best known there for his cover skills. That's remarkable when you think about how little experience he likely had. It wasn't until he rejoined Seattle that his skill as a pass rusher was rediscovered.

Normally, Peterson is the kind of talent teams do not let get away. He became a Seahawk after rupturing his Achilles tendon in 2004. When he returned to San Francisco the next season, some thought he had lost something. Tim Ruskell signed Peterson in his first big free-agent spree. Right away, defensive coordinator John Marshall saw the end in the linebacker.

Peterson would play end on obvious rushing downs, and he became a terror against left tackles. He was long-limbed and agile and could turn the corner at a speed most 270-pound ends couldn't imagine. He had 10 sacks his first season and another 9.5 his second. Before he was traded for pennies on the dollar in a cap purge, Peterson was probably the Seahawks' least replaceable player on defense.

Ruskell was signed February 23, 2005. His job was simple, but difficult: take a promising Seahawks team, one showing great promise on offense but which couldn't win a playoff game, and complete it with a functional defense. He succeeded immediately.

Ruskell was aggressive in free agency. He attempted to patch needs by signing star cornerback Andre Dyson and stud linebacker Jamie Sharper. He attempted to throw draft picks at linebacker and defense, drafting Lofa Tatupu in the second, LeRoy Hill in the third, Jeb Huckeba in the fifth, and Cornelius Wortham in the seventh. His picks were controversial from the start. Tatupu and Hill were highly productive college players who were considered too small and too slow to succeed in the pro game. That criticism of valuing character, football intelligence, and production over NFL talent haunted him. Tatupu was considered a reach. Experts were sure he would be bullied by pulling linemen.

Criticism targeting Ruskell's 2005 class magnified its success and made Ruskell look like a maverick, a trendsetter, a rogue. Tatupu excelled from the start, making headlines in training camp and starting Week 1. He was a vocal and demonstrative leader in the middle and gave the Seahawks an identity, and, more impor-tantly, a difference-making talent. Hill started as a pass-rush specialist and became Seattle's most efficient blitzing linebacker. When Sharper was injured in Week 9, Hill took over. He never relinquished the role. Seattle became a balanced and dominant team. Seattle won its first ever playoff game under Holmgren, and a week later, its first ever NFC Championship.

The 2006 off-season would be Ruskell's undoing. On Holmgren's advice he re-signed Alexander to a lengthy and cap-crippling free-agent contract. He overextended himself in free agency, transition tagged Steve Hutchinson, pursued Pro Bowl defensive end John Abraham and Pro Bowl linebacker Julian Peterson, lost Hutchinson, lost Abraham, and only landed Peterson. Peterson cost a mint, was worth it, but was a hired gun.

Hutch signed with Minnesota and continued his Canton-bound career.

Ruskell applied the same principles to the 2006 draft, with less exciting results. Kelly Jennings was polished, but possessed limited potential, and later when his lack of ball skills was exposed, he became a liability in coverage. Darryl Tapp was, is, a very good defensive end. Rob Sims was drafted right into Mike Holmgren's doghouse, and though he developed into a good left guard, he suffered from comparison. At the same time, 2005 was catching up to Ruskell. Tatupu and Hill were young stars, but Chris Spencer was a conservative pick. Drafting a center in the first isn't far from drafting a fullback in the first, and whatever his potential, Spencer developed slowly. He too suffered from comparison, and Holmgren made it clear Spencer was not Robbie Tobeck's equal. Ray Willis suffered through injury. The rest of the 2005 class disappeared into obscurity. Sharper retired. Seattle released Dyson to avoid paying a $3 million bonus.

The team pushed itself over the top, but it cost them. The offense crumbled. Alexander suffered a broken bone in his foot and was a shadow of his former self. Hasselbeck battled injury. Seattle ran through left guards, playing Floyd Womack and Spencer before settling on Sims. Tobeck was lost and later retired. Darrell Jackson battled injuries, again, and openly complained about Ruskell not offering an extension. Whitsitt had made a verbal agreement with Jackson that Ruskell had no intention of fulfilling.

John Marshall turned Peterson into a potent weapon off the edge, playing him at defensive end, and Peterson tallied 10 sacks on his way back to the Pro Bowl, but the defense was not enough to carry the team. Kelly Herndon was overmatched starting; Jennings proved serviceable in spot starts; but the Seahawks safeties, both added under Holmgren-Whitsitt, were flashy liabilities in coverage. Michael Boulware couldn't repeat his interception heroics and never learned to avoid biting on play-action. Ken Hamlin was a hitter and could grab an interception, but like Boulware was undisciplined in cover. On the leg of Josh Brown, Seattle won the NFC West but were showing cracks.

By 2007 much of the 2005 class had all but disappeared, and the core of that team, Holmgren's offense, was aging rapidly. Quarterback prospect David Greene flopped, was soon cut, soon out of the league, soon selling insurance. Too much was expected of Spencer and too soon, and without ever really struggling, he became a lightning rod for Holmgren and the media's frustration. Ruskell had traded the team's 2007 first-round pick for Deion Branch, and that decision was dead on arrival. Little did it matter that Branch was fair compensation for a first-round pick, building through the draft was en vogue. Branch struggled to develop trust with Hasselbeck and suffered injury after injury.

Eventually the details didn't matter. Ruskell couldn't save Seattle from rebuilding. He started a foil, but quickly became an enemy, and in the battle between the beloved Holmgren and the cagey and secretive Ruskell, Ruskell was sure to lose. Ruskell shouldered the blame for losing Hutchinson. Ruskell was pilloried for trading a first-round pick for Branch. Ruskell's controversial approach to drafting players, once the hallmark of his genius, became shorthand for his arrogance as a talent evaluator. The team was winning, but it's talent advantage was eroding. It ended 2007 in embarrassing fashion, losing an early 14-point lead and being run out of Lambeau 42–20.

Everything about the loss and its aftermath stung. Shortly afterward Holmgren announced 2008 would be his last season coaching in Seattle. Weeks later Ruskell announced that assistant head coach Jim L. Mora would take over as head coach in 2009. It wasn't controversial when it happened, but amid reports that Holmgren was rethinking his decision, it became first controversial and then damnable when the Seahawks finally collapsed.

Seattle was struck by a historic wave of injuries. Branch was still not healthy after tearing his ACL against the Packers. Nate Burleson tore his ACL in Week 1. Bobby Engram shattered his shoulder after just a year earlier recovering from Graves' disease. Injuries struck Hasselbeck; his backup, Seneca Wallace; its vaunted linebackers; eventually felled standout end Patrick Kerney; landed Seattle's left side, Walter Jones and Mike Wahle, on injured reserve and ended both of their careers. Seattle was desperate. It was signing street free agents to start at wide receiver. It had rid itself of Alexander in the off-season, but Julius Jones was not the man to prop up a collapsing team.

Mora took over in 2009 and proved a failure and embarrassment, not only unable to push his team to success, but known for singling out players, unabashedly calling his own team "soft," and eventually, after being fired, calling newly hired head coach Pete Carroll a "cheater." Seattle started out mediocre but sagged to bad, and amid reports that Holmgren might return as the team's general manager, Ruskell forced the issue, asked Tod Leiweke about his future, and unhappy with the answer, resigned December 2, 2009.

30 Stolen Legacy

The Seahawks' Super Bowl legacy was stolen from us. It should be of a team that fought valiantly but lost. It is of a team that was screwed, jobbed for Cowher and the Bus and a crowd that was reportedly 80 percent Steelers fans. The sickening bumper vignettes showing Roethlisberger and Bettis fondling the Lombardi Trophy still stand prominently in memory. It hurt that the Seahawks lost. It hurt incomparably more that the game felt fixed.

It was Seattle's first and only trip to the Super Bowl, and after, it felt better to forget it entirely. I was poised to give up the NFL. It was corrupt. Bill Leavy, corrupt. The Seahawks' loss, predetermined. The Super Bowl, an act, a billion-dollar charade.

Bitterness has become the hallmark of a true Seahawks fan.

Let it go.

No, I wouldn't tell you to forget. I wouldn't dare argue we should get over it. If it was corrupt, if the Steelers were aided in their victory, if there were a shred of belief in my mind that Super Bowl XL was partial, I would tell Seahawks fans, Steelers fans, and fans of all stripes, of all sports, and of all competition, to quit the NFL forever. But it was a fair contest, and the Seahawks lost.

The Seahawks fought valiantly but lost.

Did Darrell Jackson push off? I didn't think so at the time. It was a singular outrage in an outrageous game. Jackson was scrambling back for the ball and extended his arm into Chris Hope. But it was ticky-tack, right?

John Madden thought so. He said so. He said, "When we think of pushing off, that's not what we think of."

It happened during a broken play. Matt Hasselbeck and Jackson had to improvise. Jackson was running an in, but began to loop left back toward the sideline, saw Hasselbeck pointing to his right, turned, planted his hand in the defender's body, pushed off Chris Hope, and received. The infraction happened directly in front of back judge Bob Waggoner, and in his rush to flag, he first drew his whistle before re-cocking and throwing the dreaded yellow. It was almost funny, except for that knife in my belly. It was the right call. It wasn't ticky-tack, it was textbook, and it was done directly in front of an official.

Some have learned to stomach that play, but what about Roethlisberger's plunge into the end zone? It will never be fully clear whether he broke the plane or not, but after rewatching it dozens of times, I think he did. In a fraction of a second before D.D. Lewis struck him hard and drove the ball and his body back, Roethlisberger extends his arm and the ball, partially shielded by his forearm, looks at or onto the plane of the goal line. It wasn't the tip of the ball either, but the visible portion of the ball. Once it's over, it's over, and the play is dead: touchdown.

Watch 10,000 times and you would never be completely sure. I read someone triangulated the location of the ball and determined it never crossed. It was a judgment call. It could have been wrong, but it wasn't clear. It was never clear, and Leavy was responsible to uphold the ruling on the field. At that time, he was the official least likely to overturn a call. He had only overturned 23 percent of all calls. The wording of the challenge system was concrete. A play must have "incontrovertible visual evidence" to overturn. It wasn't there. Mike Holmgren went into the half in Leavy's ear, contesting the ruling. Whether the initial ruling was right, it was very, very close, and whether it was right, it could not be overturned. Had the ruling on the field been no touchdown, it would have stood, too.

Later in the same quarter, Jackson caught a pass and stepped out of bounds before he landed his second foot. At the time, I was confused because I thought the ball broke the plane, but that was immaterial. Without establishing a second foot in bounds, Jackson never had possession. It wasn't a completed pass.

Seattle was charged with five holding penalties. Each occurred on an actual hold. Were other holds not called? Yes. But that is typical in the NFL. Officials are not perfect, but we hope they are impartial.

The very worst call I saw was an uncalled push off by Hines Ward. He clearly planted a hand in the body of Kelly Herndon and pushed himself free. It was a relatively minor play, but it did convert a first. What really mattered to me was how could that penalty have gone uncalled, and Seattle's flagged? Well, I just don't think the officials saw it. I watched them, watched where they were watching, and it happened so fast that there just were not any eyes on Ward.

I was devastated when Seattle lost Super Bowl XL, not because the Seahawks lost, but because the game felt fixed. After the push-off by Jackson, and the uncalled push-off by Ward, the near-touchdown by Roethlisberger, and then the ludicrous chop-block penalty on Hasselbeck, it just felt too one-sided, too partial. Seattle did get the bad calls, and Pittsburgh the good. The game was not fixed. In the end, even if they did not play better, the Steelers won.

31 Ronin

Kenny Easley sued the Seahawks for ending his career and endangering his life. The case was settled out of court. He suffered kidney failure and charged that an overdose of Advil administered by the team trainer and team doctors was the cause. Even the great cannot control their ending. Still, Easley's ending was particularly ugly. He wasn't injured but wounded, and wasn't hurt in battle, but poisoned trying to recover.

Easley was great, everything a fourth overall pick is supposed to be and, despite the brevity of his career, one of the greatest Seahawks of all time. He was plug and play, good from his rookie season and astounding through his prime. He could tackle like a demon and was a ballhawk with bad intentions. His coverage wasn't always pure, and as his injuries mounted, his performance could be inconsistent, but it's petty to take something so amazing, clean, and beautiful and find faults.

He was an international star before breaking through as a pro. In the annual Japan Bowl, Easley set Yokohama Stadium ablaze with two interceptions and a fumble recovery. The Japan Bowl was a college all-star game, but cool. And Easley was a star among stars.

Kenny Easley looks to lateral one of his two interceptions against the Raiders during a 35–13 win in October 1987 at Los Angeles Memorial Coliseum.

He looked into Indiana quarterback Tim Clifford's eyes and said, "Stop. Stop crying. It's pathetic." But Clifford continued to sob. "I hate pathetic people. I'll have to kill you."

Japan offered Easley an early introduction to a team he knew little about but knew enough to not want to be a part of. It was

Thanksgiving 1980, and a USO station was broadcasting Seahawks-Cowboys. Dallas was winning 51–0. Tony Dorsett rushed for 107 yards and two touchdowns. I'm sure pity stopped Dorsett from twisting the knife further.

Easley joined the Seahawks in a bleak period between Patera's antics and Knox's success. He proved his vigilance right away, recovering four fumbles. Easley was an intimidator. He tackled with passion and power, and more than that, hunger. Easley wanted to make every tackle. He wanted to be everywhere. He wanted to intercept every pass.

Easley could cover a tight end in man cover or patrol the deep zone. At 6′3″, 210, he was huge for his time. That made him not just an intimidating tackler, but an intimidating presence deep. He could track the ball, extend his arms and snag stars. Joining a terrible team he didn't want to be a part of, he finished the 1981 season by promising Kingdome fans a better future. The Seahawks clobbered the Cleveland Browns, and Easley intercepted two passes, returning one for a touchdown.

His 1982 was a bit like Ken Griffey Jr.'s 1994. Easley had four picks and two sacks in just eight games. He was peaking. The Seahawks' defense was coming together. Seattle finished 4–5 in the strike-shortened season. They just missed the NFL's postseason tournament. There was promise, the feeling of something great dawning.

Like Griffey, Easley's health couldn't honor his talent. He did not miss many games, but he was constantly banged up. He had muscle spasms in his back and rib cage. He hurt his knee. He hurt his ankle and double-downed on the Advil. He suffered all that and added to his burden.

If a man can make a career out of a single season, Easley was Hall of Fame bound after 1984. He had 10 interceptions, two returned for touchdowns. He returned punts. Easley emerged as the best defender in the NFL. The Seahawks had the best pass defense in football, and despite losing Curt Warner in Week 1, despite enduring the end of Franco Harris, surged to 12–4. It was their second-best record ever. It was the best season of Seahawks football before 2005, and Easley was the team's best player.

As early as 1985, Easley wasn't the same. Things were breaking down. He suffered the ankle injury that would end his career. His interceptions diminished with his quickness.

In 1986 he hurt his knee in compensation for his ankle.

In 1987 he hurt his shoulder. Following the strike, he suffered irreparable damage to his ties to Seattle. Easley was the Seahawks' player representative. After the strike, fans booed Easley and the returning players. Easley was hardcore. He held nothing back when he heard Jim Zorn say he would cross picket lines. Zorn was out of the league, out of the union, but Easley did not care. Zorn only threatened that unforgivable act; Steve Largent actually played. The team's offensive leader and the true face of the franchise not only disrespected the union, but disrespected the Seahawks' player representative.

Then the curtain fell. Easley forced a trade to the Phoenix Cardinals, and during a routine physical the Cardinals discovered severe kidney damage. If you watch game tape, you can see his failing health hanging on him like a monkey. The man who was cover-quick, agile, and explosive into his tackles, was getting beat. I won't elaborate, though. I would rather remember Easley for when he was so good, he could never belong.

32 Greatest 3-4 End to Ever Play?

Jacob Green is the greatest player in Seahawks history who somehow is neither appreciated by the mainstream media nor his own fans. A few things work against Green. Most notably, he

Free-Agent Rush

Seattle has a long tradition of signing pass-rush mercenaries to provide sacks before they decline. The first was Chad Brown, and Brown had 48 sacks over eight seasons. Brown was a hard-nosed player who stood out on some desperate Holmgren defenses. Then came Grant Wistrom from the division-rival Rams. Wistrom was very expensive and never lived up to his hype. He had 11.5 sacks in three years before retiring. Bryce Fisher was one of the better values. Seattle got 13 sacks from Fisher in two seasons playing opposite Wistrom. Julian Peterson was a situational end and elite pass rusher who regained his college form in Seattle. He had 24.5 sacks in three seasons and appeared in the Pro Bowl all three years. Patrick Kerney was the Seahawks' latest attempt to pay for what they couldn't develop. He had a phenomenal and unexpected 2007, recording a career-best 14.5 sacks, earning his only All-Pro nod and even being considered for Defensive Player of the Year.

All except Fisher were very expensive, but all produced, at least at first. Call it the curse of Michael McCrary, but the Seahawks have not been able to develop a top-flight end of their own in over a decade.

started his career on a bad team and without much talent around him. His original position was at left defensive end in a 4-3. In 1980 that was as much a run-stopping position as a pass-rushing position. Tackle stats were not recorded at any point in his career, and so we can only guess how "active" Green was. Sacks were not recorded until his third season. Seattle never received a lot of attention, and very good players like Green didn't register with the national conscious. What really hurt Green most was that he played end in a 3-4, and 3-4 ends have always struggled for recognition.

Green was selected 10th overall in the 1980 draft. It was a good class, headlined by Hall of Fame offensive tackle Anthony Muñoz. Green was a stud at Texas A&M. He had a staggering 20 sacks and 134 tackles in 1979. Maybe if he had been drafted by the Cowboys or 49ers he would have been inducted into the Hall of Fame. Instead, Green became a great player for an often lousy franchise.

He didn't start with great surrounding talent. To his right, there was defensive tackle Robert Hardy. Hardy played just four seasons and was off the Seahawks and out of the league upon the arrival of Chuck Knox. To Hardy's right was Manu Tuiasosopo. Manu was a solid and versatile player who stuck with Seattle for a little while before moving onto greener pastures in San Francisco. Tui is best known for his progeny: Marques, Zach, and Matt. Green's first bookend partner was Bill Gregory, but Gregory lasted only a season alongside Green in Seattle before retiring. Manu moved over in 1981, and then some other players substituted in at tackle, but it wasn't until 1982 that the Seahawks achieved any kind of consistency. That year, they added Jeff Bryant, and Bryant would be Green's partner in crime for the rest of Green's career.

Seattle lost a lot his first three seasons, and losing tends to take sacks away from pass rushers. Teams can run more, and run more in pass situations. They can run shorter pass patterns and shorter drops for their quarterbacks, and that shortens the time the pass rusher has to close in and tackle. In blowout wins, especially, an opponent stops taking risks entirely, and a pass rusher plays most of the game with little chance to do more than pressure the opposing quarterback. Why risk a fumble? Check down. In Green's first three seasons, Seattle lost by two touchdowns or more 12 times. Unofficially, he tallied 18.5 sacks in his first two seasons. That's good for any 23- or 24-year-old, much less on a weak defensive line, much less on a bad team.

When the team became good, Green suffered a different setback to his recognition. Chuck Knox ran a 3-4, and ends in a 3-4 arrest tackles rather than rush passers. The all-time sacks list is populated by two specific types of players: ends in a 4-3 and linebackers in a 3-4. Whether you're Rickey Jackson or Reggie White or Lawrence Taylor or Bruce Smith, you either played end in a 4-3 or a linebacker in a 3-4. Of the 24 players that rank ahead of Green on the all-time sacks list, only Neil Smith played most of his career as a 3-4 end. If we include Green's unofficial sacks from '80 and '81, he is the all-time sacks leader among 3-4 ends. With that designation, it's arguable that Green was the greatest 3-4 end to ever play in the NFL. Maybe Howie Long was better, but it's debatable.

What really separates Green from Long is image. Long played for the Raiders, won a Super Bowl, and retired into broadcasting and movies. He was the big white guy with the flattop and the smile and the stage presence. Green was quiet everywhere but on the field. When you run a 3-4, you are supposed to have a linebacker who functions as your primary pass rusher, your Derrick Thomas, DeMarcus Ware, or Lawrence Taylor. They say Taylor changed the game forever—that he was so fast, every team had to protect the blind side like never before. Seattle never had that player. Knox never found a true pass-rushing complement to his line. Fredd Young had a couple good seasons, but that was it. Tony Wood was supposed to provide speed around the edge, but he was just average. No, it was Green, Nash, and Bryant, and those three were the heart of the Seahawks' defense.

Seattle often rushed three, and Green was constantly fighting through double teams. He would smash through the right tackle and right guard and tight end if they dared, and break through and punish the ball carrier. Fans didn't always know about Green, but opposing coaches did. He was athletic and indefatigable. You don't see too many ends who can make plays sideline to sideline like Green did. He was powerful and had great technique and could fight through blockers with terrifying ease. Green had to be game-planned around. He was that kind of disruptive force on every snap.

Seattle could win without Warner and it could win without Easley, but Green was irreplaceable. Luckily, he never got hurt. He missed two games his rookie season with a leg bruise and then not another game until Week 10 of 1989. That would be the final game he ever missed for the Seahawks, but also among the final games of his career.

There is no sure way to determine how great Green really was. Was he the best 3-4 end ever? Green deserves mention if not outright recognition. Was he the greatest defensive lineman in Seahawks history? Him or Tez; him or Tez. Was he the most indispensable player for Chuck Knox? Green, Krieg, or Largent, yeah. Green was incredible. And if you get your hands on some old game footage, he is worth watching the entire game through. He probably isn't famous enough to be inducted into the Hall of Fame, but were it the Hall of Game, there would be a Jacob Green bust where a Joe Namath bust now stands. It's all right if others don't get it, but if you're a Seahawks fan, you know Green or you don't know jack.

33 Origins of Strong

When Mack Sr. and Rose Strong named their son Mack, they named him a football player. For 14 seasons, no title better fit Mack Strong, and in turn, no man better fit the NFL. He was Mack, like a truck—no, like a knife—no, like a player, but not that kind, like a man, an everyman, any man, like every man to ever wear the pads—but stronger.

Fullback is far removed from its glory days. A starter who lead blocks and little else is a luxury in the pass-first modern NFL. If someone unearths this book 20 years from now, the position itself might seem as archaic as "wing back." One wins the title of fullback through survival and keeps it through punishment, of others, and as Newtonian physics dictates, equally of oneself.

Strong grew up in Georgia and became a Bulldog in name and function. He battered bodies for Garrison Hearst, mostly his own, battered bodies for Coach Ray Goff and Air Georgia, mostly his own, graduated in 1993, battered and forgotten. Hearst was selected third overall. Strong went undrafted, just another kid with more spirit than talent, more will than ability.

Now, he wasn't bad at Georgia. His senior season had some highlights, some sparkling numbers, a 5.7-yards-per-carry average is noteworthy of any back, much less a future fullback. The draft process is unrepentant. Minus a noteworthy miss or 10, it's pretty efficient, too. Stars and starters are selected early and all those college overachievers, guys who just know how to play football, who seduce with their skill and hustle, well, they're weeded out. Stories are for storybooks. Perseverance and patience and determination are adjectives reserved for sportswriters. Coaches prefer power, speed, and athleticism.

So Strong stuffed his shoes in a garbage bag and flew out to the one city that wanted him. Tom Flores knew a bit about not making the grade. Flores had been cut by the Calgary Stampeders. He liked backs who could catch. Strong could. If only he could stick, could survive, could straddle that pencil-thin path a free agent walks to earn a roster spot. That would be a start.

Seattle cut Strong before the regular season but signed him to the practice squad. It's a dubious honor. A forget-me-not list for the soon forgotten. But Strong survived. He made it through 1993 and made the roster in 1994.

It was a step up to be inactive, as Strong was for the first seven weeks of 1994. Inactive, but on the 53-man roster. What us workaday slobs call face time with the boss. It was a chance to prove himself. He did.

Seattle had lost six straight, and Kingdome crowds were dwindling. Brothers in misery, the Tampa Bay Bucs, rode to town on a stallion named "Yawn." It was a late-season contest for that elusive sixth win. Six, that is, between them. Tampa was 2–8. Seattle, 3–7. Rick Mirer helmed the Hawks' offense. Craig Erickson, the Bucs. Two equals divided by hype. Seattle sprinted out to a 15-point lead then watched that lead crumble. The Seahawks turned the ball over three times and lost star rusher Chris Warren to a hip pointer.

Down six, Seattle waged a desperation drive. It nearly ended but for an illegal contact penalty by corner Mike McGruder on fourth-and-12. Forty-two seconds left in the fourth, with something far greater on the line than a football game, Strong took the ball and powered in for six. The extra point sealed it.

Strong was a Seahawk.

He split time for the rest of the season, started over again with a coach who didn't know his name, was re-signed in 1996, became a starter, started over again with a coach who knew his name, was eventually recognized as an All-Pro, executed the most famous fullback draw in team history, suffered a herniated disk in his neck, was forced into retirement, and became a broadcaster.

As a Seahawk.

34 Be Irrational

It's good to be rational, right? I mean, licking a light bulb and expecting candy is no way to go through life. Feeding oneself when hungry, defecating when it's called for and in the designated place, trusting in gravity, these are good things, I think. Rational, rational is good. It helps glue the days together, it keeps one gainfully employed and out of straight-jackets, it ensures life and a certain quality of life. But too much rationality is boring, ludicrous.

Humans stay in a kind of perennial adolescence. We stay curious. We learn, forever, or as much as forever grants us. We never lose our appetite for fun or play. We turn 50 and rock out in our convertible. We believe youth is an eternal good and God-given right.

When I say, "Be irrational," I do not mean punch your neighbor in the face and expect the Nobel Peace Prize. I do not mean eat dirt and drink ball bearings. I do not mean, even, buy lottery tickets. That's dumb. I mean, never let reality stomp on your hopes.

When Seattle's down two scores in the third quarter, yeah, we get it, they're probably going to lose, but don't be that guy, don't be the self-important dude dying to declare time of death. Believe. Believe, goddamnit. Because believing in the face of certain failure is virtuous, is essential. Believe and believe, and if you're in the stands, scream your lungs out. And about that...

Don't be civil in the stands. Be a lunatic. Believe you cheer your team on to victory. Despise that rival fan arrogant enough to show up in your stadium in his colors. Revile him. Cast stones—figurative stones. Well...yeah, probably shouldn't cast real stones. Cheer every first down until the last. Go berserk on big plays: berserk, chest-bumping, voice-killing, last-day-on-earth berserk.

Love every member of the team, and like a wayward brother, have a heart-to-heart with the struggling ones. I loved you, Brian Russell. I loved your stupid face. And you sucked. Oh—oh! Did you suck. But until your very last, I wanted better for you. I wanted my every criticism to blow up in a wave of forced fumbles and pick-sixes and form tackles and good angles and *grit*. Grittygritgritgrit.

Leave it all on Sunday and take the loss to heart and let go and care again on Monday. Know every name on the roster and know, just *know* that Baraka Atkins is about to turn the corner and become beastly. Sweat the little things. Sweat the assignments and the blocking and the coverage and not just the great reception, great run, great pass.

Waste a bunch of money and buy a jersey and wear it around like a little boy, and instead of feeling shame, buy another. Own shirts and sweatshirts and vintage caps emblazoned with the Seahawks logo, the old logo, the embarrassingly outdated logo. Join a fansite, join Field Gulls, tell me I'm an idiot, and then engage in a purely rational discussion about the merits of the outside line-backer versus the stand-up end.

Don't be a dilettante. Don't be a box-score skimmer. Know the names, know the spellings, know the hype and refute it. Have a player you like too much and whose every mistake you both ignore and suffer; and have a player or two you root to get it right, one day, finally, get it right, and know they never well, but never know. Don't check in during the playoffs and be that guy during the off-season with a brain full of bad ideas and misconceptions.

We're fans. We never signed up for rational thought. We agreed to heartbreak and bad breaks and broken promises, and we did so willingly, because it speaks to our crazy soul and our crazy need to belong and be part of something big, that's unpredictable like the weather and can kill you like lightning or rain down sunshine.

So be irrational. Believe in the face of doom. Shudder in the face of victory. Love something cold and indifferent that doesn't know your name and can never love you back. Soar with the wins and swallow hard with the losses, and see someone in a 49ers jersey and hate them. Start every season with dreams of the Super Bowl and end every season with dreams of next season. Start every game with dreams of victory and end every game with dreams of next week's victory. Start every play with dreams of long receptions and sacks and broken tackles and forced fumbles and end every play with confidence in the next.

And, for it, you will suffer and suffer, and if and when winning ever happens, it will be too brief and never enough, and you'll want to snatch that feeling from anything you can before it's gone: and it'll be gone the second you search for it, but it will have been there, and it will have been better than anything you ever imagined. And you'll forget. And you'll start again with dreams of the Super Bowl.

35 1976

Critics, art critics, rock critics, critics of all kind are prone to the chronology trap. Elemental, seminal—pick your bad adjective—it may be essential, but it is not paramount. Sometimes, the first is almost arbitrary. In the warmth of spring something is sure to sprout first—a weed.

So before 1983, before 2005, there was 1976, and good God, 1976 was thorns and thistles. Seattle molded their cellar-dweller from the discard pile. It was dust to dust, indeed.

I decided to honor the Seahawks' origin not with a sequentially significant placement within the book, but an essay befitting its actual value. None of the following is an accurate presentation of the events that preceded or took place within 1976, but an extended metaphor for the season itself.

In 1972 the city of Seattle conceived a thing, a thing without head or heart, constructed from the bodies of the deceased, all arms and legs. This thing was not meant for practical purposes, but sport, and would be pitted against others of its ilk. They conjured and schemed and assembled but could not bring it to life. They tried fire, but fire was anathema to the creature. They tried persuasion, but it would not listen. Finally, they brought their creature to the gnarled and hoary wizard named Rozelle and pled, "Give it life! Give it purpose! Give it pigskin and painted lines!" Rozelle twirled his long, tangled brows and decreed, "Your creature feeds on money. Feed it and feed it, and it shall rise."

And so it was in 1972, the city first began this boondoggle we would one day call "Seahawk." It constructed an arena for its brutal games, and as millions were poured into the Kingdome, and as the concrete monstrosity took shape, the creature began to stir. The location for the Kingdome was selected, a mudflat stolen from the sea, and concrete was poured, millions of gallons, and a distant heartbeat was heard. Lloyd W. Nordstrom dedicated his riches, hired John Thompson and Jack Patera to tend to it, teach it, and give it purpose.

Seahawk took the field on August 1, 1976, to face the warped and neglected thing known as 49er. It was a troubled period for 49er. A post-Nolan period for 49er. Seahawk and 49er slugged it out, threw brutal haymakers and crushing jabs. It was exhibition football, but neither team wanted to lose. 49er feared the embarrassment of losing to a rookie team. Seahawk feared if it started losing, it might never stop.

Seahawk lost. It lost and lost, battered and splattered by more seasoned creatures, and away from battle it retired to rejected meditation. What brought its miserable self into existence? Why did others look at it and look away? It felt low. It felt ugly, and it was. It was sloppy and deficient. Parts were old, and others too young. But some things were standing out, shaping into something better. It had a left arm that could throw and two hands that could catch. Patera gave it inspiration, and what it lacked in grace and coordination, it overcame with guile.

It trudged across country and ended in Tampa. The beast known as Buccaneer was every bit its equal in ugliness, loss, squalor, and desperation. The two saw each other, saw themselves in the other, and hated what they saw. The two stepped into Tampa Stadium desperate to destroy the other and whatever they shared. It was a grueling, miserable affair. Buccaneer struck first and last, but Seahawk prevailed.

It won, and three weeks later, it won again. Not by a little, but handily, mercilessly brutalizing Falcon at home. And the Kingdome shook. And the fans poured praise and affection on Seahawk. And it stood straight up. And the action created fissures across its scaly body. And through those sores the city of Seattle could see something beautiful beneath.

36 Touchdown Alexander

We save our praise for the funeral. Shaun Alexander was broken. His foot was broken. His career was ending. Shaun Alexander was plodding toward his ending. He didn't know it, maybe Mike Holmgren didn't know it, some fans refused to know it, but it was written in every approach, every plant, every panic spin to the turf. It had been too easy, and when it left, well, that was hard.

Many braced themselves with denial. His performance had changed so suddenly, though his style looked so much the same that it was common for people to blame not Alexander but the offensive line. The 2006 line was in rough shape, but could it account for how far he had fallen and how fast? Seattle plugged in Porkchop Womack at left guard, then center Chris Spencer, and when Robbie Tobeck went down, moved Spencer to center and played Rob Sims at guard. Sims took the brunt of the fans and Holmgren's abuse. His major sin was not being Steve Hutchinson.

Alexander broke a bone in his foot, and doctors determined nothing they could do or his body could do would make it heal. It was not enough to keep him out very long, but it eroded his already depleting ability. For so long, Alexander had excelled on a knife's edge. Every dangerous cutback, every run bounced outside, every weaving, wending, unsteady, and drunken run was beautiful but fragile and, when broken, bad.

All the bad habits he had developed and obscured with his talent came to haunt him. It was no longer acceptable that he couldn't receive. His hesitant, spotty pass-blocking became a liability his rushing could not compensate for. From MVP in 2005, Alexander became one of the least valuable players in football in 2006.

For the first time in his career, he averaged fewer than four yards per attempt. He had nearly as many fumbles as touchdowns. That was probably the greatest insult for a player who had always prided himself on his ability to score.

Denial took on another form in 2007. Alexander was only getting worse, and suddenly Seahawks fans of all stripes insisted he was never very good. It wasn't Alexander, but the offensive line that blocked for him. And true, Walter Jones and Hutchinson formed an unparalleled pair, but Alexander was the essential complement that revealed their ability. Jones and Hutch excelled at blocking in space, and Alexander's cutback ability and vision maximized their pull-blocking.

The real shame of the 2007 season was that Holmgren fiercely denied Alexander's decline. The 2007 Seahawks were the last gasp of a great run and were held back by not being able to run at all. It wasn't like the team lacked an alternative, either. Maurice Morris averaged 4.5 yards per carry. He couldn't block any better than Alexander, but he could receive. Morris allowed Seattle to start a full 11 on passing plays. Alexander offered so little as a receiver and blocker, for hundreds of downs the Seahawks were playing a man down.

He was cut in the off-season, given a charity run with Jim Zorn's Washington Redskins, cut after 11 rushing attempts, and then excluded from the league. Occasionally, a story would percolate about how Alexander still wanted to play. It was just sad. He wanted to play, but no team would offer him a contract. He had hit that wall that eventually all rushers hit, and because it had been so natural for him for so long, and because he got away with bad habits blocking and receiving, and because he had always been a gifted rusher, losing his wheels hit Alexander extra hard. He was great, and then he was gone.

37 The Gargoyles of Jargon

Jargon has a common linguistic root with gargoyle, and the two serve a similar purpose. The stone beasts that sit atop walls serve a practical purpose, yes. They are water spouts that channel rainwater off a roof and away from walls. Football jargon serves a purpose, too. It creates a common language and encapsulates dense ideas into words and phrases. A gargoyle could take on any form. It could be beautiful, mystic, even welcoming, but that is almost never the case. The towers, cathedrals, fortresses, castles, and temples populated by gargoyles are strongholds, places of import, prominence, authority, that need to be protected. And so gargoyles are grotesque, frightening, intimidating.

The elephant playing the five needs to rip the blind-side protector's outside shoulder, tear through the fullback, and lay the wood on the scatback. Maybe grip and rip, or wrap and await the gang tackle.

Jargon usually conveys a kind of phony expertise. If something is meaningful, it should be intelligible. If something is bluster, it's better to couch it in jargon and intimidate and overwhelm. Coaches do this. Football commentators do this without reason. Calling a middle linebacker the "Mike" or referring to a smaller running back who is equally skilled at receiving a "scatback" lends weight to otherwise shallow commentary. *The quarterback needs to identify the Mike.* The quarterback needs to know where the middle linebacker is. *Watch out if this shifty scatback gets free in the open field.* This rusher is elusive and probably fast. Players who retire to the booth, who know little more about describing the game than you or I, but excel at, say, tackling or throwing the football, use jargon as a living résumé. It reminds us they were there. It keeps intruders far away from their sanctum.

It's a long tradition. Some readers probably got a whiff of it from a former or current coach. It filters up, and like everything, gets more attuned, more esoteric, and more specialized with each stop. Unfortunately, it then filters out to the football-watching community. Visit a football message board and you'll surely find someone named "Coach" with a BA in BS. One might more easily determine if Achilles will catch the tortoise than understand these people. Maybe he will, but only if he can identify the Mike.

The best advice my coach ever gave me was to cram my hands down my pants because it's warm down there. That's advice you can use. If I was told to cram my phalanges down by my femoral triangle to reduce convection, my hands would still be cold. But in a rare moment of clarity, he told me something I could understand. Then he told me the team needed some power pigs, and I should consider using the four-point. *The four-point lets you anchor, son, and anchorin' is good. Anchorin' frees the Ted to hit the lead blocker in the hole and set up the Mike for some rippin', grippin', strippin', flippin' nonsense.*

If it were but a poetic font of babble, set to the tune of "American Football," it could be a kind of jabberwocky that assisted the game's atmospherics without intruding into the action. But football is hard enough to understand as is. It is, by mathematical definition, chaos. Did the center snap the ball before the quarterback was entirely ready? Could that fraction-of-a-second confusion influence which receiver he perceives as "open"? Of course. Did the quarterback then move left and did that move left make it hard for his right tackle to protect him? It happens all the time. Every play is amazingly dense with information. How to make sense of it all? How to enter the cathedral encircled by gargoyles of jargon?

Here's how: understand the game and not the lingo.

Football is a game of possessions. When one team scores, the other team receives the next possession. That is, they go on offense. It's surely a rudimentary concept for anyone reading this book, but it's worth mentioning. Ideas like tempo and momentum are largely irrelevant and disproven. By definition of the word, a team cannot carry momentum into something that has ended. Yes, success tends to show itself in squared shoulders and smiles, and failure in dropped pads and grimaces, but anyone who's made it as far as the NFL puts it all out there, every play. Likewise, playing fast or slow doesn't affect total possessions, which are almost always equal. Understand that tempo and momentum are common buzzwords deployed by coaches and commentators, but are largely false constructs. The 2009 New Orleans Saints, for instance, were accused of not carrying momentum into the playoffs after losing their final three games. Somehow, they survived. I guess all that momentum returned when they smacked around the Cardinals 45–14 in the divisional round.

Tube Boobs

I was watching a game commentated by Merle Harmon and Jim Turner, and there were quite a few really funny foibles. Both seemed very uncomfortable being on the television. When they introduced themselves, Harmon held a mike to Turner, only for Turner to reveal a second later that he himself had a mike.

There was a real radio feel to the announcing. It was rich and full of detail. It makes me feel that much more frustrated with modern booth crews that are often incompetent, and sometimes worse. Nothing grates quite like hearing Joe Buck make it perfectly clear he is not excited or invested in the game.

One thing Buck would never attempt is to completely mischaracterize the action. On one down, Harmon attempted to credit John Harris for a play he was clearly nowhere near. When they showed the replay, he credited the player who actually made the tackle, but then credited Harris again. Makes me wonder what it was like when you had to listen to a game and trust what the announcers were telling you was true. I bet I would have never realized that it wasn't the line's fault but Shaun Alexander's.

A team wins by winning possessions. This is where the idea of momentum derives from. To win a possession, a team does not need to score. It needs to gain field position, and if it can't turn that field position into points, it must retain that field position after giving up possession. Field position—that is, the yards gained and kept from a drive—is worth points.

Think of it like this. A team takes the ball down to their opponents' 1-yard line. Over four possessions, they fail to convert the touchdown and then must turn over possession. Jargon football would tell you that team lost momentum. In fact, they lost possession, but have momentum—that is, the field position they give over is worth points. Sometimes the other team will be then able to drive 99 yards and score, but this is very uncommon. Instead, the opponent is likely to drive but unlikely to score, and because they have so far to go, likely to give the ball back over and with it, good field position. Further, starting a drive within one's own 5-yard line has dangers. A safety is possible. The chance of an interception or fumble being recovered for a touchdown increases. That is partially why statisticians often endorse going for it. Not only does an additional down increase the chance of conversion, but by kicking a field goal, a team sacrifices field position.

That's a lengthy aside, but the meat of the matter is that, within a game, a drive is not zero-sum. There is value in field position and value in every way it's achieved. Kickoffs that force touchbacks are valuable, because returns typically take the ball past the 20. Punts that can be downed within an opponent's 20 are valuable, as are punts that net a high number of yards. Sustained drives that do not yield points but do lead to bad field position for your opponent are valuable.

On any given down, a team has two basic ways of achieving yards. It can run or pass. This is the strategy of football. The defense then must devise a way to either stop the run or stop the pass. While those aren't mutually exclusive, they do require different actions.

On a run, the play is linear. The ball is taken by the rusher and will travel wherever he goes. Therefore, the most basic way to defend a run is to have every defender run to or around the rusher. It's not backyard football, of course, so you don't want everyone running directly at the rusher lest he shift directions and suddenly be uncontested. Still, most basically, the ball is never going to travel faster than a human runs, is never out of play, is always exactly where it looks like it is, and is almost always going where it looks like it's going.

An offense creates a run by first creating a path, and then trusting the rusher too see that path and see his options within and around that path. There are a lot of ways this is done. Most basically, a team can simply attempt to move the defense away from the rusher, and they do this either by moving toward the desired path or moving away from it.

The defense attempts to jam that path but also contain alternate paths. They usually put players on the line opposite of the offense so that it may not move forward uncontested, but even that is not necessary. The defense is always reacting. It has formations and plays, but within those plays it has a greater amount of variability. The formation reflects the offense's formation, and the offense's formation is a clue to its play call.

Passing is the more complex and modern form of offense, and also in the modern NFL, the more vital and important form of offense. Coaches and fans still repeat tired clichés about running to win, but they're wrong. It defies common sense, too. In any given game, a quarterback will account for more than double the yards of a running back, but for whatever reason, we are told the back's yards are inherently more valuable.

The passing game "jumps." The quarterback receives the ball and then surveys the field looking for a receiver. In a basic pass, he has as many "reads," or options, as he does receivers. A good quarterback must quickly determine the right read and accurately deliver the ball to that receiver. This skill is the single most important skill of a quarterback. Without it, no quarterback can be successful. It influences every part of the outcome. A quarterback who cannot properly read a defense throws incomplete passes and interceptions. A quarterback who cannot read a defense quickly is tackled before he throws.

The defense defends the pass on two levels. It, most basically, attempts to cover the receivers by interfering with the pass, but not the receiver. Except what is deemed incidental, minor, accidental, unintended, etc., the defender cannot interfere with the receiver after five yards—five yards past the line of scrimmage. So a good pass defender must be able to anticipate and react to the receiver he is covering.

What receiver he is covering is determined by whether he is assigned man-to-man or zone coverage. Those distinctions are as simple as they sound. A defender assigned man must follow his man wherever on the field he runs. This is considered riskier, because in a pure man scheme, there is only one fail-safe before a receiver is considered wide open. In a zone scheme, a defender is assigned an area on the field. In practice, this can be confusing, because the area is defined both theoretically and actually by the defenders' quickness and reaction time. Further complicating things is that a defender could be assigned a zone that is then infiltrated by multiple receivers. Which does he defend? He must decide, and that can be difficult and exploitable. The benefit of a zone is that it is less likely to break down entirely, because defenders are spread across the field, and a receiver is unlikely to become isolated against a single defender, or completely free.

The defense playing the receivers works in conjunction with the defense that is attempting to tackle the quarterback. That is called the pass rush. A defense decides how many players it wants to tackle the quarterback and how many players it wants to prevent the quarterback's targets from getting open. Basically, defending a pass is about time. The players defending the receivers are attempting to create time by preventing the quarterback from having a good read. The players rushing the quarterback are attempting to reduce the quarterback's time to make that read. So, when a quarterback is sacked, it is neither entirely because of the rush or the coverage, but the synthesis of the two. A team would have an equally perfect defense if it either never allowed a receiver to get open or was able to tackle the quarterback instantaneously.

Passing used to be predicated off the run. This is the idea of play-action. Play-action exploits the run-pass balance. A team will mimic the action of a run play, sometimes only faking a handoff, sometimes involving blockers moving as if it were a run play, sometimes receivers faking block and then releasing into a pass-catching route, and sometimes quarterbacks running circular from the pocket like they might after handing the ball to a rusher. Whatever the particular ploy, the goal is to fool the defense into reacting to a run and therefore being less prepared for a pass. A less common tactic is to draw. A draw is the opposite of play-action: a play that is designed to look like a pass that results in a run.

If you understand these concepts, everything else about football is discernable. You do not need to understand the jargon, or why coaches tell players what to do on any given play, you only need to know that one team is attempting to gain yards and ultimately score, and the other is attempting to prevent that.

The only other thing a person needs to understand football is knowledge of a running clock and the continually changing game state. All I mean by "game state" is the exact situation both teams are in. Before a team starts, both teams are equally favored by the rules. As soon as one team is awarded possession after the coin toss, that team gains an advantage because it has the first chance to score. As the game goes on, the game state changes because of possession, score, and time.

Possession is the first advantage. If two teams are tied, the team with possession most often has an advantage. In the modern NFL, anything from the 15-yard line and out is advantageous for the offense. That team has some chance of scoring, therefore gaining a tangible advantage, or giving its opponent worse field position should it not score.

The second advantage is the score, and the score works with the game clock to provide a continually improving advantage. For instance, a team up by 10 points with 50 minutes left of game clock has a negligible advantage, because its opponent can expect to score at least 10 points in that time. Therefore, the opponent feels no pressure to play differently, is not forced to pass, which achieves yards quicker than running, nor pressure to take unnecessary risks.

As the game progresses, and the trailing team has fewer and fewer chances to recover, the lead becomes a greater and greater advantage. With five minutes remaining, a 10-point lead has a dramatic impact on the trailing team. It cannot run regularly because running takes more time to achieve less than passing, and so it becomes more predictable and easier to defend against. It also must take bigger risks, and those risks can cause a reasonably close game to become lopsided.

The winning team not only maintains the run-pass balance, but what hurts the losing team actually benefits the winning team. Because runs take more time, a losing defense can feel compelled to stop the run. That makes passing and play-action more effective. The winning team also may become more conservative, and because of this, is less likely to dramatically lose possession through an interception or fumble.

The game state changes constantly, and, for the most part, benefits the winning team. Teams can become too conservative, and value game clock above preventing yards, but even though examples of that backfiring are famous, they are also uncommon.

The above is mostly common knowledge shared by all football fans. Ideas like a run-pass balance, and the pressure created by a late lead, are obvious after watching one game. The linearity of running the ball and the way a pass jumps is equally obvious. It's obvious because football is a simple game accomplished through complex means. One doesn't need to understand every tactic conceived or every word stretched and abused to describe, one really only needs to know the basics. Receivers are always going to try and get open, runners are always going to try to get free, and the defense is always going to try and stop that in whatever way it can. The Gargoyles of Jargon will forever attempt to confuse, complicate, and terrify, but football will stay, sublimely, beautifully, simple.

38 The Pick Man

Dave Brown was good, right? He was the best player Seattle selected in the expansion draft, was taken in the first round by the Steel Curtain Steelers in 1975 and was available because that team had secondary talent to burn. Pittsburgh literally had a Pro Bowler at every starting secondary position in 1976. Getting a Dave Brown was almost like a loophole in the expansion draft. He wasn't a reject, but overabundance.

Brown arrived in Seattle, started right away, and continued starting for the next 11 years. He started for Jack Patera and then started for Chuck Knox. When Brown left for Green Bay, he started first for Forest Gregg and then Lindy Infante. In fact, after leaving Pittsburgh, Brown never played in a game he didn't start.

Sure as he started, he did something magic. In 14 years in Seattle and Green Bay, Brown snagged 62 interceptions and at least one every year. He ranks eighth all-time. Among players who played in the post–Mel Blount–rule NFL, he ranks fourth, behind only Rod Woodson, Darren Sharper, and Ronnie Lott.

It sounds like fairy tale—Brown, a hidden talent, obtained for nothing. Brown, a core player on a building team. Brown, something to watch before there was anything to watch. So what gnaws at me?

Watching a football game, it's pretty easy to see the front seven. We can see the blockers block and the pass rushers pass and linebackers tackle and runners evade. We understand receivers and quarterbacks because they produce robust stats, but also because they initiate action. For a receiver to receive, he must first flash open, and getting open is the primary job of a receiver. So yards reflect ability. Receptions reflect ability.

That hardest riddle to crack in football analysis is how to evaluate a secondary. A standard TV angle obscures the majority of their actions. In fact, we mostly see corners and safeties when they've made a mistake. We know they've made a mistake, because their receiver is being targeted. We know they've made a mistake precisely because we see them at all.

Interceptions can be had because of great coverage or lousy but lucky coverage. Some players fixate on interceptions and abandon coverage attempting a pick. Season to season, interception rates vary wildly. We can scout ball skills, but we can't anticipate the exact situation that allows for an interception. Over a career, a player like Brown surely proved his ability, but at what cost?

Brown started for 14 seasons, and yet, he rarely ever started for a good pass defense. If we use adjusted net yards per attempt as our standard, a stat that factors in sacks and interceptions, he played for two elite defenses. The 1982 Seahawks ranked third, but in a strike-shortened season. The 1984 Seahawks ranked first. No one expected Brown to make Seattle elite alone, but apart from those seasons, the Seahawks were rarely even good. In 14 seasons, teams Brown played for ranked 17th on average. Seventeenth out of 28. It wasn't just because Brown's late '70s Seahawks are dragging down the average, either. He played in just four above-average units his entire career.

It wasn't like Brown was alone. Jacob Green joined in 1980 and Kenny Easley in 1981. The line was considered the strength of Seattle's defense, and so I don't assume Brown was suffering because lack of pass rush. But maybe he was. Even if I could find sack totals from before sacks were recorded, and even if I adjusted them for passing attempts and game situations, sacks still only vaguely represent overall pass rush.

For almost any argument there is a counterargument of equal merit. He only played in one Pro Bowl. The Pro Bowl is often a lousy indicator of ability. Brown played on lousy pass defenses. We can't be sure that was because of Brown. He started for many years. Maybe he was just better than the alternative. It isn't like Seattle was content with Brown. It drafted Terry Taylor in the first round of 1984, and Patrick Hunter in the third round of 1986. Of course, a team always needs defensive backs, and how do we know the Seahawks were replacing Brown instead of another corner?

We don't.

Dave Brown's career ended in Seattle when Chuck Knox traded him to Green Bay for an 11th-round pick. The modern NFL Draft doesn't even have 11 rounds. Of course, Brown was the oldest starting corner in the NFL by 1987, so it's not like Seattle was selling high. He started in Green Bay for three seasons and had 12 more picks. Three years after he retired, he was the second player ever inducted into the Seahawks Ring of Honor. The city and team appreciated Brown, and that counts. But I can't tell you if he was a great player or overvalued for his interceptions. I can't tell you if he was good in coverage. I found an article saying Stanley Morgan lit Brown up for 161 yards receiving. The author, Michael Vega, says Brown "had just been reduced to toast." Reduced to toast, how often? Reduced to toast, rhetorical flourish? I don't know.

So is Dave Brown an underappreciated star who was hidden in Seattle? Was he the 1980s version of Deltha O'Neal? Would he have been better on another team, or was he hurting the team he was on?

I don't know.

39 Darrell Jackson

He wasn't fast. What speed he had was lost to an unrelenting run of injuries. He wasn't big or particularly strong, either. If you wanted to affix superlatives to Darrell Jackson, you wouldn't find any that would stick. Greatest. No. Fastest. No. Steadiest hands. Yeah, okay, now I'm pulling your leg.

Jackson was good, and for years—and by being good, the best receiver in the greatest era of the Seahawks, he earns a place. What that place is, where it fits within the legacy of the Seahawks, and how to best—that is, most accurately—understand D-Jack is tough. It'll take a little homework.

Jackson was a Gator, complement to the more hyped Travis Taylor, but little more than situational fodder before his junior season. Steve Spurrier issued a progress report prior to the 1999 season: "Darrell, I think, is going to have his very best year. Of course, it's not going to take much to have his very best year because he hasn't done that much yet." Which was true, Jackson had not done much in his two years at Florida. He had 30 receptions for 345 yards and five touchdowns. Respectable, but hardly the totals expected of a high school legend.

Kenny Kelly and Jackson were unstoppable at Tampa Catholic High School. They formed the core of a Crusaders dynasty. It wasn't just football, either. Kelly and Jackson teamed to win a state title in basketball. All told, Jackson left Tampa Catholic with national high school records in total receiving yards (4,594) and yards per reception (24.05) his senior season. National records—Jackson was good.

That must have been in the back of Mike Holmgren's mind when he selected Jackson in the third round of the 2000 NFL Draft. He finally had that waited-for breakout season before declaring, catching 67 passes for 1,156 yards in 1999. But his draft stock was weak, and many felt he should have returned for his senior season. If not to improve his stock, then to escape a stacked wide-receiver class. Most considered Jackson the lesser teammate to Taylor. Taylor was selected 10th overall by the Ravens, but Jackson was the better pro.

He stuck his landing, receiving for 713 yards as a rookie and surpassing 1,000 the next season. Jackson was an instinctive route runner, fluid but quick through his breaks. He developed timing and rhythm with Jon Kitna, then Brock Huard, then Trent Dilfer, and ultimately Matt Hasselbeck. Quarterbacks develop favorites, and one season's star receiver can vanish when new blood takes over, but Jackson always won trust with his timing, steadiness, and ability to get open. By the end of his first season, he had surpassed Sean Dawkins and was Seattle's clear No. 1. He was never truly overtaken.

Koren Robinson flashed on the scene in 2002, his second season, and became Seattle's big-play receiver and leading yards man, but it was a flash in the pan. Robinson's receiving totals dropped the next two seasons, and by 2005 he was in Minnesota. The troubled receiver never touched an ounce of the potential he was given. Jackson returned from injury and resumed his steady presence within the roster.

He became the face of a ruinous run of drops in 2004 and missed most of Seattle's special run in 2005. When he returned in the divisional round, he was the heart of an offense that sputtered after losing Shaun Alexander to a concussion. Matt Hasselbeck threw for 215 yards, and Jackson received 143 of them. When Seattle finally made the Super Bowl, Jackson led the charge, catching five passes in the first quarter and punishing the Steelers' off coverage.

Those were the only five passes he caught. He finished with an offensive pass-interference penalty that cost Seattle a touchdown, two passes caught but out of bounds, another incomplete, and an interception on a pass targeting him. That was the story of Darrell Jackson, good everywhere he played, but always overshadowed, first by Kelly, then Taylor, briefly by Robinson, and eventually by himself. He just couldn't be what he seemed destined to be.

Jackson left Seattle after a battle of egos with general manager Tim Ruskell. Jackson said former general manager Bob Whitsitt had made a verbal agreement to give him a contract extension. A verbal agreement Ruskell saw no reason to honor. He bloated his perceived value in 2006 by catching 10 touchdowns, but a career full of injuries had sapped his ability and worn off that vital athletic edge that made him a pro. Ruskell traded Jackson to San Francisco for a fourth-round pick, and two years and two teams later, it looked like a brilliant move. He just didn't have it anymore. The guy who was always able, trustworthy, and stable, who hadn't an ounce of flash but a ton of football ability, couldn't cut it anymore.

40 The Black Hole

No light exits a black hole. A black hole cannot be seen, but its crushing gravity can be felt. Briefly. At its center lies a singularity. It may only be understood by that which surrounds it. A black hole can bend even light. A black hole can puncture the universe.

A Black Hole can leave a Seahawks fan with a red hole from a rusty shiv.

It's been a long time since Oakland was relevant, but the Raiders' failure feeds the orcs and accountants that populate sections 104 to 107. Like black mead, honey sweet, and fizzy as stadium beer, Raiders fans drink deep their lunatic owner and his commitment to failure. Like a reanimated corpse, sallow and sunken-cheeked, Davis drinks deep Raider Nation's money. The Black Hole is where civilization dies or, at least, takes a half day and writes off the travel expenses.

Yeah, the days of working-class people taking their families to a day at the stadium are long past now. A family of four eye-blacked and armored Raiders fans would have to pay about $2,400 dollars for season tickets to the Black Hole. When the city per capita income is about $22,000, well, there're either some broke but dedicated rowdies in the Black Hole, or a whole bunch of vacationing trial lawyers and dentists. I'll probably get stabbed for writing it, but modern Raiders fans are just really into Cosplay. And by stabbed, I mean subpoenaed.

The decline of the Black Hole corresponds pretty well with the Raiders themselves. Back when the American dollar was strong and Teamsters, plumbers, and mechanics like my dad could afford a ticket, the Raiders were among the most formidable and feared franchises in football. Back when Howie Long was cracking skulls instead of hawking trucks, the Madden-Flores Raiders dominated the young Seahawks and clashed like rivals against the Knox Seahawks. They were worthy rivals, better enemies, brothers in blue collars, dock workers, factory workers, loggers. They were average people who let it all out on Sunday, screamed out the weekend-ending angst, and forgot it all for a little while. They were, once.

41 Chris Warren

I remember liking Chris Warren a ton. Always was a running back man myself. My fascination stemmed from scanning box scores as a child. Warren was my chance to have a piece of Barry Sanders.

Sanders was something special. I don't know what it was like to be a Lions fan. Watching Sanders must have been a conflicted thrill. It was a demanding style, demanding of his line and demanding of his coach's patience. On any touch there was the possibility of greatness yet the probability of futility. Fifty yards sideways for a two-yard loss.

I imagine that's what it was like watching Warren play, for a little while.

Warren was drafted in 1990 in the fourth round and putted around a couple seasons working as a kick returner and proving effective. He entered the discussion for starting running back after general manager Tom Flores demoted Tom Flores to head coach Tom Flores. It was one in a career of master strokes. Warren was to be a part of the "Raiderizing" of the Seahawks' offense. How does one Raiderize something? Does it involve broken glass? Jail time? Face paint? Maybe a shank? Or a 1040?

It meant running deep and sticking your hands up like you knew how to receive. The conceit sounded plausible. The Raiders were not a reviled and defamed organization then. It was a city of champions—angry, monochromatic champions. Storied—in a good way.

Warren beat out Rueben Mayes for the right to embody Flores' flawed but flashy offense. It was a big promotion. It would start a run of four straight 1,000-yard seasons. In his second season, Warren earned a spot in the Pro Bowl. He would return the next two seasons.

Warren was undoubtedly good even when his teams were bad. His first season starting, Seattle scored an implausible 140 points. That ranked dead last in the NFL. Seattle was also dead last in total yards, first downs, passing yards, and passing touchdowns. In the modern NFL, it's hard to conceive of a running back having such success on a team with no passing firepower. Teams would stack the box and dare their opponents to pass. But Warren slashed through, painting lightning bolts over the Kingdome's turf with his strides.

Flores won two games in 1992. The offense was cripplingly bad, averaging just 4.88 yards per passing attempt. Yet somehow Warren averaged a robust 4.6 yards per rushing attempt. Three separate starting quarterbacks were sacked on more than 10 percent of their attempts. And yet Warren made the line work, topping 100 yards three times and averaging over five yards per carry six times.

He made that line work all right, slicing and cutting back and redirecting on a dime and running to one sideline before sprinting back toward the other. It was fun football—for the fan. Like Sanders, if you saw it only when it worked, it looked unstoppable.

Billy Joe Mantooth attended Ferrum College. Mantooth, closer Bill Wagner, a kicker, a journeyman outfielder, a Globetrotter, and a coach played for the Panthers in the Dixie Conference and graduated to notable sports careers. Warren transferred to Ferrum after failing to meet Virginia's academic standards. He posted a 1.75 GPA and needed to post a 1.8 or better. Ball-breakers, those Cavaliers.

At Ferrum, Warren escaped the Wahoos' rigid educational standards and any semblance of competition. He dominated. Many of his records still stand, including career and season touchdowns, rushing yards in a season, and all-purpose yards. In 1989 he had five returns for touchdowns.

He didn't quite plaster his mansion with the entrails of defeated opponents in the pros as he did in the Dixie Conference, but he gave Seahawks fans something to watch when there wasn't much else. Under the grip of Tom Flores and later Dennis Erickson, Seattle never blundered into a winning season in Warren's six years starting. He was good, and he was entertaining, Seattle's own private Barry Sanders, and if it took some heartburn before Warren would pay off with something special, then at least something special was always possible.

42 The 12

Texas A&M sued the Seahawks for use of the phrase "the 12th Man." Sometimes sports can be very stupid. Seattle settled out of court. The Seahawks must now pay a license fee and acknowledge the Aggies' ownership of the phrase. Pat Riley did something similar with the term "threepeat." Sometimes sports can be very stupid.

The 12th Man became part of Seahawks lore when Chuck Knox applied the phrase to the rowdy Kingdome crowds in 1984. It was a jubilant ejaculation, but he meant it. He more than respected fans, he could actually empathize with them. That same year, the Seahawks organization retired the number.

In some ways, it's just a marketing gimmick. Every team enjoys a home-field advantage, and the exact reasons why are well researched but not fully known. Some theorize home teams get preferential treatment from officials. In some sports the field conditions themselves change. The strongest argument is simply that players are more skilled at home because they are more thoroughly comfortable with their surroundings.

Though it sold a ton of T-shirts, the 12th Man phenomenon has a tangible value for the Seahawks. The 12th Man creates a 112-decibel cheer that not only forces false starts but disorients and disorganizes an offense. Since 2005, Seattle had forced false starts at the highest rate in the NFL at home. But though those five yards can be crucial, I think it's the way opponents must adjust that really makes the 12th Man so amazing.

Perhaps its greatest achievement was in the 2005 NFC Championship Game. Jake Delhomme had to turn his in-helmet headset so loud, it produced feedback. Delhomme was lost. He couldn't adjust his offense to take apart the Seahawks' simple strategy of pressing Steve Smith and keeping a receiver over top. It should have been easy. The Patriots attempted the same thing in Super Bowl XXXVIII, but unlike there, on neutral ground, Qwest was so loud that calling an audible was a near impossibility. Delhomme went from the highest-rated quarterback in NFL post-season history to a crippling liability, and Smith was shut down.

43 Know Physics

Taylor Mays is a physical abnormality. His coaches struggled to keep him under 240. Yet he is faster than almost anyone in college football. He ran a 4.43-second 40 at the 2009 NFL Combine, and some think he was short-changed. Mays glides 41 inches off the ground. Some would compare him to Kenny Easley, but his future might look a lot more like Roy Williams.

In Mays, many see everything they want in a safety, but bigger. He is fast, strong, and athletic. When he combines his mass and speed, he can pop a receiver with the kind of raw force that makes pro players relive childhood terrors. In Mays, many envision a player who can be that rare professional who seems like a man among boys. To them, it would be preposterous to argue Mays' size might be his undoing.

It shouldn't be, though. That same force that makes Mays such a terror also inhibits his ability to redirect. A smaller, more spritely defensive back can stop quickly and correct his angle, but Mays is a laser-guided missile. If the target moves suddenly, Mays can't match. He is built like a linebacker, and he probably will be forced to become a linebacker. He speed, athleticism, and size are tantalizing, but his agility is just not there.

Football is ruled by physics. Every interaction is a physical interaction. One does not need to be a physicist to understand the game, but a basic understanding of physics can illuminate and cut through some misunderstandings.

Consider Newton's concept of action-reaction. DeSean Jackson was an amazing college receiver, but when he weighed in at just 169, many assumed his body could not survive the pro game. But, why would weight determine toughness? Jackson was slight, but that protected him. Like a feather, he could only absorb as much force as he could return. The true measure of toughness is determined by more complicated and less well understood things like the resilience of connective tissues. Was anyone poking around Jackson's knees to see how strong his ACL and MCL were? No, of course not. The knock on Jackson was little more than common prejudice. He was small, so he couldn't play Big League Ball. Jackson slipped into the second round, was drafted behind bigger, sturdier players, and then rewarded the team that saw what he could do with 2,079 yards receiving in two seasons. He has missed one game in two seasons, a non-contact hyperextension of his knee.

Why do fireballers so often flop? Well, the harder a ball is thrown, the quicker it arrives and the harder it is to catch. Brett Favre and John Elway were considered prospects with unlimited potential because of their cannon arms, but neither succeeded until later in their careers. Maybe they had to learn how to take something off. Maybe they just lost enough arm strength to make their prototypical arm actually worth a damn. The greatest performing quarterbacks in the history of the NFL had touch, not cannons, and yet the prototype never changes. Would Joe Montana, Peyton Manning, Kurt Warner, Dan Marino, or Steve Young have been better if they could throw a ball through a safe vault? Of course not. The touch or catchability of their passes is part of what defined them.

What makes a lineman succeed? Well, if you're an interior lineman, it helps if you're heavy. With variations in initial velocity differing by fractions, being able to do it with an extra 20 pounds sure helps. It's not enough to be heavy to be good, but the initial match-up of an interior lineman, defensive tackle, and offensive guard or center, is a battle of bodies smashing into each other. Physicist Timothy Gay estimates the impact as equal to a car crash. Being heavier might not prevent you from injury, but when a Mack truck hits a Volkswagen, it's not the Mack truck that goes flying.

The study of physics in football is as deep as one wants to explore, but one doesn't need a PhD to derive a little common sense from high school basics. Sometimes too big is too big. Is Taylor Mays a top safety but bigger? Probably not, no. There is a reason why defensive backs tend to be small. Was DeSean Jackson destined to bust because he was too light? No, he has already fulfilled the potential of a second-round pick and then some. It's not like Jackson is a defensive tackle—because, man, if he was, he would be shoved into next week. There is no way a gnat like Jackson could anchor. Luckily, his job is being quick, redirecting on a dime, and catching footballs. Which, apparently, his body was made for.

44 Brian Blades

I couldn't see the athlete in the old man. Brian Blades lived the tragedy of the historically good. By the time I truly understood football, Blades wasn't even that. It's difficult for me to be sure he ever was good, honestly. Most Seahawks fans probably know his name but not his game. Who was Brian Blades?

He was a Hurricane and before that a Bengal, a Piper High Bengal. He was a Hurricane during Miami's notorious but wildly successful "the U" period. Blades attended with his younger brother, Bennie, lined across from Michael Irvin, received for Bernie Kosar, then Vinny Testaverde, and was coached by Jimmy Johnson. He saw Flutie's Hail Mary, won a national title in 1987, and probably did some other things we'd rather not know about.

Seattle selected Blades 49th overall, their first selection in the 1988 draft after burning their first-round pick on Brian Bosworth in the 1987 supplemental draft. He was Steve Largent's successor, in a way, and better fit Chuck Knox's attitude about the passing game. Knox considered him a first-round talent. Was he? Well, Blades was fast.

This is where the story careens off the rails. I was five when Seattle selected Blades. I didn't tape record games that weren't broadcast in my area, and I didn't pore over footage in my Hypercolor shirt. Actually, we couldn't afford Hypercolor. My shirt probably had a foam spider on it. I was rad.

So I can tell you that Blades was not well known for his hands—his catch percentage was typically low, at or below 60 percent—and because of that, Blades was not a very valuable

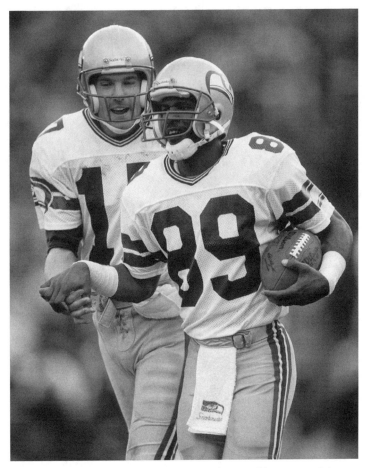

Brian Blades gets congratulated by Dave Krieg for one of his two touchdown receptions in a 43–37 win over the Raiders that secured the AFC West title on December 18, 1988, at Los Angeles Memorial Coliseum.

receiver. If Largent was the new prototype, Blades was the throwback, the play-action burner who could get behind a defense but couldn't sustain a drive, the all-or-nothing receiver who could fill out a highlight reel but never carry an offense, the Joe Namath in the era of Steve Young.

He wasn't bad, but he wasn't great, and though he had four 1,000-yard seasons, that often means nothing more than being the best of a bad bunch. It was a bad bunch. A bad bunch of receivers, linemen, and quarterbacks who could never field an even average offense. But then, maybe Blades overcame such a desultory supporting cast and emerged as a star despite it. However you want to spin it. We may never know.

Blades spent his entire career as a Seahawk. Scandal and injury ended him early, at 33. He had some superficial highs, some very real lows, was great, just not great among the great, only good. And for an outsider like me, who can never hope to be good at anything like Blades was great at football, quickly forgotten.

Toward the end, before the allegations but after his prime, Blades had his best statistical season. Seattle selected Joey Galloway eighth overall in the 1995 draft. Galloway was a younger, faster Brian Blades, but was less skilled and less trusted. Blades won Week 1, with eight receptions and 107 yards. The two went back and forth, challenging each other, complementing each, and neither ever truly surpassing the other. By almost any measure, the two were equals. Galloway finished with 1,039 yards receiving, Blades, 1,001. Blades had 10 more receptions, but Galloway three more touchdown receptions. Pro-Football-Reference.com gives the edge to Galloway, assigning him 12 points to Blades' 10. Football Outsiders considers it a dead heat, assigning Galloway 1,084 equalized yards to Blades' 1,081.

Galloway was a rookie with promise, and Blades a 30-year-old veteran. Statistics struggle to assign individual credit, and some of Blades' seeming rebound was improved surrounding talent and improved coaching. It was the first time since Largent retired that Blades had a partner. But it came much too late.

So who was Brian Blades? Well, he was one of the greatest receivers in Seahawks history, but never much more than good. He was a first-round talent according to Chuck Knox, but Knox was losing his grasp on the game. He played for some miserable teams, and his career suffered because of it. He was a one-in-a-million talent at wide receiver, and yet somehow still only good.

45 1999 Wild-Card

Seattle made the playoffs in Mike Holmgren's first season. It was the team's first playoff appearance since losing Chuck Knox, and I'm sure it felt like the beginning of something special. It was, but like a foreword instead of a first chapter. I didn't see this game when it happened. I was halfway between angry teenager and homeless teenager at the time. I tried to get my hands on a copy, failed, and then, poof, it showed up on Hulu. Rad.

It was a strange team Holmgren brought to the playoffs that year. It was mostly made by Dennis Erickson and Tom Flores. Seattle got off to a red-hot start. I mean, *red hot*. The Promise of Holmgren felt like fait accompli. Seattle started out 8–2, but ended just 9–7. It won the AFC West for just the second time in franchise history, and it was a dogfight.

The AFC West was a terror in 1999. Win-loss records do not do it justice. Kansas City was 9–7 but had the sixth-best point differential in the NFL. Football Outsiders, using a formula that adjusts for strength of schedule, ranked the Chiefs as the fourth-best team in all of football. Oakland was the third-best by the same measure. The Super Bowl Champion Broncos slumped to 6–10 but were only outscored by four points. Denver ranked 12th.

Seattle ranked 11th. They were defined by the defense. The defense that Holmgren would later dismantle. Well, it was getting old. The Seahawks had 30 interceptions. It had Tez, Adams, Sinclair, and Daniels.

I do a lot of tape work at Field Gulls. I watch and rewatch plays until I know what every player did. That's impossible on Hulu.

You'd be better off just watching the game yourself, but here's my running commentary:

It seems like the national storyline revolved around Dan Marino: whether it would be his last game, whether he was really feuding with head coach Jimmy Johnson. Seahawks fans often think they are slighted by the media, but I think it's a blessing. Seattle had a chance to make its own storyline. It was the end of the Kingdome. There was Jon Kitna, and at the time, I thought Tacoma's own was the future of the franchise. There was Holmgren, of course, and the second-half collapse.

I miss Chad Brown.

Man, why the heck did Ricky Watters bounce that run outside? Watching this, I remember just how frustrating and dislikable Watters could be. Guy had so much talent, and he ran with such grace, but like a certain back that followed him, he killed you between his touches.

Charlie Rogers' return touchdown is a great example of how difficult it is to accurately measure ability in the NFL. He muffed the kickoff, but recovered. The muff caused discord in the Dolphins, Rogers somehow split Miami's gunners while recovering the football, and that discord aided his return. Rogers more than made up for his initial error, but that play could never be repeated. I think Holmgren got that, because when Rogers walked over to the sideline, the Walrus gave him a grim look and took him under his shoulder. Killjoy.

All the funny faces and styles, the guy with the Jonathan Davis hairstyle and sunglasses, the dude with the Chuck Knox hat and a just a whisper of mustache—was it really just 10 years ago?

How did Seattle screw up that line read without Chris Spencer? I'm so confused. Zach Thomas ran through untouched, and to the best of my knowledge, Spencer had not even graduated high school yet. Kid had powers. Terrible, terrible powers.

Johnson's onside kick must have blown Holmgren's mind. Somehow, though, somehow, despite Johnson's ballsy play call, momentum was not attained. This defies everything I have ever learned about American football.

Oh, wait. Yes, it was. Seattle started inside their own 5.

F-ow-ree-uh? When did knowing how to pronounce a player's name become optional for announcers? Apparently, at least 10 years ago.

30:02. Exchange between Dolphins players regarding Kitna:

Jason Taylor: He's standing there. It's like he wants to be sacked.

Rich Owens: Yeah!

Off Camera: He's like a deer in headlights.

Must be a Seahawks thing.

I really miss Chad Brown.

30:57. That looks familiar.

Marino took a pitch on a botched flea flicker, and it was initially flagged for intentional grounding. I am sure some Seahawks fans were freaking out when the flag got picked up, but it is not grounding unless the quarterback is avoiding pressure, and clearly Marino was not.

Mike Holmgren looks thin.

Maybe it's Kitna, maybe it's because I never gave this game much thought, and maybe it is the foreign-looking uniforms, but it is hard for me to see this loss for the heartbreaker it obviously was. I guess I was lucky to have missed it. It looks like it was slow, boring, and frustrating.

46 Learn to Scout

Statistical analysis has become so precise in baseball, Sabermetricians have developed formulas that not only translate stats into wins, but stats into dollars. It's wild. If I venture over to Fangraphs.com and type in "Ichiro," I find out that not only was Ichiro Suzuki worth 5.1 wins above a replacement player, but that fair market value is $23.1 million.

How is that possible? Baseball is a simple game that produces robust samples. When the same is attempted in football, I am left with foolish assertions like D.J. Hackett is more valuable than Andre Johnson. That is because football is a complex game that produces a small and largely meaningless sample, wherein a 15-yard reception can mean the game or nothing at all.

Sabermetrics have helped feed the enthusiast culture of baseball. One can know a player's wins above replacement, his marginal value to a playoff contender, even the velocity and arc of a pitcher's curveball. Football fans are comparatively in the Stone Age. Stats can help us understand football, help us better envision what a winning football team must do, and better understand what is a repeatable skill and what is not, but we can't look at Brandon Marshall's DYAR and determine for sure whether he's a worse receiver than Vincent Jackson. There are too many complications.

The Stone Age can be fun, though. Science was once an intellectual pursuit rather than an intellectual imperative. A scientist might walk into the wilderness and keep a field journal of flora and fauna. He would take meticulous notes. Instead of quantifying the world, he qualified it. That made science a kind of art. It was fallible, for sure, but like art, precision was not the only determinant of success.

The art and science of understanding football is found in scouting. Scouting is an umbrella term that at its most essential simply means observing, understanding, and recording notes. One can scout a single player or a whole offense. One can look for individual skills or attempt to determine a game plan. One can attempt to determine relationships, fit, potential, and downside.

Learning how to do so does not take a course or a book or any such thing, but only time, patience, inquiry, and an open mind. The simplest method is to simply record a game and begin watching one player for every snap. My approach is to sit close to my television, have a notebook, fast-forward through the pre-snap hype and distraction, stop before the snap, identify the player, his position, and his opponent, and then watch it in slow motion over and over until every little detail pours out. It's time-consuming but gratifying. It creates confidence and replaces bluster. Few things betray insecurity like bragging.

When I discovered Brandon Mebane, the notion that Mebane was better than Chuck Darby was reasonably controversial. Darby had won a Super Bowl starting for the Tampa Bay Buccaneers, and that team was defined by its defensive dominance. He was a Seahawk for Seattle's own championship run. He was established and respected, and Mebane was just a rookie. But I knew Mebane was better because I had proof. Not second-hand takes, not coach speak, not semi-informative stats, but a snap-in, snap-out comparison of the two players and their ability to help their teams win.

With each game, I recorded and broke down, I became more knowledgeable. I would hit walls where I knew my knowledge was not enough. When I learned, I was able to immediately apply my learning. It wasn't seventh-grade Spanish. It was more like riding a bike. The knowledge was essential, and because I used it and practiced it every day, it became a part of my thinking.

Everyone's a Scout

Amateur scouting has become a big deal on the Internet. It's something I both love and hate. Expertise is hollow. Anyone who attempts to convince you their own opinion holds more weight is trying to sell you something. A fundamental idea of logic is that ideas can be true, but an idea cannot be true because of who said it.

However much I love the concept of a wide-open and free scouting community composed of hard-working people instead of experts, the execution is often very poor. For whatever reason, everyone wants to be the next Mel Kiper, and instead of taking a quiet and patient approach to evaluating players, they attempt to match his moxie and certitude. The product is a black-and-white view of the NFL Draft. Some players are certain busts, while others are undiscovered stars.

It might surprise some, but the NFL Draft is actually a pretty efficient process. Brian Burke of Advanced NFL Stats ran a survey of every draft pick and found a strong correlation between round and future success. We tend to think otherwise because exceptions stick in our memory, but trust me, not every Mike Kafka will become Kurt Warner.

Any person can become a scout if they are patient and work hard. It didn't land me a job managing the Seahawks. It hasn't done much more for me than expand my enjoyment of the game, but in that I have found something of worth. Something I feel both proud of and confident in.

Maybe the latter is the greatest gift of pursuing something I once enjoyed but never took very seriously. I learned not only how little I knew about football, but how little I knew about so many things I enjoyed. I learned that, like many, I was simply parroting the opinions of others without any sure idea of the truth. Recognizing how little I knew about football, but how much I could learn, allowed me to rethink everything in my life. I realized it was okay to enjoy something even if it was unpopular or critically panned. I realized that what is unpopular, what is critically unfit, can still be better, more essential, and more exciting than the biggest box-office draw or the most acclaimed Oscar winner. And I learned that if I wanted to, I could probably prove it.

47 Steve August

Steve August was the prized piece in the Tony Dorsett trade. He mucked it up for the expansion-era Seahawks and brought some stability and credibility to the Seahawks' offensive line. August played right tackle to protect Zorn's blind side, and did so credibly as the rest of the Seahawks' line was turned out and sold on the street corner.

It was probably tough being Steve August. Fans knew him as the consolation prize for losing Tony Dorsett. What do fans know? Seattle's offense took off after August signed on. But I will never know if it was because of August or a coincidence.

It is impossible for me to properly give meaning to an offensive lineman I never saw. I never saw him play, never found him in literature, and only truly knew of him because of the Dorsett trade. Older fans said he was good, and he was surely important. He would hold down the right on the Seahawks' all-time offensive line. Or maybe he would not. Maybe he was a turnstile, the very source of Zorn's decline, but you would not think so for how long he played, and how little effort the Seahawks put into replacing him.

Though it's lacking, I feel indebted to give him a spot. If nothing else, whether Zorn appreciated it or not, the two were eternally linked, and whatever good Zorn brought to the Seahawks, August helped protect it.

48 Watch College Football

College football is inferior football. That was my thinking for years. College football is sloppy, loose, and dominated by singular talents rather than great teams. I committed enough time to football. I was not about to sit in all Saturday and watch USC dismantle Washington State.

The game is bad, and the process to determine champions downright dumb. For years the champion was simply voted in. That is mind-blowing. That is determining a season the same way the NFL determines the Pro Bowl rosters. If a team was well-known and didn't screw up too badly, it was sure to finish with a respectable ranking. It created a disincentive to play tough games, and college teams recognized and responded to that. When the voting process was marginalized because of mass disgust, the NCAA introduced the BCS system. Teams are ranked by an arcane formula. It isn't true competition, but it fulfills the public's need for truthiness.

The BCS is still in effect, and on most Saturdays, singular talent still dominates. USC still wears out Washington State. My beloved Huskies are finally peeking out from their worst run in my lifetime. The game is still comparatively sloppy, but, you know what? Saturday in, enjoying wall-to-wall college ball is perhaps my happiest time of the week.

College football is a chance to enjoy football again without the stomach-wringing agony of competition. I want the Huskies to win, but I do not *need* the Huskies to win. In most games, I can simply sit back and watch the talent.

College football is a chance to see the great professionals of tomorrow. Where I once dreaded watching a bigger, faster, stronger player overmatch his opponent, I now watch with quiet fascination. These are the players who will be pros, and knowing their roots allows you to know their potential. Instead of cringing as Gerald McCoy smacked down and ran around opposing guards, I started to audit his dominance.

That idea is essential to appreciating the college game. Talent and teams must not only win, they must destroy, and the competition is not just with their opponent, but with themselves. It's not okay for McCoy to just play patty-cake with Levy Adcock. He must surge, get a violent hand punch, club him into a sister-world, and create a ripple through time that undoes his existence. McCoy must dominate and show pro tools.

I watch college football searching for pro talent and can spend entire quarters watching one or two players, auditing their every snap. How is his first step? What pass-rush moves does he possess? Does he pursue action outside his space, or does he stop and observe? Is he lean and broadly built, or has he maxed out his frame?

Then, when the scouting is done, I just sit back and enjoy a little football that I know is full of the passion and power and drama of the pro game, but is looser, less meaningful, and able to be dominated by singular talents. Sometimes, it is what you initially hate that eventually seduces you. College football is not the dense Modernist prose, it's the readable nonfiction you take to the dentist's office. College football is not a heartbreaking character portrait, it's a special-effects wonder. It's not a culinary masterpiece you savor with eyes closed, it's Ben and Jerry's on the riverfront. It's fun, and why hate fun?

49 The All-Anti-Largent Team

Seattle traded an eighth-round pick for Steve Largent because the Houston Oilers were convinced Largent was neither big enough nor fast enough to play in the NFL. It was a great moment in team history and one of the great lopsided trades in NFL history. There is nothing like seeing gold in another's rubbish. In the highly competitive NFL, winning a personnel decision can be as satisfying as winning a game.

Seattle fleeced Dallas by turning Joey Galloway into two first-round picks. Holmgren won by turning the 10th overall pick into Matt Hasselbeck and Steve Hutchinson. Seattle somehow, inexplicably, duped the Bears into offering a first-round pick for Rick Mirer. Holmgren signed Bobby Engram for loose change and turned him into a zone-busting bomb. The Seahawks added Dave Brown through the expansion draft, and Brown turned into a ball-hawking corner, perhaps the best in team history.

Of course, they didn't win 'em all. Seattle had some bad coaches who made some bad moves and lost some good talent because of it. It had to have talent before it lost talent, and so it was mostly unscathed through the '70s and early '80s. To hear experts from the period describe it, losing Theotis Brown was a mistake. Yeah, what a loss. Seattle didn't lose much of anyone of note under Knox. Without a salary cap, teams could keep the players they wanted, and the players they didn't want were guys like Wilbur Strozier and John Eisenhooth.

The first noteworthy cap casualty was Jacob Green, but Green was at his end. Seattle didn't miss him. The first casualty that hurt was Andy Heck. Chicago offered Heck a big free-agent contract, and Seattle didn't match. From that point on, they were scrapping for tackles until Walter Jones arrived in 1997.

Losing a player through free agency is a part of the post-salary-cap NFL. But that's not who we're looking for. No, we want good players Seattle simply didn't appreciate and so let walk—anti-Largents.

It wasn't until Tom Flores that Seattle started letting talent go. First it was Michael Bates. Seattle couldn't turn Bates into a decent receiver and so let him walk. He stopped in Cleveland for a season before joining the Panthers. There, he went to five consecutive Pro Bowls for Carolina. Losing talent is often about seeing what a player cannot do, rather than what they can. Bates couldn't receive, but, boy, could he return kicks.

The Seahawks dropped Lamar Smith early on, and Smith became a pretty productive rusher in Miami. Small beer, all in all. Smith was modestly talented. Kevin Mawae was an immensely talented offensive lineman, but raw. Seattle selected Mawae with an early second-round pick but gave up on him after his rookie contract. A season later, he would be an All-Pro center for the Jets. Mawae did not slow down until 2009. For his career, he was named All-Pro three times and has gone to eight Pro Bowls.

On the same roster as Mawae was Michael McCrary. Dennis Erickson was convinced that McCrary was too small, and to hear orthopedic surgeon Pierce Scranton tell it, "You might as well put a funnel over his mouth." McCrary languished on the roster for three years until a run of injuries practically forced Erickson to start him in '96. He had 13.5 sacks in 13 starts and signed with the Ravens the next season. He had 35 sacks his next three seasons and got his ring with the all-time great Ravens defense of 2000. Fatten that kid up.

The problem wasn't that Erickson was a jamook, though maybe he was, but that any coach who has a narrow definition of what does and does not work on his team is certain to lose good players. Mike Holmgren had a great eye for offensive talent, but he lost Ahman Green because he could only see Green's limitations. He lost Sam Adams and Phillip Daniels because he didn't know defense. That pretty much explains how he landed and lost Levon Kirkland, too, but Kirkland was mostly done.

Things settled down from there. The Seahawks lost Heath Evans, but did not need Heath Evans. They let Ken Hamlin go, and Hamlin was elected to the Pro Bowl the next season, but most Seahawks fans would agree it was an undeserved honor. Hamlin has a way of excelling when you see him and appearing at the edge of your screen, trailing a receiver streaking into the end zone. Finally there was some cohesion in the front office, and if Seattle lost talent, it was because they were priced out, as with Ken Lucas, or because that talent was named "Taco." They lost Chike Okeafor, but Okeafor was replaced by better talent. It lost Michael Boulware—well, traded away Boulware—but he never figured it out. The Vikings excised Hutch, but no one doubted his talent.

Yep, amazingly enough, under Bob Whitsitt and Tim Ruskell, players were properly evaluated. Seattle was freeing itself from the dogma of scheme. Free agents matched need, and lost players disappeared as quickly as Darrell Jackson. You could almost breathe and believe the stupidity had come to an end.

Then it lost Leonard Weaver. Weaver went to the Pro Bowl the very next season and then was re-signed by the Eagles, making him the highest-paid fullback in league history. Weaver was Largent, McCreary, Mawae—a good player, with obvious talent—lost, given up, because of a fixation on fit and scheme. Greg Knapp needed his fullback, and so Seattle brought in Justin Griffith and dropped Weaver and never stopped regretting it.

50 Elway

You, your dad, by the fireplace, Sunday; you played catch; he remembered your name; Sunday with the boy. Dad's so busy these days. Dad and I don't see eye to eye 'bout too many things. But you could share some things, football, the Seahawks. And perhaps, perhaps, one Sunday evening, Mom filling the house with smells of home-cooking, Dad leaned close and said, "My boy, that's John Elway on the television screen. Elway, m'boy. Some say he is the most talented quarterback that ever lived. I say I wouldn't drag his children from a burning orphanage."

Hating Elway is a proud tradition among Seahawks fans. He was hype incarnate, playing in our own division, both a rival and an enemy, the very horse face of evil. Elway was everything the common man learned to despise. He was good-looking, in an equine kind of way, easily athletic, confident, sublime. What you would fight all your life for, Elway could pick up and do. That girl you've done everything to impress, Elway could pick up and date. He was the übermensch, an American Adonis, may he die a slow death.

Elway was supposed to be a Baltimore Colt. The Colts drafted him first overall in 1983, but Elway refused the honor. He decided Baltimore would not allow him to succeed as he was destined to and told Baltimore owner Robert Irsay that, if the Colts would not trade him, Elway would simply choose baseball over football. Oh yeah, Elway was also a Yankee. I shiver writing the word.

Irsay was over a barrel. Baltimore was forced to trade the greatest asset a downtrodden team can be given, a franchise quarterback. Not a mediocre one, but a Jake Locker with horse teeth. Elway's ploy worked, but despite his Machiavellian intentions, he could not destroy the Colts. Not singlehandedly. Baltimore received Denver's fourth overall pick, left guard Chris Hinton, along with backup quarterback Mark Herrmann and the Broncos' first-round pick in 1984 in exchange for Elway. It was Irsay who destroyed the Colts, moving them from Baltimore to Indianapolis a year later.

Elway quickly became the most hyped player in the NFL. I can only imagine how disgusting that was. Wait. Wait. Oh, yeah. Like a golem born from vomit. Horse vomit.

He was one of the first great villains in Seahawks history. Elway had a necromancer-like control over fair-weather fans, and his

Old Horseface, John Elway, coughs up the ball after being hit by the Seahawks' Rufus Porter in the fourth quarter of a 42–14 Seattle win over the Broncos in December 1988 at the Kingdome. Porter also recovered the fumble on the play.

hordes flooded Seattle like a plague. Denver was the established franchise. It had been godawful for most of its history, but had a modest run of success from 1976 to 1981.

Before the Seahawks were established, the Broncos and 49ers made inroads with Seattle football fans, and when the Seahawks were suffering the embarrassing travails of an expansion franchise, the Broncos were taking off. Then, as surely as the Broncos sagged a bit, the 49ers became the team of the decade. San Francisco and Denver had the two most famous quarterbacks in football, Joe Montana and John Elway. Montana was good-natured and humble—hard to dislike. Elway was brash, and for many years, his performance didn't match his reputation—easy to hate.

He earned a special place in Seahawks fans' hearts: the right ventricle. What cardiologists refer to as the "hate ventricle." The cool thing was that for a few years, Elway sucked. Hard. And the Seahawks owned him.

As a rookie, Elway escaped the bench just in time for the Seahawks to plant a couple sacks on him and limit him to 134 yards passing. He didn't play two weeks later, but Seattle won neverthe-less. In the wild-card round, the Seahawks stomped Denver 31–7 to start their miracle playoff run.

The next season, Seattle beat the Broncos, but Elway put together a good game. Then the Broncos stomped Seattle in Week 16, but Elway threw four picks. Go figure.

For years, hype would ride high on the horse named Elway, and for a few years the Seahawks bucked the rider and put down his charge. It didn't last very long. Seattle finished the '80s 7–7 against the Elway Broncos. Elway kept getting better, and the Seahawks became gnarled and inept. In the '90s Elway was 13–4 against the Seahawks. Then there were the two Super Bowl wins and the "For John" crap, and Seattle wasn't even noteworthy as a rival, but hating him never went away, never got old, never gets old, even if Elway got the final neigh.

Wanted: Despised Rival

Every team needs villains. Since joining the NFC West, Seattle has not had many. The Rams were the first and only rivalry, but the Rams cratered and became more pitiable than fearsome. Rivalries with the 49ers and Cardinals have never taken, because the three teams have never been good at the same time.

So for Seahawks fans, the new John Elway is probably Ben Roethlisberger.

Many things about Roethlisberger peeve Seahawks fans. He beat them in XL. He beat them without actually playing well. He maybe never crossed the goal line. He went on to win another Super Bowl, and that stings for an entire franchise that has yet to win one.

Of course, rivalry with the Steelers seems less relevant by the year. The Seahawks rarely play the Steelers, and when they do, it's out of conference and does not inordinately impact the playoffs. By now, both teams have turned over much of their respective rosters, and so it's strangers against strangers with little understanding of history, what little history there is.

I have always wanted a good rivalry, like the ones that permeate the NFC North. My Bears-fan friends seem to genuinely hate the Packers and Vikings, and most of all, Brett Favre. You just can't force it, though. Soon enough.

51 Rebuilding

Rebuilding. It's the dirtiest word in sports. It's a concession of defeat. Rebuilding. May you not wish it on your worst enemy.

Seattle has spent most of its history rebuilding. Not building, no, rebuilding like what one does to a collapsed church or devastated city. Before the rebuild comes the collapse, and the collapse stings more, but it's almost savory compared to the rebuild. One can derive a masochistic thrill from the team collapsing. Rebuilding is like a Kafka parable.

The Seahawks were legitimately rebuilding before building much of anything. In their third year, Seattle had crawled from the primordial ooze, had a character, a core, a leader with some name value, even a little prestige. Jack Patera led Seattle to its first winning season and did so in the most fan-friendly manner: through a litany of gadget plays. Yes, the Seahawks were free-wheeling, fun, breezy West Coast, but with a blue collar, timber-and-dock charm.

By the fifth year, they were rebuilding again. Oh, boy. There were all the signs. A rookie quarterback with a little buzz, Dave Krieg. A defense that couldn't stop a ladybug with a quart of Raid and an atom bomb. The death spiral. Oh, the death spiral. Seattle started a promising 3–2 and then 4–3 and then lost nine straight. In a particularly pungent performance against Dallas in Texas Stadium, the Seahawks fell behind 51–0 before Zorn connected with tackle Ron Essink for a two-yard score. Seattle's little sandcastle had been kicked in by the big kids. Pity us.

Patera was a victim of the labor crisis, shuffled out after only two games in 1982, and was replaced by Mike McCormack, whom we need not dedicate any more words to. Firing the head coach is the flare shot into the night, indicating both help needed and warning, avoid.

Then something kind of remarkable happened. Seattle eschewed rebuilding and instead decided to try and win. Not later, not at some indefinite future date, but now. Right now.

Ralph Wilson did his part. Wilson is a bit of a despised man in the contemporary NFL. He has the city of Buffalo over a barrel. This might sound quaint if this book is dusted off at some future date, but the 2010-era Bills have become a rest home for failed head coaches and a minor league for other NFL teams. Within the constraints of the salary cap, Wilson spends as little as possible. Wilson's Bills were once a model organization, and Wilson a model owner: competitive, involved, and generous. There's no bad guy here, just a changing economic landscape. Western New York no longer sports a robust economy. They are, how do you say, rebuilding.

Wilson wouldn't pony up to retain the services of Chuck Knox, and so Knox and his brand of smashmouth football were recruited to Seattle. He became the Seahawks' head coach in 1983. Seattle canned rebuilding, started its best quarterback, and not simply its most accomplished, traded up for a rusher named Curt, and took their shot at immortality. What a concept.

Seattle charged to its first playoff berth and then made some noise before bowing out in the AFC Championship Game. They stayed competitive the next season, finishing 12–4. But enough about winning, let's get back to losing!

The Sea-Scabs enervated the Seahawks' drive to win, and though Seattle would scrape out two more winning seasons before Knox's departure, rebuilding was looming. Seattle traded Kenny Easley for quarterback Kelly Stouffer. Lean Cuisine was supposed to be something special, and he proved as much by sitting out his entire rookie season. Special gets paid special money, screw football. Easley discovered his kidneys were shot and was forced to retire. It was a win for all involved. And an epic triumph for the forces of rebuilding.

The rebuild was finally consummated when Knox used a buyout clause in his contract and left Seattle to join the St. Louis Rams. General manager Tom Flores made the hard decision to hire himself as the next head coach of the Seattle Seahawks. He knew right away what he had to do: rebuild.

Rebuilding is full of fancy buzzwords like "Raiderizing" and half-smart tactics like running-back go routes. It usually features at least one failed quarterback prospect and the forced departure of a successful one. Stouffer wasn't the big success he promised, and he couldn't ever overtake Dave Krieg. Krieg was facing the ravages of age and injury and couldn't keep himself on the field. Even the great Steve Largent faded in the late '80s and retired in 1989.

Seattle upped the rebuilding by cycling through not one, not two, but three failed quarterback prospects. Stouffer started the season injured and ended his Seahawks career with a separated shoulder. Seattle's newest quarterback of the future, Dan McGwire, all 6'8" of him, was sacked seven times in 37 drop backs and was injured, as well. Sacks undid McGwire, he barely played again, and when he did, subbing for an injured Rick Mirer, McGwire suffered 13 sacks in 105 pass attempts. At least he finally survived a start.

Mired in rebuilding and looking for a way out, Seattle rolled the dice on another can't-miss prospect, the Bill Walsh–approved, next Joe Montana (though Joe Montana was not the next Joe Montana), Rick "Golden Boy" Mirer. Mirer was named the AFC Rookie of the Year.

52 The Next Joe Montana

Rick Mirer was the next Joe Montana. So said Bill Walsh. And when Walsh says something, people foolishly believe it better accords to the truth than say, when Fritz Schlitz of Climax, Colorado, says something. Walsh knew a lot about Montana, but he didn't know squat about Mirer. Remember, Joe Montana was not Joe Montana before he became Joe Montana. Montana was a third-round pick and the fourth quarterback taken in 1979. He was Schmo Montana. And he stayed Schmo Montana until halfway into his second season.

No, Mirer was always Jack Thompson, the Washington State Cougars quarterback selected first among all quarterbacks in 1979 and third overall. Thompson finished his college career the all-time leader in passing yards. Mirer wasn't quite so accomplished a passer, but he did have another title: winner. Mirer was 29–7–1 as a starter and led Notre Dame to three bowl games.

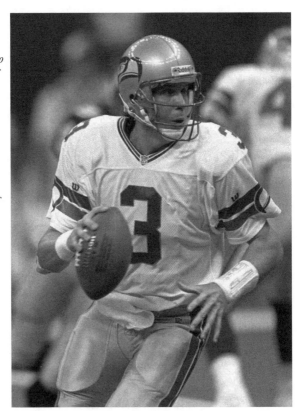

Once the "next Joe Montana," Rick Mirer drops back to pass with a look of panic mixed with confusion. Despite mediocre (at best) numbers and a losing record (6–10) in 1993, Mirer was named the AFC Rookie of the Year.

Funny the titles one gathers and how little they tell about the man. Mirer was Seattle's prize for finishing 2–14. In 1992 Seattle couldn't even lose right. The Seahawks were the Patriots' equal in failure except for one important fact. Seattle edged out New England in Week 3, giving the Patriots the tiebreaker and first overall pick. That meant Seattle missed out on another Cougars legend: Drew Bledsoe.

It was preposterous to compare Mirer to Montana. Montana completed a higher percentage of passes as a pro than Mirer could in college. Not by a small amount, either. Mirer completed 54.4 percent of his passes at Notre Dame. Montana completed 63.2 percent of his passes over his pro career. Montana was much better against much better competition at the fundamental quarterback skill: completing passes.

But compare Bill did, and his words moved mountains. Seattle signed Mirer to a five-year, $15 million contract. For a while, everyone was happy. Bledsoe brought his artillery cannon to New England, and the Patriots crawled over the Colts to move out of the AFC East cellar. Seattle stayed in last place but bested New England six wins to five. Mirer started 16 games and set rookie records for completions and passing yards.

One accomplishment created another. Mirer was never good; he just slung a lot of pigskins. It took 486 attempts to set the completions and yards record. After factoring in his league worst 47 sacks, Mirer averaged just 4.9 yards per attempt. The sacks dried up a bit after his rookie season, and he threw for the lowest interception rate of any quarterback, but those were hollow achievements. Mirer avoided interceptions and sacks at the expense of a functioning passing offense. His completion percentage dropped to 51.2 percent, and despite fewer sacks, he still only averaged 4.9 yards an attempt. Mirer was low-risk, no reward.

Dennis Erickson took over as head coach in 1995. Mirer reverted to 1993 form. His sacks and interceptions skyrocketed. He was three years into his professional career and on his second head coach. The Seahawks were giving up on him. Journeyman John Friesz was in the mix. Friesz outplayed Mirer but had none of the supposed potential. Mirer was given every opportunity but never seized one, and eventually, his exit from Seattle became inevitable.

By October 1996 Seattle was actively shopping Mirer. They attempted to send him to Atlanta for suspended quarterback Jeff George, but George dragged his heels, and eventually the trade deadline elapsed. Seattle was spared. It had offered George $30 million over six years. That trade goes down, and a lot of great Seahawks history is unwritten. SoCal Seahawks history.

Mirer retained luster. Many thought, like Steve Young before him, Mirer was not the cause of, but victim of Seattle's futility. His sacks were evidence of the Seahawks' ineptness. Research has since shown that avoiding sacks is one of the most consistent abilities a quarterback shows throughout his career. Mirer was not taking sacks, but making sacks through a slow read and poor pocket awareness. He was busted, no good, a mistake, a botched pick, sunk cost, and Seattle knew it. The Seahawks continued to shop Mirer in the off-season and found an amazingly robust market.

Chicago has always been enamored of bad quarterbacks. Sixty years ago the Bears drafted Sid Luckman. Jim McMahon is probably Chicago's greatest quarterback since. It started a Lujack, a Romanik, signed George Blanda for $600, demanded a refund the day he reported, and ran him out of the league by playing him exclusively as a kicker. Chicago had a Bukich, a Concannon, and later, a Kramer, a Miller, a McNown, and a Grossman. It had a place for Mirer. The Windy City needed Rick Mirer. Dave Wannstedt needed Rick Mirer. And Mirer, them.

On February 18, 1997, Seattle sent Mirer to Chicago along with a fourth-round pick for the Bears' first-round pick. Wannstedt had his man, and together with Mirer, the two crushed Chicago between their iron jaws, rendering the Bears lame and lifeless and easy prey. Seattle turned Mirer into Shawn Springs.

53 The Expansion Draft

In an effort to make an expansion team less pathetic, the NFL holds an expansion draft. In an effort to punish and exploit those expansion teams, but in the name of goodwill, the expansion draft is populated by players other teams don't want. Tampa and Seattle didn't get the good players, didn't get the mediocre players, didn't get the proven players or even the players with pro potential. Tampa and Seattle got the old players, the talent-poor players coaches didn't have the heart to cut, the injured players, and the malcontents.

Teams could protect 32 players—*32!*—and each time Tampa or Seattle selected one, that team could protect another player. It wasn't even the extras from the best teams. No, no. As good teams were plundered, they could protect more and more, and eventually Seattle was forced to add talent from the bad teams, too.

If this process wasn't insult enough, the Players Union nearly filed suit to stop it entirely. That would have made the Seahawks and Bucs little more than college all-star teams. But it might have helped. Sure, it would have been ugly to start. It *was* ugly to start. Tampa lost 26 in a row. But instead of the aged, rejected, broken, and soon retired, at least the Bucs and Hawks could have grown up together.

Instead, it went like this: Seattle selected Wayne Baker. Baker was a lumberjack's son, so you can see the allure. Baker never played another down of organized football. Seattle selected Carl Barisich, and Barisich lasted one season. Seattle drafted Dwayne Crump and his mean Afro, but Crump couldn't make the squad. It added young Bill Olds, but Olds' pro career was ending. Seattle drafted Neil Graff, and really, no one knows who Neil Graff is. And so forth.

The First, Worst Seahawks

Before there were the Seattle Seahawks, there were the Miami Seahawks. They were an inaugural member of the All-America Football Conference. The AAFC eventually merged with the NFL, but long after the Seahawks had disbanded.

The team ran through two coaches and finished 3–11. Their first regular-season game was against Paul Brown's Browns, and it was a lopsided shutout. Miami lost 44–0 and totaled only 27 yards. Before they could fold, the Seahawks faced Brown's Browns again and lost 34–0. This time they squeaked out 46 total yards, but also gave up nine turnovers. Still, however inept, and however short-lived, in 14 games the Miami Seahawks outscored Tom Flores' 1992 Seahawks 167–140.

It wasn't all bad, of course. There was "Happy Days" Ron Howard. I'm sure he appreciates that nickname. He stuck for a while and wasn't terrible. There was "Sudden" Sam McCullum, and Sam was excellent for a little while and facilitated the exit of Jack Patera. Thanks for that, Sam. There was Dave Brown, and Brown turned into a pretty special player for the Seahawks. Maybe never great, but good and for a long time.

The expansion draft. Sure, it wasn't the right or fair way to start a franchise, but it was the way it was done. Seattle and Tampa Bay took other teams' scraps, slapped a logo on them, and called it a team. They weren't proud, they weren't skilled, and they weren't great—heck, most of them never even made it—but they were Seahawks and Buccaneers. Those players scrapped and fought through some of the worst football the NFL has ever seen. Those players took the dream and promise of NFL football, nurtured for so many long years by desperate football fans in Seattle and Tampa Bay, and made an absolute mockery of it. They left it all on the field and didn't clean up after themselves. They got no respect and earned no respect but were probably paid pretty well. They retired to jobs as insurance salesman and gym teachers and bouncers, but they could always say, "I was almost good enough to be a Buccaneer."

54 The Kingdome

For my generation, the Kingdome was a dilapidated piece of garbage. Its finest moment was its implosion. That day, the first home of the Seahawks and first home of the Mariners reached self-actualization. Always an eyesore, a burden to its teams, an architectural blunder, noted for its falling roof tiles, noted for the repair of those roof tiles killing two men, noted for being the physical manifestation of years of losing, bad management, and irrelevance, it emerged from its impermanent shell and metamorphosed into a pile of rubble, became actual garbage.

Was it ever anything else? At some point, someone not only authorized the building of the Kingdome but poured millions of dollars into it. Someone, sometime, like the mother of Jeffrey Dahmer, must have looked upon the still-fresh, still-clean Kingdome and felt some kind of pride. Even typing it, it's hard to

The Seattle Kingdome was the home of the Seahawks, Mariners, and SuperSonics from 1976 to 1999, before being demolished on March 26, 2000.

believe. The millions: $67 million to be exact. Inflation-adjusted, the Kingdome would cost $176.2 million today. Numbers like that are sure to inspire a little working-class outrage, but stadia cost money, even the ugly ones. So let us not fret or sharpen out pitchforks, not yet.

Construction ended in 1976, when we must assume engineers looked at their great creation, decided money still spends, success or failure, fled the scene, and remembered to leave the Kingdome off their résumés.

It had one good quality: the Kingdome was loud, crazy loud. Sixty-six thousand football fans could get the walls shaking. Seattle fans screamed like the buried-alive, and the Kingdome reverberated like a concrete tomb. It was a home for prayers. People prayed for field goals, free throws, and strikeouts. It was a home for great players, great plays, Dan McGwire. It was the site of Bo versus Boz, Refuse to Lose, losing, and a thousand more times, losing. It housed a great valley of Astroturf, and that horrible pseudo grass probably cost Junior his hamstrings. It certainly made it impossible to sign free agents. Turf burned knees, buckled knees, and invented the phrase "turf monster." The turf monster drags careers to their graves.

I'm sure it had a homey kind of charm for the regulars. Maybe if I sat there and lived with the team, I could look back at it with nostalgia. Instead, I will forever see the Kingdome as an ugly mistake that needed to be replaced little more than 30 years later. The Kingdome was the stadium that best represented the teams that lost there. The Kingdome almost cost Seattle the Seahawks. It wasn't just Ken Behring, after all, who demanded a new stadium; Paul Allen held out on purchasing the team before a new stadium was approved by the state. I will forever see the Kingdome as not only one of the ugliest and least successful stadiums in American sports history, but as the worst-case scenario for Qwest Field. If 20 years from now, the state is again forced to demolish and replace the

Seahawks' stadium or face relocation, I will cry. Literally, in my drinking glass full of false teeth and Efferdent, cry.

55 When in Revelry You Drown Your Sense

Coaching an expansion team is a career-killer. Ownership says nice things, the right things, about patience and buying into a philosophy, but when that invariably fails, when fate crushes a newborn franchise under its wheel, it's always the coach who goes. That should be in the job description: "Seahawks franchise seeking coach and future scapegoat."

Since the Seahawks joined the league in 1976, the NFL has added four franchises: the Jacksonville Jaguars and Carolina Panthers in 1995, the Browns in 1999, and the Texans in 2002. Jacksonville began under head coach Tom Coughlin. Coughlin had some success in Jacksonville and later won a Super Bowl with the Giants. He's the exception. Carolina started under Dom Capers. He succeeded in his second season and was fired after his fourth. Four years later, he was hired to coach the Houston Texans. Four years later still, he was again fired. Chris Palmer coached the expansion Cleveland Browns and was gone after just two seasons.

Seattle entered the league with the Tampa Bay Bucs, who had John McKay at the helm. He suffered a longer career filled with more losses and more heartache than an average expansion coach, but like most, it about finished him. He never coached again. After his death, his son told the *Los Angeles Times* that he knew within the first week that he had made a mistake leaving USC. Money—when it seems like you're being paid too much, it's only because you underestimated the enormity of the task.

Head coaches of expansion franchises are paid handsomely to lose, and lose, and after an arbitrary grace period, be blamed for losing, be vilified by fans and media, be fired, and often, retire. It's just the way it is. Maybe it's league-mandated. One gets their few years of prominence and pay, then one day a knock comes at the door, and from under it a sulfurous smoke pours in.

Patera played the Seahawks' Faust. He was signed after making a name coaching the Purple People Eaters. He taught advanced techniques like running and running toward the quarterback. Patera packed Benchwarmer Bob with him and set off for Seattle, ready to undertake the task that would grind him down and end his head-coaching career.

He was a great fit for Seattle and a surefire failure. He was quotable and projected the steely resolve of a general. Patera was creative and knew that winning in Seattle wouldn't happen because of three years of talent acquisition, but by exploiting every angle. Trick plays became a staple, and trick plays always have entertainment value, even when they fail. But for the most poorly executed plays, fans typically enjoy razzle-dazzle. Seattle became a respectable franchise in just its third season, finishing '78 and '79 with 9–7 records.

Then, as always happens, the old players acquired through the expansion draft began to fade or retire, and the young players were not ready to step in. The offensive line turned over multiple starters, and players like Louis Bullard, Tom Lynch, and Bob Newton were at or near the end. Lynch went on to Buffalo, but was a backup. Jim Zorn took sacks, threw picks, was harassed, and struggled.

Things didn't get better the next season, and part way through the strike-shortened 1982 season, Patera was fired. Losing facilitated the move, but problems cut deeper than that. He had an adversarial relationship with the press and was very private at a time when people expected greater and greater access. He once infamously started a press conference by saying, "Let's get it over with. I don't want to be here any more than you." Maybe he didn't get that becoming a head coach also meant becoming a celebrity. It never pays to pit the media against yourself, but Patera made himself an easy target with a drunken driving arrest on September 11. By the time the case went to trial, Patera was defamed and jobless and any hope of a fair trial was likely lost. His attorney, Doug Cowan, even went as far as accusing the prosecution of aiding in Patera's dismissal.

He had problems with players, too. He refused water breaks during training camp. Less outright stupid but more inflammatory, he cut Seahawks Players Union representative Sam McCullum and provoked talk about the Seahawks' players holding an individual strike. McCullum was in his peak seasons, and his replacement, Roger Carr, was on the decline. Patera's steely resolve and old-school style was backfiring on him, and just in time, because his expiration date as an expansion team coach was at hand.

56 Play Catch

My wife throws a mean spiral. Alanya doesn't have a gun, but she could make a great quarterback in a West Coast offense. Slants, digs, quick outs: she's nails. We don't play contact, and we can rarely coordinate enough people to play a game, but we get out and toss the ball around every few weeks. It's fun, like watching football can never be, and it keeps you engaged with the game even after your cleats and pads days are long over.

Yeah, I've played Madden, I've beat the system and abused the computer, spent hours and hours, and winning 98–0 is not as fun as one well-thrown pass. One run and reach and dive and, oh yeah, I caught it. Before it was a preoccupation, most of us were kids, and we probably looked at our dad all hunkered down on the couch, chip bowl and beer nearby, and wondered, *What is he doing? If he likes football, why not play?*

It's a great question. I am passionate about the Seahawks, and, man, when they win, I soar. But no touchdown, no sack, is ever as fun as winging the ball—as running, jumping, striving, playing football. You don't have to be athletic. You don't need equipment and pads. Just get a ball and some friends, or a friend, find a field, and let loose.

Some years back, in some Portland neighborhood I scarcely remember, sometime late, 3:00 AM, I was party to a party departing a party, pigskin in hand. We found a field and started to play. We weren't in our best minds. Some of us were in no shape to drive (we didn't). Some were worse off than that, and when I evaded a rusher and scrambled for 20, yeah, I stiff-armed a butch, and that was a little awkward, but it was cool, because it was in the name of sport, play, and it was fun. And fun is impervious. Fun knows no shame.

Nowadays it's mostly just my wife and I. We don't walk too far, and what little speed I ever had, well, I still mostly have, but I'm sure it's fading. We have no score or rules or goal or time clock, but the soreness in our shoulders. It's fun and light and like bait: catch attracts strangers. Then there's more hands and more running and different throwing styles, and that one dude that's way too good, and the kid—better not swear (much)—and throw together a game of touch football, and that one dude dominates, and after a while people break off and leave, and maybe they're replaced, or maybe you thank everybody and go home.

57 NFC Worst

Football fans are proud. We wear our team's colors like a coat of arms. We don't talk about the Seahawks winning, we talk about ourselves winning, ourselves losing, what we need to do win, what we did to lose. A win is a chest-thumping occasion. We swell with pride. It's discomfiting to our pride when our division sucks, but for over a decade, the Seahawks have played in the NFC Worst.

Some of it was unshakable. The Cardinals are among the most benighted franchises in not just football history, but sports history. They've had bad coaches and worse management. In 2008 they barely escaped a bad division and then made a lucky run into the Super Bowl. Larry Fitzgerald was exceptional. The defense was suddenly capable. But that short and sudden success does not redefine them. They came close to winning it all but nearly as close to missing the playoffs entirely. What put them there was not their own ability but the resurgence of Kurt Warner and the good fortune of playing in the NFC Worst.

The 49ers collapsed into the new millennium. Like an aged hippie barely able to see through his memories to his dirty retched present, the 49ers mortgaged their future for years until the cap destroyed them. They are the worst member of the worst division in football. For years now, they have been held back by Alex Smith. Their quarterback entering the 2010 season? Alex Smith. I doubt the 49ers understand that not every quarterback turns himself into Montana or Young. Their big triumph after their big collapse was scraping back toward respectability in 2009. Will it last? We shall see.

Ten years ago, the Rams were the most exciting team in the NFL. The Greatest Show on Turf rode a grocery-store-clerk-

A Kick in the Teeth

Josh Brown went from hero to villain in record time. He was Seattle's kicker for most of the good seasons and enjoyed the halo of success. In 2006 he set new standards for good timing and was perhaps the most important part of Seattle making its fourth consecutive playoff.

Brown was known not only for his clutch kicking, should such a thing really exist, but his tackling ability. Brown was that rare breed of macho kicker who seems to savor contact. His most famous tackle came against the inimitable Devin Hester. He threw down and then hulked out.

Ruskell offered to make him the highest paid kicker in the history of football that off-season. Brown declined and instead signed a similar contract with the rival Rams. The move was met with boos and hollers. Funnily enough, it worked perfectly for Seattle. Brown brought his kicking to a team that needed everything but, and Seattle signed Olindo Mare. Mare, then derided for his accuracy, not only outperformed Brown as a field-goal kicker but wiped the floor with him as a kickoff specialist.

turned-MVP into the Super Bowl. They had Marshall Faulk, one of the great all-time, all-purpose running backs. They had Torry Holt and Isaac Bruce, and Mike Martz to guide them. They had the only left tackle with a legitimate argument with Walter Jones for greatest of his generation, Orlando Pace. And for all that, for all the winning, the high-flying, the improbable turn-of-century dominance, they are now the worst team in the NFL. Few teams can claim to have won three games in a season, two the next, and then one, but the 2007–2009 Rams did just that. Making their win totals that much more humiliating is that they play in the worst division in football.

I read a lot about East Coast bias and how Seattle is not properly respected. I read a lot about how Seattle would not have reached the playoffs in five consecutive seasons if they played in a more powerful division. You know what? It's true. I think we just have to accept that, and remember, however much they disrespect us, and whether they are right or not, there is always a playoff spot to be won in the NFC West.

58 The Bit Players

Franchises need both great people—great personalities and great players—and minor actors, forgotten but essential. For example, Rod Rutledge, the starting tight end for the 2001 Super Bowl–champion New England Patriots, caught Tom Brady's first pass. Had he dropped it, Brady would have gone 0-for-3, maybe fallen back behind Michael Bishop, maybe never had a chance to prove his greatness.

Mike McCormack was an offensive tackle who played in the '50s and early '60s. He was one of those old-school run-blocking road graders who could dominate the pre-modern era. He went to six Pro Bowls, five as a right tackle for Paul Brown's Browns.

McCormack was elected to the Pro Football Hall of Fame in 1984, two years after he relieved Jack Patera and became the Seahawks' head coach. He was instrumental in signing Chuck Knox. He reached out to Knox, and Knox was happy to work for a former offensive lineman. Until 1989 he was the Seahawks' general manager and worked with Knox to create the first consistently successful Seahawks teams. That was when it was assumed general managers and coaches would work together to determine a roster. Of course, it was McCormack who wagered a first-round pick to draft Brian Bosworth in the 1987 supplemental round.

Randy Mueller worked under McCormack from 1983 to 1989. He would stick with Seattle through the 1999 season. Mueller did two things that forever changed Seahawks history. He traded Rick Mirer to the Bears for a first-round pick, an accomplishment that startles me every time I type it. And he helped Seattle wheel and deal to move up and draft Walter Jones.

The final minor player who deserves recognition if not acclaim is Bob Whitsitt. Whitsitt made his name as the general manager of the Portland Trailblazers. It was not a distinguished name. Nor is he remembered for his great work with the Seattle Seahawks. But if he was never great, and if his moves never helped make Seattle a contender, he was nevertheless vital.

Maybe Whitsitt was just a better businessman than talent evaluator. His draft classes were weak, but his deeds were great. He helped negotiate the creation of Qwest Field, and Qwest Field is a jewel on the NFL landscape. He also signed Mike Holmgren.

McCormack, Mueller, and Whitsitt did great things for the Seahawks. They also committed great folly. They were not the stars, they were never revered, and I am sure even most diehard fans hardly know their names, but they were power players in the annals of team history. Each one was minor but essential.

59 Record a Game and Rewatch It

I know what you're thinking. *That dude totally dropped the pass.* Rewatch it. The pass was behind him. *That tackle totally blew his block.* Rewatch it. The quarterback ran into the defender. *That end was shut out.* Rewatch it. He was playing in the offense's backfield.

Football is chaotic. Football is visceral. It's felt, not understood. Add a little beer to the mix, a little company, maybe a kid, someone who asks too many questions, and you're liable to miss the whole thing. A whole game unfolds in about 11 minutes. Twenty-two players with 22 separate jobs, all unfolding in increments of seconds, and Bill in maintenance has opinions to last the week. The wide receiver's a bum. That linebacker's a gamer. That rookie quarterback, total bust.

Love is understanding, right? Didn't Hallmark copyright that? Or did I read it in *Chicken Soup for the Leper's Soul*? Wait, no, love is never having to say you're sorry.

No, love is that delicate line between knowing and not knowing: the place where we settle when we understand enough to love but stop before the autopsy. Most football fans are merely infatuated. Infatuation is capricious. Infatuation is heartsick for someone one second and sick another. Most football fans know, broadly, what it takes to win or lose, know, for sure, that they like winning, but know nothing about what it takes to win. Instead, they resort to empty platitudes about heart, grit, and the spirit of a champion. It's really quite revolting.

So if you love, truly love your football team, stop a second, put aside your judgments, and instead do what true love does: ask questions. Record a game and rewatch it. Pick a player, and focus on him for a series. Rewind, watch that same play, but watch another player. Who finishes their blocks? Who finishes their routes? Whose fault was that drop?

I started football commentary the easy way: bad statistics and overwrought opinions. Speak strongly and you'll blunder into a few truths, and those seeking easy answers will remember your accuracies and forget your failures. But opinionated and ignorant is no way to go through life. So I decided to hold myself to my own standards. I started recording games and piecing through them.

The first thing you notice is how amazingly complex everything is. Every play involves incredibly delicate and complex interactions. I had to create new ideas just to know what was happening. And those ideas survived or died with more and more exposure. I was attempting to unravel the game and forced to learn it by doing so.

It may not appeal to everyone to attempt to know everything about a game. It should appeal to every fan to attempt to know what really happened in a game. Somewhere between a first viewing and a 15th, I think every fan can find a point that satisfies their needs. Maybe you just need to audit the officiating. Maybe you just need to watch the final minutes again, and see if it could have ended differently, better. Whatever you need, the answers are on the tape. It's free, but for the time and effort. And it will save you from being the guy who trades loudness and the semblance of certainty for actual knowledge.

60 Lawyers, Puns, & Poison Pills

Tim Ruskell made a habit of waiting until the off-season to negotiate contracts. If you can command the English language, and, by command, I mean string together words into a halfway intelligible whole, you could postulate on why he did this. And, by postulate, I mean speculate. And since we're speculating, what matters most is our internal biases toward the man.

If you respected Ruskell, went so far as to express an "in Ruskell we trust" mantra—*ugh*—you might extol the virtues and pseudo-virtues of waiting. Waiting allowed Ruskell to have the full picture of the player. It supplied the most important evidence to predicting their future ability, their most recent performance. It allowed Ruskell to sign a player when their health had stabilized and wasn't in permanent flux as a playing player's is. Sign someone to a million today, and they blow out their knee tomorrow. Oops.

If you had a rosy but realistic picture of Ruskell, you recognized the above, but also understood that it shouldn't be a rule. Ruskell was pretty cutthroat, fully willing to go back on his word if it was prudent. Before releasing Shaun Alexander, Ruskell gave the broken running back his public support. He would share his opinions of players, unfiltered, gave a less-than-glowing assessment of Marcus

Marcus Trufant's Peak Season

For a long time, Torry Holt was the bane of the Seattle Seahawks and especially Marcus Trufant. He had five 100-yard receiving games against Seattle and four since Seattle drafted Tru in 2003. His most thorough butt-kicking was in 2006, when in Week 6 he had eight receptions for 154 yards and three touchdowns.

Things change, though, and sometimes suddenly. In 2007 with the Rams and Holt fading, Trufant emerged as a complete corner. Long known for his pure cover skills but not for his ability to snag picks, Marcus combined the two skills and began showing the rare ability to play the ball without losing the man.

Instead of facing Holt, Trufant mostly matched up against Isaac Bruce. On one play, he ran Bruce up the sideline, maintaining his normal close cover, but when the pass arrived, he showed a new ability, something tantalizing. He broke cover, leapt, and intercepted the pass. It was all part of a spectacular season for the corner. It's too bad that might be as good as it ever gets. He signed a free-agent contract in the off-season and has never shown that kind of special ability again.

Trufant before signing him to a long-term contract, and knowingly used the media and its ability to shape opinions to leverage negotiations. It might be a rule of thumb to sign most players only after their contract had expired, but certainly there should be exceptions. That was just good business.

If you had a jaundiced but fair opinion of Ruskell, it was obvious that he sometimes leveraged against his own sometimes incorrect opinions. He had a figure for his player's value and would rather not overspend if he could let the market reinforce that figure. Ruskell was notorious for letting a player test the market, sure that player would crawl back discouraged and willing to negotiate. It worked sometimes. He got a deal on right tackle Ray Willis and pulled an absolute negotiating coup in the signing of LeRoy Hill. It also failed miserably sometimes.

If you hated Ruskell's guts and wouldn't sit in the booth he vacated because the warmth of his backside ruined your appetite, you thought he was a moron, and whatever plausible explanation there was for his actions, it was nothing more than further proof of his half-smart scheming and abundant arrogance.

That particular opinion was sewn into many a Seahawks fan's heart after Ruskell lost Steve Hutchinson to an elaborate bit of back-door dealings. And at the hands of an arbiter who rivals Roger B. Taney for judicial miscarriage and overall buffoonery. No, arbiter Stephen Burbank wasn't a "stooped, sallow, ugly...supple, cringing tool of Jacksonian power" as Connecticut law professor R. Kent Newmyer described Taney, and he didn't set the civil rights movement back a hundred years or unleash a corporate monster still unvanquished, but he did deprive Seattle of a Hall of Fame–bound guard, the best of his generation, and render the transition tag impotent.

In football terms, Ruskell called a controversial play, one with moderate upside and potentially damning downside, and managed to fumble, watch his quarterback toted out on a stretcher, and then lose half his fanbase to spontaneous combustion. Ruskell envisioned a Super Bowl contender he could improve into a dynasty. It's not unprecedented. The 1971 Dolphins lost the Super Bowl but rebounded to win the next two.

Ruskell was never shy about spending his owner's vast fortune to add talent through free agency. He believed he could retain Hutchinson and also add elite talents in defensive end John Abraham and linebacker Julian Peterson. If he did, he would no doubt have been deemed a genius of Newtonian proportions. That team could find the playoffs blindfolded and would have been a clear-cut Super Bowl favorite. But Ruskell became the kid caught with his hand in the pickle jar.

Hutchinson made it clear he didn't find Ruskell's decision to wait until the off-season particularly complimentary. Like many athletes, he equated pay with respect, and Ruskell's unwillingness to sign him ASAP was an indication that Ruskell was not that enthused about signing him at all. It's possible he was right. It's possible Hutch was tying together a loose straw man to deflect his own desire to leave the Pacific Northwest, it's geographical location opposite his home in Florida, and far away from his adopted home in Michigan. Peel a fable back, and one often finds no bad guys, only bad situations.

Ruskell sealed his fate when he applied the transition tag to Hutch. The stated purpose of the transition tag was simple and elegant. The transition tag allowed the recipient to test the free-agent market by being able to negotiate a contract with other teams, and the team applying the tag the right to match any contract and still sign their player. In theory, it was a masterful application of Ruskell's belief that even the best player was not priceless, and that instead of competing with oneself to sign a player, a general manager could allow the market to determine the player's worth.

In reality, it was Ruskell waxing the slue on Hutchinson's farewell slide to Mosquito Boot. Seattle did its best to overcome that first blunder, appealed to sympathetic NFL commissioner Paul Tagliabue, and appealed the contract to arbitration, but it had already extended itself too much. Burbank was likely to rule as a litigator should, to the letter of the law and not to its intent. He did, and Hutch was a Viking.

Seattle cleverly negotiated themselves into an unfillable void on the offensive line. Abraham signed elsewhere, and of Ruskell's targets, only Peterson and Shaun Alexander were attained. One was good. Another was the pyrotechnic ash of a copper halide prime.

61 Engram

It will shock latter-day Seahawks fans to read, but Bobby Engram entered the league a bona fide No. 1 wide receiver. The Bears drafted him in the Greatest Wide Receiver Draft Ever, as determined by

Bobby Engram gains 14 yards on a reception before being tackled by New York Giants cornerback Ralph Brown during a game at Giants Stadium in September 2002.

God and Kiper. He was not drafted in the second round because he fit the position of slot receiver and third-down specialist but because superstar talents like Keyshawn Johnson, Terry Glenn, and Marvin Harrison hogged the first. Receiver talent drowned Engram's class like water over a flood plain: Eddie Kennison, Eric Moulds, Amani Toomer, Terrell Owens, and Joe Horn—afterthoughts and consolation prizes in the Johnson-Glenn sweepstakes.

Had Engram declared a year earlier or later, he could have breached the hallowed first round. It's laughable to think of Michael Westbrook or Ike Hilliard topping their respective draft classes when Engram was the 10th receiver drafted in 1996. Westbrook and Hilliard made a career out of what Engram declined into: a possession receiver.

See, the kid was good. Trawl the Internet, and one can still find love letters written to Engram by former Penn State students. Men enwrapped in appreciation for Bobby. Bobby Engram, the man who dusted off the record books and scrawled his name atop: first in receiving yards (3,026), second in receptions (167), first in receiving touchdowns (31), and second in punt-return yards (786). Engram was the first-ever Fred Biletnikoff Award winner in 1994. Penn State was undefeated that season, but fell short of a national championship in a split vote. He had the athleticism, achievement, and production of a first-round pick, but fell, fell, fell to the Bears.

Engram never broke out in Chicago. Dave Wannstedt, and later Dick Jauron, wanted Engram to be a star, a stud, a difference-maker, but paired him with busts, retreads, and Kramers. Well, just one Kramer, but one is enough. Engram caught for Dave Krieg on Krieg's farewell tour. It was his last stop starting. Engram received for Shane Matthews after Matthews returned from the balmy climes of North Carolina and back to the team foolish enough to make him a pro. That same team later drafted Cade McNown, and McNown fluttered a few passes toward Engram before benching himself, being benched, benched again, banned from the Playboy mansion, and finally traded to Miami. You know what they say in Chicago about McNown: he's no Akili Smith.

Bobby tore his ACL in 2000 and for that offense was cut August 29, 2001. Mike Holmgren signed him two days later. Engram signed a two-year contract that paid him less than $500,000 annually. He was the 101st highest paid receiver in 2001. He got a $60,000 raise his second season and took on punt-return duties to compensate. He averaged 10.7 yards per return and returned one to the house. That was the season Engram became the darling of Football Outsiders metrics. Targets to Engram ranked 26th in total value and 13th in value per target. He was ninth and second in 2003. Engram received a raise before that.

The Outsiders crew came to call Engram "first-down machine," and the title was earned. Engram didn't waste a reception. He didn't receive for six on third-and-7. He packed value into every curl, slant, and out. In his first five seasons in Seattle, 77 percent of his receptions achieved a first down or touchdown.

It was more elegant than stats can describe. Hasselbeck-to-Engram took on pneumatic precision. Hasselbeck would drop back, throw, and as surely as the camera panned to his target, there was Engram snatching the pass, continuing the drive, bewildering the defender, all unassuming and easily athletic, death dealt seven yards at a time.

And so it was for the next five seasons. B-Easy was the biggest little thing in Seattle: a watermark for true fandom, the glue in Seattle's greatest offenses—so steady, his full name became "First Down Bobby Engram."

Engram's 1,000-Yard Season

Mike Holmgren was always able to create incredible value through his slot receivers. When the Seahawks would split three or four wide, opponents were in a true fix. The power of the Seahawks' rushing attack made them want to avoid nickel coverage, but assigning someone like Bobby Engram or D.J. Hackett a linebacker or safety was a bad mismatch.

It didn't matter if it was James Williams, Jerheme Urban, Bobby Engram, D.J. Hackett, or Jerry Rice. If Holmgren could play you out of the slot, you were almost unstoppable. His greatest accomplishment was in 2007, when the Seahawks abandoned the run and attempted to create an offense through Holmgren's vision of a spread. Thirty-four and recovering from Graves' disease, Engram had the first and only 1,000-yard season of his career, and became the Seahawks de facto No. 1 receiver, one 10-yard curl at a time.

Then 2007 arrived, and Engram, the surviving stalwart on those great Holmgren offenses, returning from Graves' disease, took on the role he was drafted to play. He became the Seahawks' No. 1 receiver. Perhaps the first-ever No. 1 receiver to play primarily out of the slot. Deion Branch couldn't stay healthy and never developed trust with Matt. Shaun Alexander was a broken-footed shadow of himself. The team needed an anchor, something to give its offense mooring, a counterbalance to a defense that was suddenly developing, a means to the end zone that didn't travel through Branch, Alexander, Nate Burleson, Maurice Morris, or Marcus Pollard. And so Engram, 34, caught for 1,147 yards on 94 receptions. Through him, Seattle had one of the best passing offenses in football.

Everything after is dross. Engram lost much of 2008, and the Seahawks' offense splattered like Blitz droppings. He wasn't retained in 2009 and did what soon-to-be-retired players do: signed with another team and suffered a brief and ignominious finale. But for a little while, and in his own way, Engram was great, an inseparable piece of the greatest run in Seahawks history.

62 Share the Team You Love

I live in an apartment. I see my neighbors not at all. Maybe we exchange a polite hello; maybe I see a hand closing a curtain as I walk by. I think I have a neighbor who's a Seahawks fan, but it's so hard to say sometimes. Fans shrivel or disappear entirely when the team goes bad. I've certainly never had a meaningful conversation about team needs, or defensive strategy, or David Hawthorne versus Lofa Tatupu.

No one ever owns a football team. With all his money and all his influence, Paul Allen can no more own the Seahawks than I can.

It's community property. We go when we can, give what we can, take what we can, and love it like a child.

If you are separated from Seattle but still bear a passion for the Seahawks, you can follow the news, you can listen to the radio, and in most places, you can even watch the team play, but you can also talk about the team. You can fulfill the second need of a fan: community. Without community, there is no Seahawks, not really. You can savor the action, but with whom can you celebrate? You can die with the ending of the game clock, but with whom can you commiserate?

I would be a liar if I told you I enjoyed every second I spent on Field Gulls. When I started, I honestly bristled at being called a blogger. The word sounds stupid. I worked for a long time without compensation of any kind.

I would be a liar if I told you I understood or appreciated every opinion from every Seahawks fan I ever encountered. I think many are entitled. Maybe they signed on in 2005 and never loved football until the team started winning. When the Seahawks began to sink, fingers emerged for pointing, and blades for goats sharpened.

I would be a liar if I told you that reaching other fans, having somewhere to celebrate Brandon Mebane, somewhere to bash Brian Russell, somewhere to stop every day and talk Hawks, did not take me from fan to disciple. It saddens me how modern man is Balkanized. Maybe it's a West Coast thing, but all this land, this separation makes life feel very hollow sometimes. It's important to have somewhere to feel comfortable, to relate, and to connect with people who think obsessing about Jamar Adams and Jon Ryan is not so dang foolish.

I cannot speak for everyone, cannot tell you that finding a community will make being a fan more fulfilling. I can only invite you to stop by. I would be a liar if I told you it does not still sound kind of foolish to me, but it's the truth: sharing the team you love makes you love it more.

63 The Joey Galloway Trade

The Dallas Cowboys' dynasty was collapsing. Oil tycoon and owner Jerry Jones couldn't stomach it. His beloved quarterback needed weapons. Troy Aikman was winding down. He was entering his middle thirties, had swapped Michael Irvin for Raghib Ismael, Jay Novacek for David Lafleur, and Emmitt Smith for old Emmitt Smith. His completion percentage was down, his health failing him, and the dynasty he quarterbacked was crushing Aikman as it crumbled.

He needed weapons. Joey Galloway needed out. Mike Holmgren needed an aspirin. Holmgren inherited Galloway and all his airs. He was a star on a star-crossed team. Galloway had elite speed. He could scare defensive coordinators, if never crack the Pro Bowl. He could catch anything and had to, receiving for busts and retreads—saved, *saved*, by quatragenarian bomber Warren Moon.

Galloway was the kind of player a kid like me loooved. He was a one-man team on the highlight reels. Galloway for 59. Galloway for 81 and the score. Galloway for 86 on the end around. No one's catching Joey. All deep routes and burnt corners. All busted coverage and touchdowns. All highlights every play, and not an ordinary completion between them. (Highlight reels edit out the incompletions.)

In four years in Seattle, Galloway was targeted for more incomplete passes than completions. He never cracked even a 50 percent catch rate. Galloway could take it to the house but rarely sustain a drive. He didn't play Holmgren football. He was a Cowboy by birth and a Seahawk by accident.

Paul Allen offered Joey an impressive salary, enough to make him the second-highest-paid receiver in the NFL, but never enough. Galloway held out through training camp and into the season. It was a godsend. Seattle traded Galloway to Dallas on February 12, 2000. Seattle traded Galloway to Dallas for their first-round picks in 2000 and 2001. It was lunacy. Unforgivable the second it happened, and it only got worse.

Galloway tore his ACL in the fourth quarter of his very first game. Boom, pop, burner broken. It's not like I ever wished harm on Galloway, but there's a shameful satisfaction in not only winning a trade, but dominating. Galloway was gone for the rest of 2000. Aikman suffered his 10th concussion…ahem, *diagnosed* concussion. He was waived before the 2001 season and retired.

Maybe if it wasn't the Cowboys I wouldn't feel such warmth and smug satisfaction typing this, but it was the Cowboys, and screw them. Jones decided that he would replace Aikman with series of surprise quarterbacks, each more surprising than the last. He drafted Quincy Carter, and Carter introduced himself to the league with two sacks, two fumbles, two picks, nine completions and a benching in Week 1. Carter was No. 2 incarnate. Then there was Anthony Wright, but Wright went wrong, and so Carter returned, briefly. Eventually, Clint Stoerner and Ryan Leaf joined the mix. Galloway threw a pass and completed it for one, and everyone agreed that apart from punter Micah Knorr, Galloway was the best quarterback of the bunch. He understandably struggled as a wide receiver.

Seattle turned those picks into Shaun Alexander—*hooray*—and Koren Robinson—*glug, glug*. Alexander was sensational, good enough to be underappreciated, and Robinson, well Robinson careened off the straight and narrow and eventually out of the league, but before all that liver damage, accomplished more than Galloway ever accomplished in Dallas.

And so it was, for one transaction, the good guys won, and the hated Cowboys lost, and it was good. It wasn't Tony Dorsett good, but it was good, and deserved, and may I end with: screw the Cowboys.

64 Trading Tony

Seattle had a shot at Tony Dorsett in the 1977 NFL Draft. Unlike most tales of what-if, Dorsett was not a low-profile sleeper who burst into his own upon reaching the NFL. He was big-time. He won the Heisman in 1976. Dorsett was fast, powerful, had hands and health, and now has a bust in Canton. Seattle selected second overall. The Seahawks were starting the serviceable but by no means sensational Sherman Smith. Dorsett could have been ours. His four Pro Bowls, his 12,000 yards, his Super Bowl ring: ours, ours, ours.

Like most what-if stories, losing Dorsett is only worth suffering if you really dig that kind of thing. Smith wasn't sensational, but he was good, and Seattle had drafted him in the second round just a year earlier. Smith was only a part-time player, and by 1980, most of his value had been chewed up. More importantly, Sherman Smith was good enough. Smith averaged 4.2 yards per carry. Dorsett: 4.3. Dorsett was joining an established winner with a defense, a quarterback named Staubach, and a coach named Landry.

Seattle needed everything. It didn't need a show-stopper, it needed starters. Through a series of moves, general manager John Thompson turned Dorsett into Steve August, Terry Beeson, Pete Cronan, Geoff Reece, and Duke Ferguson…

Wait, who? I was kind of expecting a more impressive list of names there. Like Largent or Zorn or something. Geez, it really sucked not drafting Dorsett. I mean, Tony Dorsett, in the Silver and Blue. How sweet would that have been? You don't turn that down.

That is the kind of move that gets you fired. And it did, too. Thompson left with Patera, and the two took their losing loserdom with them. "Good process"—*pfft*, that's nerd code for "loser football." Process don't know nothing about playmakers. Dorsett was a—play—maker. Dude was a play factory. Dude was a play Detroit, pumping out plays on a play assembly line. And a winner.

If he didn't want to play in Seattle, then he could have sat. He could have pouted. He could have cried all over his Silver and Blue, because that's where he would have played if not for Thompson. Super Bowl, that's where Seattle would have been without Thompson. Reminds me of Ruskell. He probably didn't even want Dorsett, because Tony was tooo faaast and Ruskell only wanted slow jobbers. Midgets.

Ain't it the truth, though. Look how bad this team has gotten since Ruskell took over. He just wants church boys and choir girls, and he doesn't want Dorsett because Dorsett was a winner and playmaker and fast. Holmgren would have drafted Dorsett. And re-signed Hutch! That would have been sweet. Sweet. Sweet. Dorsett exploding behind Hutch. Dorsett storming through tackles. None of this, "Oh, oh, don't touch me," you get from Alexander. What a puss.

I can't believe we lost out on Dorsett. That's the Seahawks, though, always finding ways to lose.

65 Care About the Kicker

Care about the kicker,
the return man,
the punter,
the gunner,
the up back.
Care about the backup fullback,

the emergency quarterback,
the emergency punter,
the emergency kicker.
Care about the depth,
the practice squad,
the reserves,
the next man up.

Care about the assistant head coach,
the quarterbacks coach,
the running backs coach,
the wide receivers coach,
the offensive line coach,
the defensive line coach,
the linebackers coach,
the secondary coach,
the special-teams coach,
the offensive quality control coach,
the defensive quality control coach.
Care about the head of strength and conditioning,
the assistant strength and conditioning coach,
the team physicians.

Care about the CEO,
the president,
the general manager,
the head of scouting,
the vice president of player personnel,
the director of pro personnel.
Care about the Southwest scout,
the Midwest scout,

the Northeast scout,
the Southeast scout.

Care about every single one,
because winning takes the kicker,
the punter,
the return man,
the gunner,
the up back…

Where Did All the Hang Time Go?

Hang time used to be a common measure of a punter's ability but has disappeared. In theory, a great punter should be able to kick it high to limit the return and long to increase distance. But without knowing how high and how long, we don't know for sure if some punters are flipping field position or out-kicking their coverage. It's strange that in a league where information of all kinds is being added, that this essential data would disappear.

It could certainly help all of us engaged in debates over the value of Seahawks punters. After Tom Rouen left his mark, Seattle drafted Ryan Plackemeier. Plackemeier supposedly had an ability to consistently punt the ball so it would land end down. That would cause the ball to bounce up instead of forward and allow the return teams to down the punt deep in opponent territory. Could he consistently do it? I don't know, but he did show some ability to pin teams inside their 20. At least for a little while.

Plack tore his peck, and after a not-too-heated battle between Plackemeier and Reggie Hodges, Plack was replaced, but not by Hodges. Seattle signed Jon Ryan, and Ryan's specialty was kicking the ball a long distance. But then, was he kicking it too long? I don't know. It's not completely clear whether Ryan is kicking too long or if Seattle's special-teams unit is just too slow.

66 Dan McGwire

Dan McGwire busted on impact and cost Seattle Chuck Knox, maybe not in that order. Draft experts come in the proclaimed, the bona fide, the unidentified, and then there's the unassuming but prophetic. "He's an easy target. If you beat the line, get rid of the center and try to fight off the guard, you've got him, and he can get hurt. He's there. A big guy. You can't miss him."

Spartan defensive tackle Bobby Wilson was right. McGwire was a sack waiting to happen. Once in every eight drop-backs, McGwire was sacked. That is almost beyond comprehension. A quarterback regularly passes eight or more times in a single drive. McGwire only had 169 drop-backs in his entire professional career, but 21 ended with him under a defender. If he'd lasted long enough to qualify, McGwire would have ranked 183rd all-time in sack percentage. Only Steve Fuller, Bobby Douglass, and the inimitable Rob Johnson were sacked more often among qualifiers.

Johnson was truly amazing. In 1998 Johnson suffered sacks in 21.3 percent of all pass attempts. Lest you think he was playing a man short, or behind a sadistic offensive line, teammate Doug Flutie was sacked in only 3.3 percent of all snaps. Consider that— the 6'4" Johnson, waiting and waiting, defenders closing on all sides, and the 5'10" Flutie, bobbing and weaving, scrambling away and keeping the play alive.

But Johnson had something resembling redeeming value, because he continued to start. He took his licks, got comfortable with his horizontal, picked himself up, and was entrusted to try again. McGwire was sacked into dust and then abandoned. You may never see another first-round quarterback who elicited less faith in his head coaches than McGwire. There have been bigger busts, but few bigger failures.

Regarding Knox: Chuck, like any decent human being, had a chilly relationship with new owner Dan Behring. Knox was on his last year of his contract but wanted an extension. Negotiations lasted for months. It was reported that Knox wanted to extend his contract another three or four years. He settled for one year and an option.

Knox didn't like McGwire and didn't want to draft a quarterback in the first round. McGwire was all Behring. Behring drafted McGwire. Knox favored a player he thought could be had in the second round, but only two quarterbacks were selected in the second round of the 1991 draft: Browning Nagle and Brett Favre. It's a fun fantasy to envision Favre in the Silver and Blue, but Favre was long gone before Seattle got to pick again. More importantly, the fissure opened after that draft and, after the public showing of disrespect, never healed. A year later, Knox was gone.

McGwire stuck around. Took more sacks. Got injured. Had whatever media-created luster stripped from him. Finally, under Tom Flores, McGwire finished out the 1994 season, playing extensively in the final four games. It was crazy, really. Seattle had already replaced McGwire with a comparable bust, Rick Mirer. Mirer went down with a broken thumb, and there was McGwire, all ostrich-like, ready to begin again, rewrite his unwritten legacy, and he did. He did. He did. He wrote 13 sacks onto the field, and punctuated his work with nine fumbles.

That ended Dan McGwire. Not as excruciating as Mirer, but his own kind of awful, on the down low.

67 Better to Reign in Hell

Aaron Curry was supposed to eat dynamite and belch thunder. He was supposed to be Lawrence Taylor combined with Derrick Brooks, including all constituent parts. Aaron Curry, four arms and four legs of pure, linebacker badassery. He was supposed to be a rookie sensation, the greatest linebacker prospect of his generation: a mutant, cyborg, zombie, vampire, Frankenstein composed of Butkus and HAL and Lucifer, but not fey Lucifer, but butt-kicking, sword-wielding, fallen-angel Lucifer. He was supposed to be that, because that is what a fourth overall pick is: Roger Goodell's boo-boo kiss for your team getting smacked around all season.

Aaron Curry was supposed to be that, because when you're bad, and you know you're bad, and you know you're not going to escape anytime soon, you want to be bad, but cool. Seattle selected Aaron Curry after finishing a 4–12 season. It suffered a historic wave of injuries. It lost most of its offensive line. It lost Walter Jones forever. It lost Lofa and LeRoy and Hasselbeck, and about anyone else you care to care about. It was a broken season, and it was Mike Holmgren's last in Seattle, so it lost Mike Holmgren, too.

Aaron Curry was long-limbed and powerfully built. He had a mean streak that began and ended on the football field. He could fly around and propel 260 pounds of ripped muscle into anyone, anywhere, anytime. Some said he was an excellent pass rusher, but he wasn't really. Some said he knew a lot about cover, but a couple fluke picks can confuse. About no one said he'd bust.

Curry was safe. Maybe he was just a linebacker. Maybe a linebacker never won a championship for a team. Maybe the Hall of Linebackers is half-filled with great players who never grasped glory.

But if he wasn't going to put the team over the top, he would at least be awesome to watch.

Like Cortez in the '90s. Cortez Kennedy was an indisputable point of pride for a run of Seahawks teams that frustrated and embarrassed. Tez was enviable. Any fan would want Tez. Any team could sign Tez and improve. But he was ours. And through him projected the dim rays of a better future.

Aaron Curry didn't do it. He looked lost at times. He didn't trade rookie boners with moments of great promise. Jim Mora spoke of him in veiled putdowns. Mora began limiting his snaps. Established players began accusing him of being dirty. Elder fans invoked "the Boz."

Aaron Curry was just a rookie. So no one worries too much. Speaking worries is blasphemy. First spoken and then truth. Could he be a bust? Could he be all prototypical body and bad football? Don't say it.

Don't say it.

68 Bo Versus Boz

The unsung hero of Bo versus Boz was Marcus Allen. Allen, a feature back in his prime, was relegated to not only splitting carries but lead blocking. He did, with heart, and he threw some beauties. On the famous 91-yard rush Bo Jackson ended in the Seahawks tunnel, Allen cut-blocked corner Patrick Hunter to free Jackson to the sideline.

The unsung goat of Bo versus Boz is Kenny Easley. He fell, allowing Jackson an easy touchdown reception earlier in the second. His athleticism fading, his sometimes poor instincts in coverage were exposed. On Jackson's long run, Bo exploded past

Easley easily, provoking Dan Dierdorf to comment that Kenny was "not a burner." Dierdorf was always a little loose with the facts, but that day he was right. Easley was not just easily eclipsed by Bo but caught from behind by a hustling Brian Bosworth.

The story of Bo versus Boz was not about Bo or Boz—both were gone from the league before they could justify their hype—but the fading Seahawks. It was 1987, and Chuck Knox thought the Seahawks were favorites. They beat both of the Super Bowl–bound teams the season before, and that meant a lot to Knox and the media.

That kind of logic just does not translate to the football field. No one knew it then, but Easley was near his end. So was Steve Largent. Jacob Green had turned 30. Curt Warner wasn't old, but his legs were. The team was at the precipice, and maybe if things had broken different, 1987 could have been their 2005.

Knox blamed the strike, but the Sea-Scabs finished 2–1. They had a ringer, too. Largent crossed picket lines to play in Week 5 at Detroit and caught 15 passes for 261 yards and three touchdowns. Knox thought the strike hurt team unity, but it wasn't unity, or the lack of it, that let Jackson run all over the Kingdome.

Jackson was turning the corner with ease, and only Bosworth was quick enough to get near him. He was bowled over attempting to do something no other Seahawks seemed capable or particularly inclined to do: attempt a tackle. Knox's defense was getting old, and it showed against faster opponents.

The idea of Bo versus Boz is a Bosworth-worthy fabrication. The entire Seahawks defense was crumbling. Boz could neither save nor destroy it. In 1987 the team allowed the most rushing yards per attempt in the NFL. It was not just Bo. Eleven opponents topped 100 yards rushing, including the Oilers in the wild-card. I guess "Boz versus Alonzo Highsmith, Mike Rozier, and Allen Pinkett" does not have the same sex appeal—that group of Oilers helped Houston run for 178.

It is easy to make sense of it in retrospect. Back then, no one knew Easley's kidneys were failing, or how bad Bosworth would bust. No one knew the Seahawks were winding down their best run in franchise history, or that it would be the defense that betrayed them. They just knew a two-sport athlete and overblown hayseed and how one ran his mouth and the other ran all over him.

69 Make Football an Event

Multitasking is dead. Long live the pure experience.

Maybe I am at odds with my generation, but I find multitasking to be shallow and insubstantial. Research has proven that the basic idea of multitasking, the ability to do multiple things at once, is in fact a lie. We never do multiple things at once, but instead quickly shift from thing to thing. The quality of each thing we do is reduced, as is our ability to understand, appreciate, and enjoy each thing we do.

I am not an old-fashioned guy. I do not believe in a Golden Age, a centuries-old myth; I do not pine for an era when most humans were repressed. I don't miss oil-slick hair and casual racism, something that's been a vogue reaction to our often stifling need to not offend. No, no, I am, ladies and gentleman, a futurist.

Multitasking is dead. Maybe we don't see it yet, but it is. Lag or something. Multitasking is dead, because multitasking is not progress. It is a detour, a distraction, a cowardly retreat from experience.

Yes, you can appreciate more taste in your food if you turn off the TV. You can better understand music if you close your eyes and listen. You can better enjoy football if you close the laptop, quit flipping channels, and sit agog at its beauty and complexity.

It's true. We get what we put in. Not because of cosmic justice, no, that's BS. We get what we put in because the more we look forward to Sunday, the better we plan, the more we invest, the more we care, the more it can hurt and the better it can feel.

So make football an event. Prepare a good meal. Get a grill going if that's your thing. I love a well-crafted sandwich. Gets some snacks, too. Just don't get crap to munch on, but find something that really satisfies. Spend money. Everyone has some money. Money we blow on Mountain Dews while buying gas and lottery tickets and other ephemera and crap.

Pool your wasted cash and buy some good beer. Some expensive beer. Get a beer for every quarter, not some domestic crap, but how about a wit beer for kickoff, and a stout for the third quarter? Get the beer you love, and drink like you enjoy the beer, not like the beer is a means to an end.

Love football like it's not a means to an end. Love the moments stretched to breaking. The snap. The good block on the bad run.

Invite friends. Make Seahawks friends and get together and get loud and ribald together. There is no substitute for shared fandom.

Treat every game like it's special because it is. Know your opponent and know the match-ups and the storylines and the implications. Anticipate. Get nervous. Concentrate on every moment. Savor. Don't dabble in football and disappear when things get tough. Commit. Care. Believe.

70 The Whole Sick Crew

History remembers the stars, the victories, and also the epic failures, but it tends to glance over the screw-ups, the jobbers, the last line of defense, the sycophants, the favored, the bad, the players who made those failures possible. To fans, the bad players are almost as important as the good. Invariably, a team is going to lose—and if you're a Seahawks fan, a lot—and losing produces grief. Grief is a miserable thing for a sports fan to endure. Sport is leisure, an escape, and suffering through your leisure is better left for ascetics. My leisure comes with beer and swearing and stomping on the ground and yelling: whooping, hollering, onomatopoeia of all shapes and sounds.

So how about the bad guys, the schmucks, the players whose name are most often bookended by profanity? Let's give it up for them. It wasn't always their fault, but we'd like to think it was.

To be a true scoundrel, you can't just pop and get cut. Sports fans have little concern about the fodder that graces a roster and is replaced just as quickly. No, you have to have some staying power. The true thorn of a sports fan is the player who not only sucks but inexplicably sticks, sometimes for seasons.

Seattle was short on talent of all kinds in 1976, so when Jack Patera signed his former player Bob Lurtsema, it probably seemed like a sensible acquisition. Minnesota was a contender in the '70s, and their strength lay in their defensive line: the Purple People Eaters. Lurtsema had earned a spot in Vikings fans' hearts as "Benchwarmer Bob," situational end and minor celebrity.

He had all the markings of an absolute pain in the ass. He had earned favor from his coach and was acquired not because of obvious ability but connections. Patera made the 34-year-old man and nine-year backup an immediate starter. He stuck for two seasons before gifting the franchise with his retirement. The Seahawks contended the very next season.

If you can't insert yourself through connections and good press, vengeance works. Patera signed Roger Carr to replace Sudden Sam McCullum. McCullum was the Seahawks' union rep and among their best and most respected players. Carr was on the downswing, every bit of what you'd expect from a middling, oft-injured wide receiver turning 30. He only lasted one season, but it was an arduous season, and his suckiness seemed especially glaring because of it.

After Carr and after Patera, there was Chuck Knox. Knox was good about starting the best players instead of the best-known, but even Chuck had a soft spot for veterans and legends. And so Seattle signed Franco Harris. Harris was every bit the burned-out shell of his former self the Steelers cut. Knox could be forgiven for signing Harris—after all, it wasn't the plan. Seattle had its star rusher, Curt Warner, but Warner blew out his knee in the season opener and was placed on IR.

Harris brought national attention. He was a Super Bowl legend and only a few yards short of Jim Brown's all-time rushing record. Harris had rushed for 1,000 yards the season prior, and that, my friends, is an immutable achievement. Sure, Harris was plodding where he once was powerful, and he had not had a run longer than 21 yards in two seasons, and, sure, maybe his fumbling problems were no longer excusable when his rushing couldn't match, but *this was Franco Harris*. A legend in pursuit of history.

His arrival was met with ludicrous expectations, as if he carried the Steel Curtain to Seattle atop his broad shoulders. Guard Reggie McKenzie was psyched: "When Franco came here, the first thing he talked about was us winning the Super Bowl. Not going to the Super Bowl; winning it. Oh, it's going to be such a great year." It was. It was. Right after Seattle cut Harris and his 2.5 yards per carry.

Looking backward, there was Norm Johnson, who somehow earned the eternally trite nickname "Mr. Automatic." One wonders if it was meant ironically, as Johnson, somehow, despite kicking at least half his games in a dome, finished with a 69.7 percent field-goal percentage. That's not fair, though. Johnson kicked during a time when all kickers were less accurate for various reasons. It still looks wonky to me. Even in the most hostile environment,

Johnson's 36-for-60 run from 1985 through 1986 must have been hard to swallow.

The next big disaster was probably the Boz, but Brian deserves his own essay. Seattle then crawled from a period of relevance, where disaster players could actually stick out, to a point of complete failure, where singling out any one failure is petty and beneath me. Rick Mirer.

That Mirer somehow won AFC Rookie of the Year speaks volumes about the award. He was a sack-prone check-down artist who somehow arrested coaches' interest—first Tom Flores, then Dennis Erickson, Dave Wannstedt in Chicago, and after all that failure, Bill Parcells in New York.

Almost any member of Holmgren's defense fits the Crew. There was an Isaiah Kacyvenski and a Rashad Moore. Bob Whitsitt added a couple players who put an ironic spin on their position title: safety Ken Hamlin and safety Michael Boulware. They were all pretty forgettable, though. Bad players, soon replaced, sooner forgotten.

It was not until Brian Russell that the Sick Crew got its team captain. Russell had it all: grit, determination, a fluke good season many years removed, a rapport with coaches, good interview skills, and the favor of local media. Most importantly, Russell had a secret weapon: the overseer zone. Russell took the axiom of keeping the play in front of him to absurd lengths. Every play started a minimum of five yards in front of him. He was seemingly never involved in anything but cleanup tackles. He played in 32 consecutive games and broke up nine passes. Russell had little range, and that made it seem like he was never burned, like the receiver would pop open from thin air, or the corner was just supposed to be isolated in single coverage. He took confusing angles to the ball carrier and tackled like a Crisco-glazed fourth-grader. He hit late and often, and padded his stats by jumping on every pile no matter how dead the play.

But Russell played and played and even convinced some people he was good. Some took an agnostic stance; others attempted to prove his quality through negative proof. Russell was terrible when we saw him, but when we did not, he was Ed Reed/Ronnie Lott. How else could he continue to start? Maybe the coaches saw something we couldn't. Maybe fans suffered Stockholm syndrome. Maybe Brian Russell was good.

Maybe they all were.

71 Joey Galloway

Right off, I don't know nothin' about Galloway but blurred pictures and eternal love. That puts me at odds with this entire essay. Seahawks fans do not like Joey Galloway. (I do not even know if that's true, but I think it's true.) I was a kid, and Joey was the big thing at the time. The burner. The home-run threat. The player opponents feared.

The afterimage of Galloway's Seahawks career is an ugly contract dispute with Mike Holmgren. Eventually, Joey went to Dallas for *way too much* in return. Holmgren moved on, assembled his team, and became the most-/second-most-beloved coach in Seahawks history. Galloway flopped in Dallas. He later excelled in Tampa Bay, but Hawks fans had moved on by then. It was the ultimate dis: Seahawks fans didn't even care enough to hate him.

I could go on. Joey was the ultimate boom-bust proposition. His highlights were a fraud. They made me think Galloway was a golden gift. They made me think he was unstoppable. They made me think Galloway was an exception on an awful offense.

He wasn't, though. He was good. He was Brian Blades good. He was pre-merger football good. He would have killed in the

Seahawks wide receiver Joey Galloway pulls away from the Dallas Cowboys' Kevin Smith for a 44-yard touchdown reception at Irving, Texas, in November 1998. Galloway was a good receiver who could have been great in the play-action, deep-passing game of eras past.

play-action offenses of the past. But he was mismatched. Mismatched for the changing game. Mismatched for Holmgren and the West Coast offense. And so he bounced around doing his thing. Good as he ever was, he was only good, and that's kind of sad.

Just don't tell teenage me. He would be heartbroken.

72 Bulletin 1147

It is with great regret that I am announcing today that the NFL franchise we purchased in 1988 is leaving Seattle.

—February 2, 1996

Ken Behring's son, David, thinks that his father soured on football after the 1992 season. Man, didn't we all? Seattle fell to 2–14 in its first season after Chuck Knox. Tom Flores attempted to modernize the Seahawks' offense and through his modernization created an existential nightmare. Seattle scored 140 points, the lowest total in the history of the 16-game season. If you're looking for a record that's never likely to fall, that's a safe one.

Scoring points isn't the measure of a football team or even the measure of excitement. If Seattle had allowed 0 points, well, 1992 would have produced the greatest Seahawks team in franchise history. It didn't, of course, Seattle allowed 312 points. Still, being bad is one thing, and Seahawks fans have known that feeling pretty well throughout their history, but never even scoring 20 points in a game? Averaging less than 10 points scored a game? That has to be desperate and absurd. Are you still a fan when you hate your team more than your rival?

Knowing he was responsible? I'm sure that would have burned Ken Behring if he cared. I do not think he did, though. I'm sure, like most private citizens suddenly thrust into the spotlight, the hate mail was startling and discouraging. Anonymity and entitlement bring out the worst in people. Fans expect to win, and those who write hate mail typically forego the return address.

You might notice by now that this essay is short on name-calling and recriminations. Let's see if I can fix that.

Behring was a Midwesterner. He had no connection to Seattle but the Seahawks. Injury ended his college football dreams. I think he just wanted to own an NFL franchise, and when the Seahawks became available, Behring seized the opportunity. The Nordstrom family wanted out. They sold Behring the Seahawks, knowing full well he was not committed to the area.

Nashville businessman George C. Gillett was interested. Nashville was pushing hard for a major sports franchise, and the Houston Oilers eventually relocated there and became the Titans. Had Gillett offered a little more, the Seahawks might have been relocated before Paul Allen could intercede.

In that way, Behring was a lesser villain. Maybe if he got his way, maybe if he acted earlier and NFL commissioner Paul Tagliabue had not soured on the proposed relocation, maybe I would harbor more anger toward Behring. He wanted to murder the Seahawks and steal life from the city of Seattle. Behring believed that was his right as an owner. He thought the Kingdome was a dump and pressured Seattle to spend millions in renovation or build him a new stadium entirely. The Kingdome was a dump. Paul Allen himself did not commit to buying the Seahawks before the State of Washington agreed to build a new stadium. I doubt Behring was interested in staying, regardless, but he wasn't wrong. Whoever owned the Seahawks today, the team would not be playing in the Kingdome. Maybe under it.

Some welcomed Behring when he joined the organization. He was "hands-on." He wanted to shake up the team. He demanded a winner. He wanted a more wide-open offense, and it's not like Ground Chuck wasn't getting a little stale. Time turned his intentions into folly, revealed his distance from the city, and exposed him as a selfish owner.

There is a more exciting way to tell this story, I'm sure. Maybe in the moment. Behring must have seemed sulfurous and Machiavellian at the time. Seattle could have lost the Seahawks. We didn't, though. And Behring's treachery begat Paul Allen; Allen hired Holmgren; and Holmgren helped give us 2005.

I guess that makes Behring a despicable but elemental piece in the process. He swooped in and drove out Chuck and then attempted to destroy the Seahawks but failed. The fear he wrought surely encouraged voters to ratify a stadium bill, and that built Seahawks Stadium, and kept the Seahawks in Seattle for the foreseeable future. Behring wanted to move out of Seattle but failed, and so sold the Seahawks to Allen. I guess that makes Ken Behring the fertilizer from which Super Bowl XL grew.

73 Believe

Did anyone think that Seattle would make a championship run in 1983? Of course not. It started with one quarterback and finished strong with another. It went from a castoff to a nobody and rallied behind Dave Krieg like nobody could have anticipated.

Did anyone think that Seattle would make a Super Bowl run in 2005? I guess some thought it was possible. Seattle was a playoff team in 2004, but a paltry one. It was the year of the drops. The year Matt Hasselbeck regressed. The year that Seattle won the NFC West, only to lose its third straight game against the rival Rams. Tim Ruskell was throwing talent at the defense, and not five-star talent, but too-small players like Lofa Tatupu. If you believed Tatupu was the ingredient that would put Seattle over the top, you were a better fan than I.

Things do not follow the miserable path so many envision. Things never follow the optimistic path some seem to survive on. Mostly, though, things just do not follow the path we predict for them. Football can be so impenetrable that great change can happen and not be perceived for months or even years.

In retrospect, the shaky and weak-armed Matt Hasselbeck who has helped sink Seattle the last two seasons first appeared in 2007. That was perhaps the year of Hasselbeck's greatest career accomplishment. The line was no longer the league's best, and the skill-position talent was comprised of whoever had hands. The running game was frightful, and the once gliding, ankle-breaking style of Alexander was now plummeting, heartbreaking. Hasselbeck moved and distributed and used all his weapons and helped construct a top 10 passing offense. He was also slower, had lost his deep range, and needed wider and wider windows to throw through. For a season, there was a mesh point where his knowledge overcame his fading ability, and his fading ability perhaps brought his decision-making to the fore. So, though Hasselbeck was becoming inexorably worse, he was briefly in a place where he played better.

I watched every game of the 2007 season with meticulous note-taking, and though I could see he was slowing down, that his arm was weakening, I did not see that he was fading so rapidly. No one did. No one could.

Injury was to blame for the team's 2008 collapse. I guess. The team had shifted. It had realized a decline that was following it for years. Some of that decline manifested in injury, but the injury was not unnatural, a fluke. It was more like a tether breaking that had been strained so long.

As surely as that is depressing, the currents run in both directions. Seattle sprung into its own in 1983 and 2005. No one could see what it would become, but it wasn't chance or the product of great and wise decision-making. It was an emergence. It was a blooming where before there had not even been a flower.

If there is one thing every fan must do, it is believe. Believe your sorry team can get better. Dramatically. Believe it might already be happening. Believe it can happen without warning. It happens all the time. Believe, because hope and faith is a fan's sword and shield against the inevitable fact that every team but one ends the season a loser.

74 John L.

Football has progressed from its smashmouth roots. Time of possession took on a whole other meaning before Walter Camp introduced the play clock. Banning the wedge opened the outside and forced teams to take advantage of the 53.3-yard width in the pursuit of the 100-yard length. Steady and incremental refinements and rule changes have opened passing to the point where it dominates the modern game.

Fullback is one of the oldest positions on the football field, but in the modern game, its existence holds on by a thread. A designated run-blocker, the primary role of a fullback, is a luxury that teams dedicated to spreading the field with passing can rarely assume. Modern fullbacks are utilitarian. They can block, they can rush a little, and most importantly, they can receive. Mack Strong emerged from Air Georgia, and his ability to rush and receive earned him a place long before he could deliver brain-damaging run blocks. Much missed and undervalued former Seahawks fullback Leonard Weaver was a tight end in college, and though he never became a great lead blocker in Seahawks blue, he was a potent pass blocker and a dangerous receiver.

The receiving fullback is an antipodal combination of history and utility. It is those contrasts that make the receiving fullback so valuable. Defensive coordinators cannot help but cover a fullback with a linebacker lest they sacrifice their run defense, but most linebackers could never hope to cover a player like John L. Williams. So Williams cut the opposition to pieces in nine-yard increments.

Williams, like Weaver, was in some ways a fullback in name only. He was an accomplished rusher and receiver, and in another system might have played tailback. Williams was an accomplished

Seahawks fullback John L. Williams carries upfield in a 43–37 win over the Raiders in December 1988. Under "Ground Chuck," Williams was one of the last great running fullbacks in the NFL.

rusher at Florida. He was a surprise first-round pick for Seattle. Well, surprise for those who didn't know Ground Chuck.

Knox wanted to run it and run it and run it. Warner was excellent, but after his injury in 1984, emphasis was put on protecting him. He started splitting carries, but Seattle did not have equal talent to share the load. Knox gave some carries to Randall Morris and David Hughes, but they were also forced to throw more. It wasn't just about protecting Warner, but that with Warner less effective, Seattle was stuck in more third-and-longs.

Williams let Seattle reinvent itself as an offense. Rather, it allowed Knox to run the offense he wanted. After passing 113 more times than running in 1985, the Seahawks re-embraced Ground Chuck in 1986. It rushed 60 more times than it passed, and Williams absorbed 129 of their 513 team carries. It continued in 1987, this time with 91 more carries than passes. Plus-80 in 1988 and another winning record. It wasn't until Warner started breaking down that Knox resorted again to a pass-first offense, and he hated it. Seattle sunk all the way to 27th in scoring offense.

It wasn't all about Ground Chuck, though. Williams was a heck of a receiver. In his third season and with the NFC West title on the line, Williams caught a 75-yard pass for a touchdown. That put Seattle up 37–20, and as it turned out, they would need every score. The Raiders roared back and scored 17 from late in the third through the fourth. Seattle won by six and captured their first divisional crown. Williams had 180 yards receiving that day. Williams is still the Seahawks' third leading receiver in receptions and sixth in yards.

It was a surprise even then to draft a fullback in the first, and nowadays it would make Seattle the laughingstock of the league. Drafting a fullback in the first is like Oakland drafting kicker Sebastian Janikowski in the first, except teams still use kickers. But if the talent was there, did playing fullback diminish Williams' value or importance? I guarantee you Knox never regretted the move.

75 Visit Training Camp

You drive into Renton, but it gets better. You drive into Renton and find a shopping mall, never a challenge. You drive south and then north, and you enter Renton, but you stop there, yes, and I know that's crazy talk, but you drive into Renton and park at a place called The Landing. At The Landing, you're going to want to find parking, and it's going to be tough, because The Landing is the kind place that unabashedly brags about its urban ambience, where little sanitized chunks of culture come housed in faux brick, and where little sanitized chunks of humanity come and go. But you're going to want to park there, and then, and I stress this, get out of your car. You drive into Renton, park in The Landing, get out of your car, see a pilgrimage of Blue, and belong.

You drive into Renton because the VMAC is in Renton. It's on Lake Washington. Near the stately center lies a practice field, and it spreads like Elysium from Renton's Underworld. The air smells good, in every direction there is a view, and the grass is always fresh, no matter how many cleats dug at it the day before.

You drive into Renton, but it gets better. You park, wend down the parking garage stairs, see a pilgrimage of Blue, and belong. You register. You wait on the curb and board busses and sit among the faithful.

On the bus, there is spirited conversation. Conversation about triumphs and casualties, and maybe you disagree about this and that, but the spirit is shared. Everyone just wants to win. Everyone bleeds Seahawks.

Off the busses you walk, and there's some fanfare, a gauntlet of sponsors, and a path that wends up a hill.

The other side is where the Seahawks hold training camp. Speakers blast top 40. Players split into small groups organized by position. Everyone is running drills.

To your left you might see blitzing and blocking drills. And that's where Aaron Curry tore through not Julius Jones, not Justin Forsett, and not Owen Schmitt, but everybody. It was my first chance to see Curry close up, and he was every bit the prototype reported. The defender charges, and the offensive blocker charges to meet, and the two collide—if the blocker is lucky. Some players are so quick they just run around the blocker, and that's embarrassing. As a fan you feel the embarrassment. There are no enemies at training camp.

The receivers run routes and catch. They line up and run identical routes and run to the other side and line up again. It looks like high school practice. Just a bunch of grown-up kids running around and stomping and playing football. There's nothing professional about it but the money. There's the talent, and the talent pops. There's the high-effort players, yessir-yessir-yessir, who do everything they're told, and they are typically the least talented

Discover the Next Great Seahawk

If you ever visit training camp, you have two basic options to get the most of it. The first is the sampler. You can walk around the hill and try to get a look at everything and everyone. This is the typical path. One might spend a little time seeing wide-receiver drills and then move on to locking and passing drills.

The other is what I suggest for anyone who thinks of himself as a true enthusiast. Instead of walking around and just breathing it all in, pick a player or two and just track them all day. See how they do in every attempt in every drill. It helps if this player is unestablished.

It might seem silly to wander around and scrutinize someone who is likely to be cut, but if someone did that in 1991, they could have been the first person to talk up Michael Sinclair. Discovery is probably the truest joy of the enthusiast. And championing a player from obscurity to stardom is something that just cannot be matched.

players on the field. There are the veterans and the soon-to-be cut. There are the bad days for the players who cannot afford a bad day. It broke my heart to see Derek Walker, shoulders slumped, carrying four helmets into the locker room. So I yelled, "Stick with it, you're doing good out there!" and he turned and looked. Of course, he probably wondered, *Who the heck is that?* But he made it. And if you think tracking a player from the draft to starting gives you a connection, try tracking a player from fighting for his job to making the 53-man roster.

Players line up and scrimmage. It's contact, but for the most part, no one wants to hurt anyone else. Every so often there's a scrap, and it erupts in predictable ways. The early-round picks who haven't established themselves but are safe chafe the practice fodder fighting for a job. I watched Josh Wilson and Michael Bumpus go at it, and you know there was some epic trash talk that preceded. Bumpus had some limited experience in the regular season but was fighting for his football life. Wilson was a second-round pick from 2007 and, if not firmly entrenched as a starter, not in any danger to be cut. Wilson is mouthy. The two took it to the turf, but everyone broke and swarmed and broke it up. You hate to see bad blood among teammates, but at training camp, teammate is battling teammate for a job.

If you take notes, you are going to get a little extra attention from security. I sat on the hill and recorded names and performances. An officer walked up to me and asked me who I was. And I said, "Nobody. A fan." He told me that they had to be on the watch for advanced scouts evaluating their schemes and talent. I guess I was, but I was reporting only to Seahawks fans. Attending is about the only way you'll ever know what happens in training camp. Along the sidelines you can see press, but when the day is done, they all file the same story.

It's fun, and none of it matters much. If you've never been, maybe you imagine a heated contest between veterans and up-and-comers, clashing of pads, scrapping in the pile, and epic match-ups that determine jobs. But it's nothing like that. Players run drills, and many of the players most adept at running drills are least able to play football. Some players practice well and get through an entire career by impressing coach after coach with their discipline and hustle, but when it's game time, the best players play. Training camp gives coaches a look, but it's preseason and innate talent that typically defines who sticks and who is cut.

It's fun, and for the most part, your fellow 12 are good people who just want to talk Seahawks. A couple people come with an agenda, and that can be annoying. Last year, one guy had a real bone to pick with Matt Hasselbeck. All day, he was slagging Hasselbeck, deriding his game, his baldness, his past failures, and at the top of his lungs. What's worse, he had a really confused impression of Seneca Wallace. He championed Seneca like he was doing Wallace and all of us a favor. Training camp lasts about two hours, and most people talk quietly among themselves, so anywhere you went, this guy could be heard.

It's fun, and it's over fast. If you stick around, players walk over and sign autographs. The veterans are impassive. They stand, deflect questions, and are friendly, but have been here before. When Patrick Kerney walks over, you understand just how huge Patrick Kerney is. He's not just tall or built, but every part of him is bigger and broader than a typical human. His head is big. His hands are big. And when he towers over everyone, he's not awkward or gangly, he's alien. The young players eat up the attention. The Brandon Mebanes and the Josh Wilsons of the world are still pretty new to the fervent fans and the kids, and you can tell it's still a thrill. Others are shy, and that's lovable, too. Some are hammy and some are humble, but they're all human, and that sounds trite, but you can never appreciate that across a television set.

You get back on the bus and watch the VMAC fade behind the tree line and know you're going back to Renton and feel sad. Heady conversation percolates about the day and the season. Who impressed, who disappointed, and of course, *Who was that who did that? That was who did that? I thought it was him. No, Logan Payne is white.* Most around you are not going to be back tomorrow, so this was their day. Enthusiasm fades into reverie for some, and others are already back into their lives, talking shop or making business calls.

76 Cheney

The Seahawks held training camp in Cheney, Washington, 20 times. Cheney is one of those big small towns that people settle down in and doom their children to misery and alcoholism. It's bucolic and boring.

It's where Chuck Knox first connected with his kids. Gave them water. Looked them in the eye and promised them they could be good, even if he knew he was fibbing.

It's where Jack Patera stole away. Suffered the media. Denied the players water because of outdated ideas about toughness and good football.

It's where Tom Flores first Raiderized the Seahawks. Undid Ground Chuck. Hatched the schemes that would destroy the Seahawks' offense.

It's where Dennis Erickson did whatever Dennis Erickson did.

It's where Holmgren looked out and first saw a champion. And where he eventually pieced it together.

It's where 2,500 fans first dreamed the big dreams of a new season.

After 20 seasons of Seahawks football touching down in eastern Washington, taking the field of Eastern Washington University, Seattle upgraded and moved their camps a little closer to home.

I have never been out to Cheney. Eastern Washington has that tough temperate climate I grew up on. It has mountains and desert and gorges and farmland packed into every space in between. There is no night life, I figure, but X-box Live and hard drinking. It probably was extra special when the Seahawks came to town.

There was a lot of sadness and nostalgia when the Seahawks moved to Renton. I guess Cheney became the kind of place that somehow contained not just land, but action, people, and memories.

77 Silver

Warren Moon awoke in me a Seahawks passion. He brought exciting football to a moribund franchise. It wasn't all great. It never was once in Moon's career. And teenage me, full of contradiction and venom and discontent wanted Kitna. Jon Kitna was just 25, and Moon, he was a kind of old that I couldn't smell, see, or understand. Moon was 41.

Which was all part of the experience. Moon made me love the Seahawks, tune in to see him shell opponents, not grind and survive, but blow out the Colts and 49ers. The 13–3 49ers. Moon found Galloway for two long scores, Pritchard and McKnight for two more, and in a moment of portent and promise, Kitna substituted in, completed eight straight passes for 88, and scrambled for the finishing score.

False portent. False promise. Kitna proved less than stellar. But Moon, in his unintentional yet inestimable fashion, brought excitement and controversy. A quarterback controversy. Real football teams had those. Morton-Staubach. Montana-Young. Kitna-Moon.

It put the Seahawks on *SportsCenter*, and *SportsCenter* was my lifeline to Seattle sports. I lived in New Hampshire and followed my love from afar. Like any long-distance relationship, moments of connection were wonderful, sun-kissed moments of profound agony that I played over until my heart was sore.

The Seahawks mattered again. After a retched stretch, Seattle had crawled from the primordial ooze and clawed itself toward relevance. A vestigial Unverzagt stuck through camp, but he was shed, too. This team was going to be good. Walter was beginning his legacy at left. Joey Galloway was straight running past defenders. The kids, Kevin Mawae and Pete Kendall, weren't getting it, but the talent was there. Dennis Erickson would teach them. Dennis Erickson would lead the way.

Moon was charismatic. He was big-business, big-city, wide-smiled, important, and legendary: a real living future Hall of Famer in the Silver and Blue. His passes escaped gravity and reentered the atmosphere with big plans and bad intentions for opponents. Moon to Galloway was football as it was never meant to be—easy and graceful, a rank affront to football's smashmouth origins. It was too beautiful to describe. It was too big to comprehend. It was American football at the apex of its evolution and was happening in the Kingdome.

If you were a kid like me, that is all it ever was. It never began and never ended but existed outside of time like a dream half-remembered. I never knew Seattle signed him, and I was not paying attention when he moved on. He retired a little while later, and maybe I remember that. Someone named "Warren Moon" does broadcast work for Seahawks radio, but that voice is a stranger to me. The Moon I know is still hanging 'em high over Joey's shoulder as regular and unstoppable as the tide.

78 The Stage and Its Actor

Football produces plenty of villains, but it's short on cartoonish super villains—players who talk big, have a bigger persona, and fail hard. Fail hard, then fail, fail again.

That is the unspoken charm of a super villain. For all their showboating, dash, and flair, they're losers. Bruce Wayne is a charming, billionaire playboy with talent, charisma, and connections to burn. The Joker is a deranged fool in a clown costume. Wayne is almost alien in his rectitude. The Riddler could run a puzzle shop at Pike Place Market.

The Boz, alter ego of Brian Keith Bosworth, was a late-'80s super villain and Seahawk—in that order. He touched down his helicopter in King County in the summer of 1987. The smoke machines billowed, the strobes flashed, and from the hull of Sooners football emerged the biggest joke of a bust in franchise history.

His hair was a joke: a bleach-blond flattop that melted into a straggly late-'80s mullet. It stood atop a manly visage—all chin and brow.

He looked football, as interpreted by a sugar-addled eight-year-old: huge pads, thousand-yard stare, jaw like a shovel, and body like an action hero.

The Boz was branded, patented, and sold. He hucked product like a second calling. He called out John Elway and then covertly sold "Boz Buster" shirts to angry Broncos fans. He challenged Bo Jackson and lost. Jackson ran for 221 yards and three touchdowns. You can still watch Bo drag Boz into the end zone on YouTube.

Of course, he wasn't dragged. Brian Bosworth hit Jackson at the 2, stood him up, attempted the strip, and held on as the two fell

A Star Is Stillborn

Chuck Knox talked about Brian Bosworth with the quiet patience of a father. The mainstream media finds ways to take potshots at the long-irrelevant athlete. I wonder if what would really kill Bosworth is if everyone just stopped talking about him?

His career was short and undistinguished. Apart from the hype, he had one good season, and two seasons of sudden and cataclysmic decline. He had one movie of note, *Stone Cold*, and it was of note because people still cared about Bosworth when it was released. If you have seen it, you are among the dozens. It's amazing what total crap $25 million can buy.

I had never considered Bosworth before writing this book, but the guy really does cast a long shadow. For someone who failed at football and failed at acting, he holds fascination like few ever have. I don't think Bosworth is evil or scum or anything as marginalizing as that, but I figure he is a heck of an egotist. He was a self-promoter of historic proportions, and it was his self-promotion that is his legacy. Instead of calling Bosworth a bust, perhaps the ultimate act of cosmic justice is to call him what he truly is: irrelevant.

forward into the end zone. Strip off the hype, and it was just another slipped tackle. Bosworth wasn't dragged. He wasn't blown up or broken down. He hit his man square but lost.

Strip off the hyperbole, the caricature Bosworth wrought, and No. 55 was a promising young linebacker who played big as a rookie before breaking down and fading away. Bosworth hit hard and fast, played hard, and tried harder. In Week 14 of the 1987 season, facing the declining but still great Ditka-led Bears, Bosworth flew across the field, from outside the left hash mark to the right flat, smashed, stripped, and recovered a Neal Anderson fumble and returned to it to the 1. Curt Warner soared into the end zone on the next play. Seattle would never trail again.

He wasn't great. He wasn't likeable. He was polarizing, galvanizing, and good. The Boz was run over, through, and around. Bosworth had four sacks his rookie season and two forced fumbles. The Boz inflated his physique with 'roids. Bosworth twice won the Dick Butkus Award as the top college linebacker and deserved every

Brian Bosworth and his mullet take a phone call from his agent, or possibly one of the coaches in the booth, during a 16–10 win over the Cleveland Browns in October 1988 at Cleveland Municipal Stadium.

cent of his 10-year, $11 million contract. The Boz adapted his look and shtick for a short and ignominious career as a Hollywood action hero. Brian Bosworth lost his career, his talent, and his passion on the operating table.

He retired after only 24 games in the NFL, all starts. His image collapsed on him. Bosworth's self-idolatry came to haunt him like a specter; the hype he created was used to retroactively define him as a legendary bust. And so it was with some consternation that people read about the Boz rescuing a woman from an overturned SUV in 2007, and later, saving a man's life with CPR in 2009.

I mean, villains don't save. Cartoonish super villains like the Boz are crafty and despicable. Could it be that Brian Bosworth was just a man, and as any man faced with crisis, beholden to his humanity—his innate need to do right? Could it be the Boz was just a fiction, and like any fiction, as real as we need it to be? And that, where the two meet, there was nothing more than a good linebacker whose body never let him be great?

Nah. That's a terrible story. One not even the Boz would sign on for.

79 Buy a Jersey

I was drunk. Not loaded, but not able to legally operate machinery, either. I was blasting "This Time Tomorrow." It's a habit when I've had a few. I was wailing, "This time tomorrooooo*oow*!" It's a habit when I've had a few. I was inspired, by beer. Beerspiration. Now, that's just bad. It's the same way I got my first cat. I was drunk, sitting beside my future wife, and I said, "Let's get a cat!" and she said, "No way. You're drunk." She was right, but as Hemingway said, always do sober what you said you would do drunk. The next day we adopted Houdini.

I was in front of my laptop. I was drunk. Not loaded, but optimistic. I was saying, "I should buy a jersey," and my wife said, "You should." Bad idea.

I was on NFL.com. I was in front of my laptop. I was drunk. I was wailing "This Time Tomorrow." Jerseys are crazy expensive. For the price of a jersey, you could attend a game, and games are crazy expensive. I was on NFL.com. The jerseys bored me. Matt Hasselbeck? No. Aaron Curry? Too early. Shaun Alexander? You must be kidding me.

I was on NFL.com. I was in front of my laptop. I was drunk. I was about to buy a Brandon Mebane jersey.

And man, I have never regretted it.

What compels a grown man to buy a player's jersey? It's all kinds of silly. It's juvenile. Walking around with a "Largent" or "Jones" or "Tatupu" on your back. It looks like a desperate grasp at lost glory. Pale dude, buck-sixty soaking wet, with a Pat Williams jersey on—it looks foolish, incongruous, puerile.

But stupid has a calling. It plays in our hearts, it's charming and inviting and totally unlike smart, which is distancing, threatening. Maybe it's the Homer in the human soul, but embracing your dumb, your irrational, your primitive self, and boldly declaring, "I am Seahawks! You can find me stuffing my face and screaming crumbs this Sunday!" has an undeniable savor.

Jerseys from Goodwill

Goodwill is a great place to find Seahawks memorabilia and jerseys. I have a Ricky Watters, and my wife has a Deion Branch and Shaun Alexander, all authentic, that we got from Goodwill. Jerseys at the Goodwill cost less than $10, and if you are concerned about this kind of thing, look worn in.

Not only do I have two jerseys, but multiple Seahawks mugs, Seahawks glasses, Seahawks tees from different eras, a Chuck Knox–style ball cap, and some Seahawks sweaters. I think part of the charm is that it's cheap and supports a good cause rather than crass commercialism. That is what's kind of cool about buying anything at Goodwill, you know you are doing more than recycling, you are taking garbage and making it a treasure again.

The other part of the charm is that it's a bit like antiquing, I guess. Goodwill cuts across eras, and so you get the good, the forgettable, and the gaudy. My wife and I do not make a ton of cash, but leafing through the Goodwill lets us have a robust collection of Seahawks stuff. She is on standing order to buy me any jersey I can fit in.

And so I bought it and spent too much and maybe thought about that a little between the time of ordering and arrival, but mostly embraced a giddy anticipation. I pestered the UPS lady, and she reciprocated with a world-weary stare. I, 11:45 sharp, opened my front door and said, "Hello, Mr. Sun," with a smile, and he burned on hot and indifferent. When it arrived, I tore off the packaging like Christmas wrap, saw the embroidery and the "Mebane" and the "92," and slid it on. It was cool and soft and lazily hung over my shoulders. I put on pants and walked to the store, and every few blocks I shouted out:

Me!

Bane!

80. The Arrhythmic Dance of Quoted Unmentionables

The Internet is a wonderful place to argue, and don't my readers know it. It affords all sorts of advantages over an actual, tangible, in-your-face argument: time to collect your thoughts, time to fact-check, time to edit, time to figure out new angles to argue long after the point is settled, a decreased risk of being punched in the face. I am personally not fond of it, but some of it is just part of doing the job. Never muck it up with another, and you let the braindead megaphone take over.

It was in one of those classic battles of resolve that someone suggested to me that you can take a lot from a press conference if you translate coachspeak. I realized he's right. There is a lot said like, "We need to play better," and, "This player needs to play better," and, "That other player needs to play better," and, "I prefer it when the team wins," and the always-informative, "I will offer no information about that subject because it would compromise myself, my team, and/or my family."

Coaches have never offered more than Crash Davis, ever. NFL coaches are particularly secretive because, unlike most coaches, what they think and decide actually impacts the game. Baseball coaches smack asses and keep curfew, but their in-game decisions could be decided by a rhesus monkey. Bunt, run, you go out, you go in, pick lice off that catcher, fling feces! Fling feces! Hold up at third.

Maybe football fans have been beat down by bullcrap, because so many hang on every word. They clamor for the postgame, savor the coachspeak, and reread it all week as it's peppered into articles. It confounds me.

Every coach is intent on "executing" because "executing" simply means "doing your job." The right tackle didn't execute? Well, shoot, he probably missed a block or five. Every coach wants to force turnovers, because that's good, but surprisingly, there is no "force turnover" play in the playbook. You have to execute to force turnovers. If you force enough, you can "establish the run," and every coach wants to "establish the run" because winning teams run the ball to kill the clock. Rush attempts correlate strongly with wins. Yards per rush, almost not at all.

It is not hard to avoid coachspeak. Coaches typically dispense injury updates at the beginning of press conferences and then field softball questions for an hour. If you're there for the start, you get the important information. If you stick around for the softball questions, you're sure to learn about the team's need to establish rhythm in the passing game and create pressure with the front four. I find the latter tiresome. I want the Seahawks to create pressure with the front one. I want Nick Reed to tear through five blockers and decapitate quarterbacks with the whoosh of his sonic boom.

It isn't hard to turn off, and it doesn't hurt anybody. Coaches do not enjoy dishing out the daily bull to the press corps, but it's the way it's been done, so they do it. I am sure they would rather take that time and instruct or game-plan an opponent or, I don't know, see their kids.

Sometimes obsolete practices continue through sheer force of inertia. It wasn't that long ago that the press had a monopoly on distribution. Want to know the injury lowdown? You had to buy a paper. Nowadays, teams distribute injury information through their own websites. Teams distribute transactions through press releases. It's everywhere, and anyone with Internet access can find it.

So ignore the coachspeak, because it is and always has been just one thing: the least amount of information that can possibly be conveyed while still speaking in sentences.

81 Seneca Wallace

Seneca Wallace could make you scream and make you suffer, and for all his purported scrambling ability, I hated it when he took off. Seneca Wallace is the great receiver who wasn't, who maybe could have never have been a great receiver. He had the most peculiar habits as a quarterback, but burrowed his way into perennial second-string status and, because of that, has started 14 games in the last four years.

Like a lot of people, I wanted Wallace to figure it out. There were a lot of reasons to doubt him. He is short, and short enough that it seems to honestly hurt his ability to see the field. He has dyslexia, and some think that damages his ability to read a playbook. He succeeded in college through sheer athletic gifts.

Those gifts beguiled me into thinking he had unlimited potential. It is the classic trap of equating tools to upside. I thought if his

What If? Umm…Maybe Not

One of the great what-ifs we will never know is how good Seneca Wallace could have been if he played receiver. Mike Holmgren thought he could be special. Matt Hasselbeck said he wore out the Seahawks corners in practice. His slant-and-go route in the 2005 NFC Championship Game is still the thing of legends. He didn't just shed Ken Lucas like dirty laundry, he caught an underthrown pass by pinning it against his left shoulder.

The truth is, while Wallace maybe could have been a great receiver, we can never be sure or even really believe it was likely. In 2008, when Seahawks receiver was the most dangerous job in football and Seattle was signing street free agents, Holmgren finally swallowed his convention and took a risk by playing Wallace as a returner and receiver. Well, he tried. Wallace injured himself during warm-ups. It's a reminder that receiving in practice involves a lot fewer bone-jarring tackles.

head could catch up to his arm and legs, he would be unstoppable. Maybe if it was that simple, he would be.

Like so many things cast off as free choice rather than God-given ability, Wallace did not struggle because he didn't want it enough. He did not fail to develop because he was not committed to the system. His head could never truly catch up to his arm and legs because his head was a tool like everything else.

Wallace never learned to read defenses. He would instinctively make one read and then want to run. He never learned how to feel comfortable within the pocket, and he created sacks by getting jumpy. His drop-step was curiously long, so that he would be almost 10 yards behind the line of scrimmage before he stopped to look out at the field. That made him toast for edge rushers who could run in straight lines to beat the tackles. Even after years of study, his understanding of Mike Holmgren's offense was rudimentary, and when Holmgren retired and Seattle signed a new offensive coordinator, what little gains in confidence and knowledge he made were lost entirely.

Even so, and despite all his deficits and limitations, he was a good backup quarterback for a few seasons. His 2006, in all its herky-jerky and heart-stopping beauty, was solid enough. The Seahawks managed a 2–2 record without Matt Hasselbeck. I will always remember that long pass to Darrell Jackson for the score. Whatever his passing ability, Wallace has an awesome arm.

Holmgren worked him as a receiver occasionally, and when Greg Knapp took over, he created the SeneCat. Both were perfect summations of Wallace's career. Good, gimmicky, and equally scary and exciting. He was never good, never what you envision in a starter, but he brought something exciting and different as a backup. If nothing else, Wallace was a heck of a lot better than Charlie Frye.

A Threat with His Legs, and Hands

Before he became a Seahawk, Seneca Wallace was an Iowa State Cyclone. His success there tells us a lot about the difference between the college and pro game. On one famous play, affectionately known as "the Run," Wallace ran left, then right, then back, then forward, then left all the way back across the field, and then forward into the end zone.

His scrambling and mobility were assets in college, but never proved valuable in the pros. Wallace would take long drops that made it very hard for his tackles to block the edge. He has only averaged four yards per attempt and has only run for one touchdown. Matt Hasselbeck has averaged 3.8 yards per attempt and rushed for five touchdowns.

Watch any game Wallace starts, and the announcers are sure to tell you that he is a threat with his legs, but Seahawks fans learned his legs were a greater threat to his team. He fumbled 17 times in his Seahawks career. He also had a habit of running out of bounds behind the line of scrimmage instead of throwing it away. That meant Wallace was essentially sacking himself. He just is not fast enough to regularly outrun professional linebackers.

82 Watch an Old Game

It took a lot of searching to find copies of old games. Eventually, I found people online who would share. It's a wonderful thing that someone who once lived and died Seahawks-Broncos or Seahawks-Chiefs can share that with someone who wasn't alive or was in diapers or wasn't sure even which team to root for.

What I've learned is that, in 30 years, the essence of the game never changed—the snap, the drop-back, the scramble, the completion, the pressure. Players have gotten bigger and maybe a little faster, but football is still football, and a fan of any era can peek into the past and instantly feel the rush. I knew who to root for and, after a little while, why. I could tell right away that Paul Johns was probably a headache for his short stay in Seattle. Dude dropped passes like they were hot.

Then, for how similar everything was, there were also the cool and sometimes subtle differences. The offensive and defensive lines were smaller, and it seemed to make running the ball a lot easier. It wasn't just that Curt Warner was bowling over players his own size. It actually looked like bigger holes appeared more naturally in the spaces between players. I never saw teams throw quick outs or wide receiver screens. In that sense, the passing game was more pure. It was vertical, all long routes and big receptions. And incompletions. No one fretted over a minor cold streak, and quarterbacks didn't regularly string together runs of 10-for-11, and 18-for-21. The pass was a high-reward gamble, and you could tell some of the older coaches wished they could avoid it all together.

Watching old tape gives you roots. It gave me a sense of where the Seahawks had been, but also where football had been. It made

Best Game Ever

If anyone ever asks you what the most exciting game in Seahawks history is, you can provide them something approaching an objective answer. In 2005, after falling to 2–2, the Seahawks ripped off a six-game win streak. People were really starting to believe in the team, but at the same time, it wasn't like Seattle hadn't been here before. In fact, 8–2 was exactly how Seattle had started in Holmgren's first season.

The NFC West was already declining into a pitiful division, and though the Seahawks were 8–2, they had fattened on teams that could not tie their cleats without supervision. The 7–3 Giants were the exact test Seattle needed to prove their playoff mettle.

The game turned out to be not just important, but exciting. Win probability assumes 100 percent is sure victory, but between a 50–50 starting point and the inevitable victory, the probability itself can move wildly or almost not at all. Consider the butt-kicking the Vikings gave Seattle in Week 11 of the 2009 season. The game was over before the half, and so the sum movement was only 160 percent, or a little more than three times the minimum. Seahawks-Giants moved an astonishing 1,030 percent.

Well, astonishing if you did not watch it. Each team owned a lead for a little bit, but New York looked like it would prevail with a late drive to end the fourth quarter. The Giants closed to within the Seahawks 22, and with four seconds on the clock, attempted a 40-yard field goal. Jay Feeley hooked it wide left, and the game went into overtime.

Overtime only upped the excitement. The ball changed hands multiple times, and Feeley attempted another field goal but missed again. Eventually, Josh Brown nailed a 36-yarder to end it. The game not only gave Seahawks fans the quality win they needed to believe, but determined something more tangible. The Giants hosted Carolina and lost in the wild-card round. Had they won, they would have owned the tiebreaker with Seattle, the No. 1 seed, and a first-round bye. No one knew it then, but the Seahawks were playing for the Super Bowl.

me realize the modern need for bigger and bigger isn't all that great, honestly. Something about seeing man-sized competitors doing incredible things seemed welcome after growing up on 300-pound players who don't move and get paid for it. Football is always changing, and when you jump around its history, the changes can be striking. I cringe when I see a team run a reverse or an end-around in today's game, but again and again, those plays were safe, successful, and explosive for the '80s-era offenses. Maybe that's why they're still in the playbook.

Football didn't start when I started watching. The Seahawks weren't born when I decided I was a Seahawks fan. The game will change continuously throughout my life, and where it ends is not clear to me. Maybe things will reverse, and smaller, quicker players will once again rule. Maybe the passing game will become so pre-eminent, rushers like Warner can once again take the field and school players their own size. Maybe, just maybe, the Seahawks don't have to always be bad. No team is destined to failure or even mediocrity. San Francisco and Denver endured decades of some-times good but never great football before the right mix of coaching and talent turned them into champions. Did the 49ers know what it meant to draft Joe Montana? What I know is so small, and what can be is endless, and I knew that, I did, but I didn't understand. Seeing Warner and Krieg and Largent run around on the too-too green Kingdome turf like every play was the Super Bowl, and every down their last, made me realize there's a lot of football left for me to see, a lot of changes, and maybe a time when the Seahawks achieve true greatness.

83 The Walrus

He knew offensive talent. He could see great things in Darrell Jackson, Steve Hutchinson, Bobby Engram, Shaun Alexander, and Matt Hasselbeck. Mike Holmgren knew the West Coast offense like few will ever know anything. He could design great plays and get his players to buy in. He was a great coach, with a great eye for offensive talent and a historic résumé of great quarterbacks developed, but

Head coach Mike Holmgren stands on the sideline before the kickoff of a preseason game in August 1999, his first season with the Seahawks after guiding the Green Bay Packers to two Super Bowls and one championship.

I think I will always know him best for the silent films he enacted on the sideline.

Maybe it was the mustache, or the tall, rotund frame, but Holmgren always looked like a Walrus to me. I think everyone saw it, in a way. Commentators would talk about him barking, and, oh, he did. Holmgren had a huge temper and shot off multiple times a game. He seemed hot and cold, steely and focused one second, and then liable to explode into an angry tirade the next.

You could tell his players and coaches feared him. When he popped up, bodies would retreat from him in waves. It was all in the moment of anger. I never saw him chew anyone out, not like that, not with the red face and barking.

Instead, he would pull an arm around a player and hold them in his private chambers. I am sure it scared the bejesus out of them. He was the kind of coach who scared most with a long, hard, disappointed look. You always knew whom he was angry at during the game, but he was cautious in the postgame. He chose his words well with reporters. Holmgren was not above singling out a player, but you never felt he disrespected them.

He was a devilish red-zone tactician. His routes were supremely crafted to free players. Holmgren shied from gimmick, from change, adhered to the principles of good coaching he grew up with, but within that palette, he painted beautiful plays. He understood how to pick out a defensive back without incurring offensive pass interference. His routes were well timed, and when the Seahawks were on, their efficiency made them seem unstoppable.

I think Holmgren was like any great composer, somewhat set in his ways, but ruthless with detail. He came to Seattle and dismantled what might have been a good team, but only because he wanted to remake the Seahawks exactly to his own specifications. The 2005 team was so locked in, so coordinated and graceful, it was an absolute joy to watch. That effortlessness and grace was surely won through hard, tiring work, frustration, and failure.

Mike Holmgren was the greatest head coach I ever had a chance to appreciate. The more I learned about football, the more I could see his fingerprints on everything I loved. By the end, I think the game had passed him by. He was still working the basic Bill Walsh offense when others had expanded on it and teased out new plays, better plays. Maybe it was a little outdated, and maybe it was demanding of resources, of his players, of his fans' patience, but I think I can say, for all Seahawks, the reward was so worth it.

84 Marcus Tubbs

A player is important both for his duration and value. The best contribute great things for decades. Most simply stick around, have their days and their off days. Those are the stars and the punch-card players, respectively, and the two comprise most of the NFL. There is a long history of sensational talents who burned bright but burned out before we could fully appreciate them. It's common among running backs, where even the best players rarely last even a decade. Terrell Davis and Jamal Anderson had concurrent runs of dominance and both disappeared after debilitating knee injuries.

Marcus Tubbs knows a little something about debilitating knee injuries. He was a boom-or-bust pick by the Holmgren-Whitsitt brain trust who boomed before his body busted. Tubbs had the size and athleticism, but was inconsistent. He was soft-bodied, and fellow players openly questioned his desire. In the unwritten history of Seahawks could-have-beens, Seattle was targeting Vince Wilfork but couldn't move up. Wilfork was selected 21st overall by the Patriots. Tubbs was picked 23rd.

Tubbs didn't flash and burn out. He was valuable by contrast and because of need. Seattle had a hole at defensive tackle. A hole the size of Sam Adams. Mike Holmgren lost Cortez Kennedy in his second season in Seattle, but Cortez was grinding down, and he wasn't lost because of a personnel blunder but because of retirement. Tez hung 'em up.

Adams was lost for no good reason at all. In his second season with the team and first real run at free agency, Mike Holmgren lost Adams and defensive end Philip Daniels. Daniels signed with Chicago. Adams signed with the Ravens. The Bears had the top-ranked defense in the NFL in 2001. The Ravens perhaps the greatest defense in NFL history in 2000. Seattle sagged to 25th in scoring defense and last in yards allowed. Seattle allowed 6.3 yards per play, .5 yards worse than second-ranked Denver, and the same distance between Denver and 23rd-ranked Indianapolis.

Seattle eventually upgraded over Riddick Parker. They signed 34-year-old John Randle to a very risky and very expensive contract, but nevertheless struck gold. It re-signed aged end Michael Sinclair and sold the fans nonsense about scheme adjustments. It ponied up bucks for Chad Eaton. All contributed briefly, but as rent-a-players do, were soon lost to age, injury, and retirement. By the time the offense developed, Seattle was starting over, starting Cedric Woodard and Rashad Moore.

Tubbs was food for a starving man. That's the real story of Marcus Tubbs. He wasn't great. He never got a chance to be. Tubbs was invaluable because of whom he replaced. With him around, every member of the defense played better. He wasn't Merlin Olsen, but he could force a double team. Lofa Tatupu and LeRoy Hill thrived playing behind Tubbs. Without him and before Brandon Mebane, the Seahawks' run stuffer was Chuck Darby. Darby could slice in and disrupt, but was impotent against a double team.

Tubbs' career was short. He was never a great value for a first-round pick. He struggled to become a starter before injury took it all away. But the best season in Seahawks history was built on offense and a surprise defense, and though many players were better, many players did more, no player was more essential than Marcus Tubbs. In his own way, and if only for a season, Tubbs achieved greatness.

85 Understand Probability

Football is in a fix. Its season is silly short, and its postseason shorter. It's full of uncommon but important things like interceptions returned for touchdowns and last-second field goals. The parity within the league, coupled with the difficulty in understanding the quality of a team, coupled with the extreme difficulty of guessing the outcome of one game, has created the phrase "any given Sunday." It is a beautiful, essential part of football, but it confuses the crap out of most people.

Football is entertaining, but its entertainment is predicated on competition. Nothing is more exciting than a close, well-contested game. Great comebacks are their own kind of incredible, and for one's own team, kicking the snot out of an opponent can be better than either. However, whether the game is hotly contested, first won but eventually lost, or owned from the first snap, football fans need to have an appreciation of why.

We need to know why the Cowboys and 49ers were once unbeatable. Why the Lions are always bad. We need to know that football isn't just scored chaos. That is what puts football in a fix. With so little hard evidence, and so much variability game to game and season to season, it can feel like just that: scored chaos.

To do that, and to understand football, one needs to understand probability. It's not so foreign when you think about it. Football is full of numbers. Completion percentage, yards per carry, down and distance, etc. Football doesn't translate readily into statistics, though, not meaningful statistics, anyway. It's a team sport, every stat measures team ability, and that makes individual stats fun but hardly representative. However, stats aren't the matter that interests me.

I am instead talking about the game itself, and understanding why it can seem so mercurial. Consider the lowly field-goal kick. Analysis indicates that a kicker has little ability to consistently kick field goals. Is he lucky when he kicks 10 in a row? Is he unlucky when he only kicks 60 percent over a season? Not really, no.

Luck is a bad word for it. Josh Brown kicked four game-winning field goals in 2006. Was he lucky to kick those field goals? No, he, his long snapper, and his holder worked with his offensive line to accomplish something special when it mattered most.

A better way to understand it is this: go outside, pick a target, and throw a football at it 10 times. Most people will miss some and hit some. Even those good enough to hit every time will have good throws and bad throws. Even those that miss every time will have better throws and worse throws. Even the greatest, most practiced athlete in the world will have good throws and bad throws. What we are doing is executing a coordinated set of motions, and at each step, something can go wrong.

Brown was not lucky to kick four field goals, but he was lucky that he never misfired with the game on the line. It's not like Brown ever intends to miss kicks, but he still does once in about every five attempts. Sometimes, in attempting to do the exact right thing, something goes wrong. Sometimes, the same happens for his long snapper or holder. No one is lucky or unlucky when it happens. In fact, consistency is what allows a quarterback to become a pro, a pitcher to throw strikes, a golfer to hit the green, and so on—but in a sport with a constantly evolving game state, a team can be lucky *when* it happens. Brown never attempted to miss. Seattle was just lucky that he missed in less-important situations.

Football is full of these kinds of interactions.

Many times a game, an offensive lineman is slow off the snap, and therefore at a disadvantage against the defender. But we as football fans are never likely to notice this until it coincides with the defender doing something right. So, even if it only happens once, if it coincides with the defender timing the snap perfectly and sacking the quarterback, it seems worse than if it happens five times, and the defender is never able to exploit it.

If a quarterback throws a pass inaccurately, most times the pass is missed by the receiver, or, the receiver is able to catch it, anyway. A little behind him, a little in front, a little over his head, but the receiver tracks the ball and catches it. Take that exact same pass but direct it at a receiver with slightly worse hands. Now, we have more incompletions, and every so often the receiver will attempt to catch it, deflect the pass, and it will be intercepted. People are quick to blame the quarterback, because he was in fact inaccurate, but the outcome is dependent on multiple variables he can't control.

That is why football can seem so confusing and unpredictable. Players have skills, but skills only influence the outcome. Things like fumbles and fumble recoveries and interceptions and drops are dependent on complex interactions of singular events that will never be repeated. This is where understanding probability becomes essential to understanding football.

If I were to race someone slightly faster than me, that person would beat me every time. That is because it is a simple skills competition: two people, unable to influence the other, running a designated length. If we know that one person can arrive more quickly to, say, 100 meters, we can be pretty sure that that person will beat me in every race.

If we run the same race, but now decide irregularities will appear randomly on the track, I could win. Maybe my opponent trips after 10 yards, and I don't. Now we are not only introducing chance—we never assured the irregularities would equally influence both runners—but we are also introducing a very hard-to-measure skill: the ability to avoid random irregularities on the track. Now, if we run the same race again but have coordinated irregularities, and

I still win, all we have measured is my ability to negotiate one particular type of course. Run the race again with different but again equal irregularities, and either racer may win.

In the NFL, we have 22 athletes interacting. Every play ever performed is wholly and totally unique. The position on the field, the time on the clock, the stamina of the players involved, the weather, the game state, the condition of the field itself, the players' alignment, how cleanly they execute, the discrepancy between their execution and the execution of their match-up are wholly and totally unique to that one play. That is why when a quarterback throws an interception or a defense fails to recover a fumble, we can attempt to analyze core skills, but we can't take the outcome as evidence of an inability to avoid throwing interceptions, or ability to intercept a pass, or inability of the defense to recover a fumble or ability of the offense to recover a fumble. They did or did not, in that one, never-repeated play.

Football is not hopelessly random. Despite its short season and single-elimination playoff format, the NFL has had multiple dynasties. Surely, there are core abilities that make some teams consistently better than others. But approximating these core abilities is about as accurate as you can ever get in the NFL. We know that completion percentage approximates a quarterback's ability to throw accurately and to the right receiver. We know that yards-per-carry approximates a running back's ability to see and run through a hole, but also the offensive line's ability to create that hole, along with other factors. We don't, however, ever create a sample large enough to truly know what the next play will be like, or the next 10 plays, or the next game.

Wild, huh?

86 Michael Sinclair

Teams draft punters in the sixth round. Long snappers. Teams draft practice dummies in the sixth round. And kickers. Being drafted in the sixth round is a curse and a certain insult. At least an undrafted free agent can pick his team. Players drafted in the sixth round are marked for failure. They have little chance to prove themselves because the coach has already put a sixth-round stamp on them.

Michael Sinclair probably should not have made it—at least not as a Seahawk. He was drafted in the sixth round of the 1991 draft to play behind Jacob Green. Green was entering his mid-thirties, but his production was holding steady. The season before Seattle drafted Sinclair, Green notched 12.5 sacks. He wasn't just behind Green, either. Seattle had former first-round-pick Jeff Bryant, who split time between tackle and end. Seattle had drafted Tony Woods in the first round in 1987, and Woods was an under-sized pass-rush specialist like Sinclair.

Sinclair struggled through his first training camp and was cut but signed to the practice squad. And that was his first season in a nutshell: practice at the precipice. Eventually injury landed him in the starting lineup. He was the last defensive end Seattle developed from scratch who was truly good. He was a bargain Grant Wistrom, but better. For his career he recorded 73.5 sacks. His peak was special. From 1996 to 1998, Sinclair had 41.5 sacks for the Seahawks.

I am not sure where he fits in the big picture. His peak was short and for Seahawks teams that could barely scrape respectability. Maybe current Seahawk Darryl Tapp could approach something like what Sinclair did. For all the hope I have for Tapp, and for how much he would have to grow to reach Sinclair, it puts into perspective just how awesome Sinclair was. Teams draft punters in the sixth round, and sometimes, when they take a chance, teams draft Michael Sinclair in the sixth round.

87 Sea Hawk

Seattle is named after the osprey. The osprey is a beautiful bird of prey that Seahawks fans can truly be proud of. Loving your mascot is a small but important thing. I would be horrified to have to root for the Redskins or Chiefs. Both are old teams, teams that were founded before it seemed taboo to name a team after a racial epithet, but both are nevertheless stuck with an offensive and ignorant team name. I guess like so many things, fans become inured. Certainly the name does not make the fans or the franchises themselves racist, but "Redskin" and "Chief" are nevertheless unsavory.

The osprey is a fish-eating raptor. Raptors are noteworthy for hunting in flight, and when you combine hunting in flight with fishing, you have one of nature's great coordinated acts of grace. The osprey is actually the only species of the genus Pandion and is found all over the world. One place it is not often found is Seattle.

The most Seahawk-like Seahawk of all-time is Dave Brown. *Raptor* derives from *rapacious* and Brown was a true ball hawk. The all-raptor team for Seattle would include Brown, Eugene Robinson, Kenny Easley, and John Harris. That is actually very close to the starting secondary for the 1985 Seahawks.

The modern game is turning airborne, and though the name is incidental, something derived from a contest, it is cool to be a fan of the Seahawks. They are not dogs, not miners, not sheep, never will be victim to changing mores, but something elegant, skillful, and predatory, like a great football team.

88 Husky Stadium

For whatever reason, Husky Stadium inhabits a terrifying nook in my subconscious. I remember thinking it was ugly and intimidating. The seating looked too steep. It made me think of El Castillo in Chichen Itza. There, the steps are high and must be climbed on hands and knees. It was built for ritualistic sacrifice, the bodies cast down its steep sides.

When I started researching this book, a few things stood out to me. First, Husky Stadium is widely considered beautiful and scenic. That baffled me. Well, it didn't, because I knew my memories were irrational, but on a gut level, it did. The other thing that really startled me were black-and-white pictures from the 1987 north deck collapse. The sound of twisted metal is horrifying. Seeing the bent and collapsing structure reinforced my foolish fear.

Husky Stadium housed the Seahawks for three regular-season games in 1994 and two seasons before the completion of Qwest. Seattle finished 10–9 in Husky Stadium. Maybe the Huskies themselves left a little suck lying around, and it got on the Seahawks. It was loud like every good Seahawks stadium should be. Maybe if I could see it as a haven from the Kingdome, something that let Seattle find a better home, I could love it, too. But I don't. I fear and hate it and assume I always will.

I guess superstitions die hard.

89 Eugene Robinson

Every doubt I harbor writing about Dave Brown doubles when writing about Eugene Robinson. The safety, the last line of defense: how do we know when he's good? How can we know? Is it enough to never see them get burned, or should they, like Troy Polamalu and Ed Reed, be active parts of a secondary?

Robinson made the Seahawks' roster as an undrafted free agent out of Colgate. Even as a reserve and situational player, he displayed his dangerous hands and return ability. In his first season, Robinson picked two passes and returned them for 47 yards. By the next year, he was firmly entrenched as the Seahawks' free safety. He would stick there for the next 10 seasons.

That is academic, recorded, available through NFL.com and other sites. What really was Robinson? Was he a ball hawk who abandoned coverage like Michael Boulware? When Boulware was starting, I never dreamed he was such a liability. When he picked a pass in Super Bowl XL, I thought the talented, toolsy former linebacker was emerging, would become a great, all-time Seahawk. Then he was traded for a first-round bust, benched by the Texans, and has never regained a starting spot since.

I watched Boulware, and I did not know that. Sure, I remember he broke coverage sometimes. Or at least he was the closest player to the free receiver. But I was not watching tape then. I was just a fan who got high in the big moments and remembered how awesome he was in his rookie season.

I watched Boulware and still do not feel comfortable saying exactly how good he was or could have become. So what I can say about Robinson? He deserves a place, I think. He is second all-time

Seahawks free safety Eugene Robinson, in action during a game against the Washington Redskins in November 1995 at RFK Stadium, ranks second all-time for most interceptions by a Seahawk. Photo courtesy of Getty Images

on the Seahawks' interceptions list. It was not long ago that I thought RBIs were the ultimate measure of a batter's production. Now I know RBIs are a hollow stat, indicative of a team's total skill, and a stat that can badly mislead. Robinson played for a long time and earned the trust of multiple coaches, just like Jim Rice. When the day comes that we have a concrete measure of range, reliability, and coverage skills, maybe I can tell you Robinson was great, but until then, I will tell you only that he was noteworthy.

90 Josh Brown

You won't find too many kickers listed among a team's all-time great players, but you won't find too many kickers who did what Josh Brown did.

Brown was a star athlete in high school. He was a letterman in basketball, football, and track for the Foyil Panthers in Oklahoma. It is a subtle reminder that the oddball kickers we love to revile are in fact gifted athletes. He finished Foyil with 9,136 all-purpose yards and 51 touchdowns, but Brown's future lay in kicking.

He attended Nebraska and distinguished himself as an NFL prospect. Brown was a heck of a kicker. Of course, that's a bit of a matter of perspective. Brown only converted 69.4 percent of his kicks in college, including a sophomore season in which he was 5-for-10. That's enough to get someone run out of the league in the NFL, but in college long snappers are less skilled and hash marks wider. Further, Brown kicked 'em when they counted, or whatever. He was carried off the field after a 29-yard field goal to beat Colorado, and that win kept Nebraska in bowl contention. The Cornhuskers would finish the season stomping the piss out of Northwestern in the Alamo Bowl. Brown made the embarrassment of a million Wildcats fans possible. He helped turn the Alamo Bowl into an unwatchable travesty of entertainment.

It was all about good timing and better luck for Brown. There's little evidence that a kicker can control when they're accurate and when they're off. Retrospective psychology applied by beat reporters and fans invented concepts such as "clutch." Brown got lucky at the right time. It would propel him to NFL millions. It would save the season like a kicker never should.

Seattle drafted Brown in 2003, and for his first few years, he was an ordinary kicker of little distinction. Then came 2006. Seattle was cursed. The Super Bowl losers' curse. It dragged teams to their graves, fans to the bottle, coaches to their antacids, and reporters to their thesauruses. The curse was booming in 2006, supported by the unimpeachable proof of recent history, believed by the unimpeachable intellect of Joe Sports Fan, Esq.

The Seahawks avoided this cosmic curse because they didn't actually lose the Super Bowl. The Steelers watched their quarterback motorcycle his face off. It was good times. A correction of sorts. An IOU from God, delivered six months too late and a few dollars short. Sort of a "Sorry I ran over your dog, but here's a gerbil."

By ordinary stats, the 2006 Seahawks were ordinarily bad. They were outscored by six points. They ranked 19th in offensive yards and defensive yards allowed. They lost the turnover war 34–26.

Ordinary stats neglect quality of opponents, and the NFC West was brutally bad that year. The 49ers, Cardinals, Rams, and Seahawks combined were outscored by 209 points. Seattle squeaked out an NFC West title on the leg of Brown.

Bad Day at Lambeau Field

One of the more heartbreaking losses in franchise history came in the 2007 playoffs. After squeaking in on the leg of Josh Brown in 2006, the 2007 Seahawks were a legitimate, if not favored, contender. They hosted the Redskins and turned a close game through the third quarter into a lopsided victory after interceptions returned for touchdowns by Marcus Trufant and Jordan Babineaux.

They then traveled to Green Bay to face the 13–3 Packers. Things started out amazingly well, as two quick turnovers allowed Seattle to build a 14–0 lead. With 8:43 left in the first, the Seahawks had already pushed their win probability to 88 percent. What followed was a massacre. The Packers had pushed their win probability to 70 percent before the quarter was over. When the dust settled, Seattle was blown out 42–20.

91

82 Percent

Josh Brown kicked four game-winning field goals. To get what that really means, let me use Brian Burke's win-probability metric. Burke broke down years of data to determine how much every play, in every situation, time, score, etc., is worth. Brown's first kick, a 42-yard strike to beat the Lions in Week 1, was worth 16 percent. Seattle went from an 84 percent chance of winning to a 100 percent chance of winning. Minor drama compared to what would come.

Brown's next feat was a 54-yard, game-winning field goal against the St. Louis Rams. Kickers convert about half of all attempts from 50-plus yards. Brown nailed it, adding another 40 percent to his win total. He again beat the Rams two weeks later, but this was a chip shot from 38, so only worth 10 percent. Brown notched another 50-yard game-winner against the Broncos. The 50-yard shot broke up a tie and so was less valuable than his dagger against the Rams, thus 26 percent.

All told, Brown's four field goals accounted for 82 percent of win probability, or a bit less than two wins. Ignoring home-field advantage and team quality, both teams start with a 50 percent chance of winning, and so 50 percent must be gained to achieve victory. Brown's two wins carried Seattle, and that those two wins came against the division-rival Rams proved decisive in the NFC West. Seattle finished 9–7. The Rams finished 8–8. Brown became a cult hero, was franchised, eventually signed to the Rams for *way too much* money, and became the enemy. For a season, Brown was chicken bones and slumpbusters and salt over the shoulder.

92 Labor

I have been on both sides of a union. I was a Teamster for a little over a year and managed Teamsters for about that same amount of time. *Manage* is the technically correct way to put it, but I imagine it's a lot like coaching million-dollar athletes. You can attempt to intimidate, you can befriend, you can just try to do right, but you are never truly in control.

When you're a Teamster, there is a true camaraderie unlike anything I have experienced outside of sports. You meet complete strangers, and all the friction and awkwardness of being new or strange is just not there. That might sound idealistic, and maybe it is a little polished by memory, but it felt that way. I think it was a combination of factors that made everyone so tight. Pay was pretty good where I worked, and there were benefits. It was the first time I had health insurance in about a decade, and it wasn't scummy state insurance, but good, honorable insurance—and dental. People felt safe in their jobs. Removing competition between workers removes a lot of the mistrust. More than anything, I think when you are in a union you have a common enemy.

When you are managing a union, no matter how fair you try to be, or just or tolerant or respectful, you are that enemy. It's not subtle, either, or misguided: the union thinks you're their enemy, and the management reminds you that you are. It's everything you could expect in a racial squabble. The management mistrusts union members without question, and union members reciprocate. The management thinks the union is lazy, entitled, and slow. The union thinks the management is crafty, greedy, and dishonest. Both sides wish the other did not exist. Management thinks anyone who has had their job too long is compromised by the union, and the union sees management the same way. If you try to walk the line, not take sides, you become a man without a country.

That is pretty much what I did. I joined management because my wife wanted to go back to nursing school. I didn't understand. Without the union, I was almost immediately transferred, and where I landed I was viewed with hostility. I was put on the kind of line they put you on when they want to promote you or they want you to quit. It was all old-school union guys, and they didn't have any reason to respect me, but they had plenty to assume the worst. I worked it out with them the best I could and won respect, if never trust. I wouldn't trust me. Not with the side I was on.

The Seahawks were affected by two strikes. The first was in 1982. Labor unrest probably cost the Seahawks Sam McCullum. McCullum was the team's union rep. The position can seem abstract to anyone who hasn't been in a union situation, but let me translate: to a union member, the rep is the go-to guy for complaints and, as such, the buffer between you and management. There is no one you have to trust like the union rep, and when you have a good one, it's a true godsend. For management, the union rep is the face and body of your frustration. They are the hardest employee to work with, and the one who corrupts the most. Jack Patera made waves by moving McCullum, and even with what little I know about Patera, I understand that he would hate a union rep. That decision probably cost him his team, their trust, and ultimately his job.

Before the 1982 strike, Steve Largent and Jim Zorn cited Matthew 5:36–37 as the reason they would not strike. That might be a convoluted and convenient interpretation of that isolated passage, and it surely did not win friends among their teammates, but they were far from alone. Terry Bradshaw and Joe Montana were opposed, and Montana quit the NFLPA. It weakened the union's position, but not enough to destroy it.

Largent crossed picket lines in 1987 and played among the Sea-Scabs. If you are union, there is no greater betrayal than an employee who crosses the picket lines. That Largent was honored and established certainly made his action that much harder for others to swallow. Not only did he have less to lose from breaking the picket line and weakening the union, but because he was so prominent, his decision reflected weakness throughout.

Fans booed the returning Seahawks. Fans do not tolerate when their team stops playing because the players want better wages and more equitable treatment. That probably cost the team Kenny Easley, but also probably saved Easley's life. Easley was the successor to McCullum. When the team walked, the Seahawks scrambled to field a team. They had a bouncer, and two players who flew in on Sunday and departed on Monday. They were exactly what a group of scabs should be: completely unqualified.

But they got a ringer in their third week when Largent took the field and dominated some scrubs. That was a major slight to Easley. He was fighting to convince Jim Zorn not to return to football and take the field. He convinced Zorn, only to be betrayed by Largent. So he demanded a trade before the 1988 season. No disrespect, no booing, and Easley probably would have stuck around. That might have cost him his life.

93 Sam Adams

The Revolutionary was a radical. I am not sure anyone called Sam Adams "the Revolutionary," or "the Radical," but I surely would have. There is nothing like good line play, and Adams was a bull. He was 350 pounds of run-stuffing, guard-battering interior power.

Seattle started Adams and Tez and wished opponents good luck. Or so is my rosy memory.

Seattle drafted Adams in the first round of the 1994 draft. He was the powerful, huge complement to the unblockable Cortez Kennedy. I always think of interior line play as the single most important part of a good defense. It clogs the run game, blocks interior passing lanes, and creates the fastest arriving pressure. A player like Adams was such a load that, joined with Tez, teams were helpless to defend the Seahawks' ends. Michael Sinclair and Michael McCrary, both considered too small, broke out beside the Tez-Adams interior.

Strangely enough, though, with Adams did not come great defensive play. By Football Outsiders DVOA, the Seahawks ranked 14, 25, 24, 17, 8, and 8 in Adams' six years with the team. When the Seahawks drafted Aaron Curry, I was critical of the team taking a linebacker so high. I reasoned that linebackers, no matter how great, could never truly make a team great. For six years, Seattle had what every defensive coach wants: a great defensive line. Yet they could not build a great defense. It only became truly good when the offense began to match it.

I wonder, can any one player make a defense great? Can a defense itself even seem great with an offense that can't take pressure off? Like many things, the more I learn about the game, the more questions I have. The more I recognize I don't know.

Adams helped a run of bad Seahawks teams stay respectable and was honored for his duty by being let go by Mike Holmgren. It worked out, though. Adams landed in Baltimore, and with Baltimore he won a ring. That offense is constantly derided, but while it had Dilfer, and we know Dilfer was lacking, it also had Jamal Lewis, and Lewis was the kind of back you could build your entire offense around. I wonder, if Seattle had that kind of back when it had Kennedy and Adams, would we look back and think those late-'90s Seahawks teams had some of the greatest defenses of all-time?

94 Let Go of Winning

If you can accept losing, you can't win. —Vince Lombardi

That's right. That is *right*. Lombardi was a champion, and he knew that you can never accept losing. Losing must be repellent. It must fill your stomach full of maggots and brain full of flames. You must never accept losing even if you lose. You must always, always want—no, *need*—to win. You must need to win like you need to eat—as if, without winning, you'd starve.

If you can't accept losing, you can't win. —Vince Lombardi

Wait. Huh? He said that, too? No, I think I get it. I get it! You must accept losing to win because loss is the path to ultimate victory. You must lose and lose and fail and fail to become good, to become a champion. You can't exhaust yourself losing. You must forget the loss and concentrate only on the victory. The next victory! Ultimate glory!

Winning isn't everything, it's the only thing. —Vince Lombardi

Now I'm lost.

Lombardi only lost 34 times in his 10-year career. He never endured a losing season and lost only once in the playoffs. He did suffer six ties but failed to make a memorable quote about the affair, real or imagined. Lombardi knew a lot about football. He knew everything about being a coach. He was an incredible motivator, and even his apocryphal quotes are moving.

Lombardi is not a legendary fan. He never had the chance to step back and love from afar. He died a young man, at 57. Lombardi died after a lifetime of indigestion.

Fans must accept losing. They have no choice. They accept losing or become a Yankees fan. Yankees fans, but for the few true, are the living dead. Fans in fair-weather. Fans with more dust than sweat on their ball caps. Fans for the playoff run. Not fans at all.

We don't win when the team wins or lose when the team loses, but it feels like we do. It feels like it so much for some that winning indeed becomes the only thing. It isn't, it can't be, and if it becomes as much, you're losing yourself. Love your team. Love it when it loses. Love it equally when it wins.

The Legend of Charlie Frye

Things got so bad in 2008 that the Seahawks started Charlie Frye. Frye was a failed quarterback acquired from the Browns for a sixth-round pick. Seattle overpaid. The former Akron Zip was in the league for one reason, the tired concept of "prototypical." Frye looked the part of a professional quarterback, even though he couldn't throw worth a lick and sensed pass rushers from other dimensions.

Seattle was hosting Green Bay, and since it was starting Frye, it was really counting on its running game to step up and carry the offense. That is when I started to notice that the Packers were planning to stop just that, and that Seattle didn't have a hope of running with Frye playing quarterback. Every snap, the Packers linebackers crashed the line. When it was a run, Julius Jones was running into a hornets' nest. When it was a pass, well, the small disadvantage of losing coverage linebackers did not seem to hurt Frye's opponents too much.

Humans need to compartmentalize things for our sanity. We need units like the secondary and the linebackers corps, and we need to assign very specific duties and stereotypes to the players who populate those units. Football is too messy for all that. Everything impacts everything. Peyton Manning has never had a struggling run game. Who would bother defending the run when they must desperately attempt to slow Manning? Charlie Frye didn't earn that same kind of respect.

The Seahawks have lost 277 games. They have been blown out, edged out, screwed, and humiliated. They have suffered questionable touchdowns and uncalled play-clock violations. They have lost 10 or more games nine times. They've had two good head coaches, three barely worth mentioning, and Jack Patera. They are not a legendary franchise or even a particularly successful one. They have never ended a season anything but a loser: failing to make the playoffs or being bounced by a better team.

It would not be too hard to abandon them. Technology allows fans to watch whatever team they want from about anywhere. You could be a Saints fan today and a Steelers fan next season. You could support one preseason contender and hedge your bets with another. You could be a fan of the league and never suffer losing at all. Someone always wins.

Or you can be a fan.

95 Maurice Morris

Maurice Morris did what Shaun Alexander refused to do. When Alexander became Touchdown Alexander in 2005, he traded touchdowns for receptions. Morris and Mack Strong picked up the slack. For many seasons, Morris proved to be a more valuable per-play rusher. He was more versatile, and had better top-end speed.

I am not an Alexander denier. I can see the guy was a special talent. But I'm not pig-headed, either. Morris wasn't chopped liver. Holmgren spent a second-round pick to draft him, and he was a standout rusher at Oregon.

Sometime in 2007, when my backing had shifted from Alexander to 100 percent Morris, I began to wonder what the history of the Seahawks would have been if Alexander, for whatever reason, lost it all before 2005. What if it were Touchdown Morris? Would we call him "Mercury"?

He sort of saved the season. Morris did not start until phantom injuries felled Alexander, and by then the season was close to lost. The Seahawks were 4–4 and had just suffered a grueling overtime loss to the Browns. Somehow, Seattle made Derek Anderson look like a great quarterback. Holmgren was stubbornly sticking to Alexander and blaming the line, but if the optimist could see a twinkle of the Old Shaun in 2006, it was wholly and completely gone by 2007. Morris took over the next week, Holmgren declared that he had officially abandoned the run game, and the Seahawks finished out 5–1 in games Morris started.

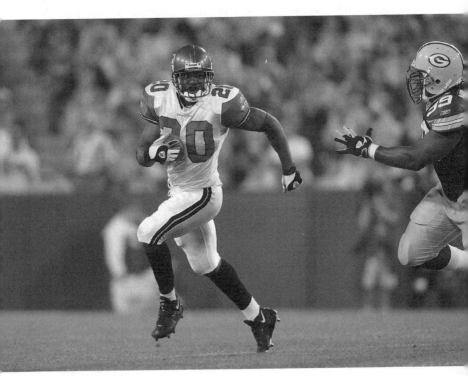

Seahawks running back Maurice Morris takes it outside during a 21–3 victory in a preseason game against the Green Bay Packers in August 2004 at Lambeau Field.

Football is full of what-ifs. What if Barry Sanders could have run behind Emmitt Smith's offensive line? What if Jim Brown played in a time when he wasn't simply bigger than the defenders? I think this one merits. Morris was not a better rusher than Alexander until the very end, but he was a more skilled and versatile receiver. Could Morris have been better than Alexander? Probably not as a rusher. But here is another question we will never be able to answer: would the Seahawks have been a better team starting Morris? They certainly were in 2007.

96 Be Completely Wrong

Before the 2008 season, I was championing a little-known receiver named Courtney Taylor. Taylor had been a standout receiver for a run-first Auburn team and had fallen to the sixth round in a loaded wide-receiver class. It was not easy finding good information or tape on Taylor, but I did my best and liked what I saw.

He was a fluid athlete, powerfully built, and seemed to understand the subtleties of receiving. I did not know how good he could become, but after Matt Hasselbeck had constructed a potent offense through the likes of Leonard Weaver, Marcus Pollard, and Nate Burleson, I thought surely Taylor could rise up and establish himself as a stop-gap No. 1. I thought he would become my new discovery.

Courtney Taylor barely made it through a game before he was benched. He dropped easy passes in a game against the Bills that would set the tone for the entire season. Before the game was over, not only had Seattle been embarrassed by a mediocre team, but it had lost starting right guard Rob Sims for the season.

The team went from attempting to build an offense around Taylor and rookie tight end John Carlson, to benching Taylor and holding open tryouts for street free agents. Eventually, the entire offense crumbled. How was I so wrong? I never knew. I only knew I was.

It turns out Taylor was diagnosed with multiple sclerosis in the summer of 2008. It was private, as it should be, but Taylor himself admits that eye twitches hurt his ability to track the ball. The disease was caught early, and Taylor received treatment that should help him lead a normal life.

97 Chris Gray

Chris Gray was one of multiple players who frustrated the crap out of me in 2007. He was 37 and on the true downside of a journeyman's long career. Gray had been a mobile finesse blocker—the kind of guard who did a lot of little things well, never killed you, but was never a presence, either. When the strength fully and truly went, he was little more than a body between the defender and the ball carrier.

When an offensive lineman is said to be able to play multiple positions, that is often code for a player who cannot play any one position well. That was not the case with Gray. He was a natural center, and when Seattle signed him 1998, that is the position he filled. Gray played there for three seasons before moving to right guard to accommodate Robbie Tobeck.

When Hutch went down in 2002, he even played some left guard. That's because Gray was a very polished blocker, with good feet and great awareness. He was the rare do-all lineman who can actually do most. His career was certainly more long than distinguished, but he was a part of some of the very best Seahawks teams ever. I think what someone like Gray proves is that even great teams need a few good, cheap players to fill out their roster.

98 Sudden Sam

Seattle seemingly always had a burner. A player who played behind the defense. A wide receiver who could threaten secondaries deep. That all started with Sam McCullum.

McCullum was one of the very few good players to find himself in Seattle because of the expansion draft. The process was so stacked against the Seahawks and Buccaneers, the only way a talented player could slip through was if they had not yet been discovered.

McCullum started his NFL career with the Vikings. He had been a flanker at Montana State and was somewhat known on the eastern edges of Seahawks country. McCullum had been the Vikings' third-string receiver behind Pro Bowler John Gilliam and semi-accomplished youngster Jim Lash. He ended up outperforming both over the next few years. Fran Tarkenton just never got the breaks.

He was the Seahawks' first No. 1 receiver in the generic sense. McCullum was the explosive deep threat to Steve Largent's steady hands. Like Blades, Galloway, and Robinson after him, McCullum may have excited more than he produced. He had great deep speed, but at first, not a ton else. His snaps were cut way down his second season in Seattle, but by 1980, the players voted him the team MVP.

Some might question if McCullum was valuable to the team or just valuable to his teammates. He was cut prior to the 1982 season, and the Seahawks players were sure that it was because he was the team's union rep. On November 23, 1983, Judge Bernard Ries agreed, and ruled against the Seahawks organization. The ending was ugly, but his career was sweet if short. And unlike a lot of players, McCullum was smart with his money, and his brief NFL career helped him to a comfortable retirement.

99 Be Passionate but Never a Completist

Sometime after I have sorted through the draft, scouted the picks, and let go of the players I wanted but Seattle did not get, things get extremely quiet in Seahawks country. It is perhaps the happiest time of the year for me. I love the Seahawks, but we all need a break.

I do not need to know about Matt Hasselbeck's personal life. I do not need to know where he shops with his kids or even if he has kids. Football players are celebrities, but they are celebrated for their talent, not the minutia that fills their life. I do not know when it happened, it seems like it has been around my entire life, but sometime in the history of sport, the athlete merged with the man, and fans needed to know not just that they were rooting for a great player but someone they could have a beer with.

Professional football players do not owe us their personal lives. They do not have to be upstanding citizens, though of course I would rather they be. They are paid for being fast and strong and skilled, not for being good people.

What creeps me out is less that we expect the players to be good people but more that we expect the players to be likeable. Football players are strangers. We know them as athletes, like we knew

Picasso from his paintings. The narrow and twisted perspective we are fed about who is a good guy, who is a family man, and who is distant, disagreeable, or whatever, is nothing more than a proxy created by the mass media. In the twisted world of popular culture, a player tied to murder is somehow more likable than someone who is recalcitrant.

When there is not news, there just is not news. The 24-hour news cycle cannot stand that. It needs updates all the time. Fans who want to think of themselves as hardcore, pride themselves on knowing every little bit of trivia that can be known. But there is knowledge, and then there is marginalizing your life for a reputation.

Fans should be passionate, informed, questioning, concerned, and curious, but never nosey or invasive. I despise sites that survive on shame. I do not need to know who got drunk and did what. I do not need to know that Jimmy Clausen was punched in the face or why, because I know I won't know, anyway. At best, I will get a take. I will get a slant. I will get the perspective that serves the provider the best. Too often, the perspective that serves the news media is scandal.

When early June rolls around and players get back to having a life, fans should, too. It is okay to not know who was seen shopping where, or who left a drunken cell phone call with whom. If you need more Seahawks, need a fix, need something that lets you feel close to the team when the season seems so far away, try rewatching a game. Try unearthing an old story about long-retired players. Try challenging the smart part of you that craves being a fan and not loading up on shame and schadenfreude. Or, maybe try this next suggestion.

100 Write a Book

What a humbling experience. Like any young writer looking for a break, when I was contacted to write this book, I jumped in head-first. And into a dark and treacherous trench I sunk. Maybe you can tell me, did I hit bottom? Have I struggled to the surface? Am I broken, bashed against hidden rocks, adrift along the surface, drowned?

This team existed before I was born. It was losing and winning and twisting emotions and breaking hearts before I ever took a breath. Jim Zorn pinned up hopes and passed to perfection and was surpassed and benched before I ever spoke a word.

You can go to the Grand Canyon and sit and feel connected to something greater or be crushed by its expanse. There was all this history and meaning and passion and loss that I could never tap into, and searching archives and thumbing through biographies, I knew I was trespassing on someone else's team. A team I could never own.

But I did it, anyway. I wrote a book. If there was ever anything that could bring me closer to a team, make me challenge my loyalty, my understanding, and my appreciation for the Seattle Seahawks, it was this. If you ever have the chance, the excuse, or the inclination, take something you love and write a book about it. You will end up changed, better. You will take something you thought you could never love more and love it more.

The Good Lord Willin', Things'll Work Out For Ya

Early in my blogging career, if I may take extreme liberties with the term, I wanted to be a regular journalist and do regular journalist things. The backbone of sports journalism is the interview. Seattle needed talent in its interior, and because I was sort of going nuts about Brandon Mebane, I thought that interior talent could do wonders for the entire defense.

It was a top-heavy draft for defensive tackles. Glenn Dorsey was the stud, certified best player. Sedrick Ellis was the more athletic player with better upside. As it has turned out, neither has impressed that much. Behind both were two players from different ends of the prospect spectrum. There was Kentwan Balmer, whom every mock draft insisted Seattle would take, and there was Trevor Laws.

Balmer was the career underachiever with loads of upside. Laws was the overachiever with comparatively limited tools. I locked onto Laws and said that Seattle should draft him in the first round. At that time, Laws had moved himself into the second through a good showing at the NFL Scouting Combine, but seemed stretched to move up any further. I pursued Laws for over a month, and finally he agreed through his brother to conduct an email interview. The readership really liked it, but the truth is, I look back and think it was pretty boring stuff. I realized sometime that summer that there is an innate conflict of interest between getting to know players and attempting to assess them accurately. Laws and Balmer are both still backups on their respective teams.

Sources

Books

Carroll, Bob, Pete Palmer, and John Thorn. *The Hidden Game of Football.* New York: Warner Books, 1988.

Gay, Timothy. *The Physics of Football.* New York: HarperCollins, 2005.

Knox, Chuck, and Bill Plaschke. *Hard Knox: The Life of an NFL Coach.* New York: Harcourt Brace Jovanovich, 1988.

Moody, Fred. *Fighting Chance: An NFL Season with the Seattle Seahawks.* Seattle: Sasquatch Books, 1989.

Raible, Steve, and Mike Sando. *Tales from the Seahawks Sidelines.* Champaign, Illinois: Sports Publishing, 2004.

Magazines

People magazine

Sports Illustrated (Peter King, Bruce Newman)

News Services

The Associated Press (Rachel Cohen, Barry Wilner)

Newspapers

Boston Globe (Will McDonough, Michael Vega)

Chicago Tribune

Ellensburgh Daily Record (Daryl Gadbow)

Milwaukee Journal

Moscow Pullman Daily News

New York Times (Samantha Stevenson, William N. Wallace)

Rock Hill Herald

San Diego Union Tribune (Jim Trotter)

Seattle Post-Intelligencer (Steve Kelley, Danny O'Neil)

Seattle Times (Greg Bishop, Clare Farnsworth)

Spokane Chronicle (Dan Weaver)
Spokesman-Review (Dan Weaver)
St. Petersburg Times
Sun Herald
Tacoma News Tribune (Mike Sando)
Tri-City Herald
USA Today (Denise Tom)
Washington Post (Leonard Shapiro)

Websites
Advanced NFL Stats (AdvancedNFLStats.com)
Alabama.com (Kevin Scarbinski: Al.com)
Becky's Seattle Seahawks Fan Site (Beckys-Place.com)
ESPN (ESPN.com)
Football Outsiders (FootballOutisders.com)
Google News (news.google.com)
Pro Football Hall of Fame (profootballhof.com)
Pro-Football-Reference.com
San Francisco Gate (SFGate.com)
Sports Illustrated (SportsIllustrated.cnn.com)
The Official Site of the NFL (NFL.com)
The Official Site of the Oakland Raiders (Raiders.com)
The Official Site of the Seattle Seahawks (Seahawks.com)

Television
NFL Game of the Week: Bo versus Boz (NFL Films)
NFL Game of the Week: 1999 Seahawks @ Dolphins (NFL Films)